DATE			

PLAYS AND PLAYERS
IN
MODERN ITALY

NOVELLI

PLAYS AND PLAYERS

IN

MODERN ITALY

BEING A STUDY OF THE ITALIAN STAGE
AS AFFECTED BY THE POLITICAL AND SOCIAL LIFE
MANNERS AND CHARACTER OF TO-DAY

BY

ADDISON McLEOD

WITH ILLUSTRATIONS

KENNIKAT PRESS
Port Washington, N. Y./London

PLAYS AND PLAYERS IN MODERN ITALY

First published in 1912
Reissued in 1970 by Kennikat Press
Library of Congress Catalog Card No: 79-102848
SBN 8046-0758-3

Manufactured by Taylor Publishing Company   Dallas, Texas

To all the good actors and gentle actresses of the Italian stage who find no place in this work, it is dedicated by the Author, who has lost more by missing their performances than they by losing a place in this chronicle.

PREFATORY NOTE

THE Author wishes to express his indebtedness to the photographers who have furnished illustrations for this work. In respect of the four illustrations from drawings, he wishes to call attention to the difficulties under which these were made : taken by the young artist—he was only eighteen or nineteen—from drawings dashed off in the course of the representation, in almost total darkness. Whatever else they are, they are really faithful and characteristic. The Author has to thank M. Ernest Flammarion for permission to use matter contained in his edition of ' Le Père Lebonnard.'

Finally, the dedication is not a formal matter, but the discharge of a duty : and the Author hopes sincerely that it may find its way to the eyes of those to whom it is addressed.

May 1912.

ERRATA.

CONTENTS

CHAP.		PAGE
I.	INTRODUCTION	I
II.	ITALIAN PLAYS AND PLAYWRIGHTS	33
III.	ITALIAN PLAYERS	175
IV.	THE ITALIAN STYLE	235
V.	THE DIALECT THEATRE	270
VI.	THEATRES AND AUDIENCES. DIVAGANDO	305
	APPENDICES	337
	INDEX	349

LIST OF ILLUSTRATIONS

NOVELLI	*Frontispiece*
'COME LE FOGLIE,' ACT I, SCENE 4	*To face p.* 74
'COME LE FOGLIE,' ACT IV	,, 76
'LA COMMEDIA DELLA PESTE,' ACT II	,, 132
'LA COMMEDIA DELLA PESTE,' ACT III	,, 138
ELEONORA DUSE, IN 'LA CITTÀ MORTA'	,, 173
GINA FAVRE, IN 'I BUFFONI'	,, 183
TINA DI LORENZO	,, 185
DINA GALLI	,, 196
TOMMASO SALVINI	,, 200
DE SANCTIS	,, 203
ZACCONI, IN 'IL CARDINALE LAMBERTINI'	,, 222
BENINI, IN 'IL BUGIARDO'	,, 288
FERRAVILLA	,, 292

PLAYS AND PLAYERS

MODERN ITALY

CHAPTER I

INTRODUCTION

A WORK dealing with the subject of the theatre stands
in less need of recommendation or apology, perhaps,
than any other. Not because the theme is that good
wine which needs no bush, but because it has a character
so well known that praise or disparagement would
be superfluous. Few men born in easy circumstances
reach the age of twenty without having tasted of it;
fewer still the age of thirty without having determined
the part that it is to play in their lives. Whether they
are to seek it out, take it as it comes, or avoid it
altogether. Whether they regard it as deep and sweet,
light and sparkling, or abhorrent and unwholesome.

Writing of the stage, then, we deal with a thing
perfectly knowable, but, perhaps, unknown to the actual
reader. Writing of a foreign stage, we turn from something unseen to something invisible: yet, though invisible,
describable on the one hand, and recognisable on the

B

other. To speak of the Italian stage is to speak of something for the enjoyment of which, as matters stand, the ordinary Englishman is only half equipped. It is to supply him with the lacking moiety that the present work is undertaken.

The subject has such an obvious interest that it is strange that no English writer should have touched it before. A description of Italian plays and acting might conceivably be lacking because no Englishman felt himself in position to write with confidence on the subject. But with regard to the past there would be no difficulty, even for a foreigner, in writing from authorities. Yet Addington Symonds himself, in his comprehensive 'History of the Renaissance,' has passed the subject by, except in so far as it touched on the domain of literature ; although the stage was a most important factor in the court and social life to which he gives so much attention.

The present writer must confess to having little taste for research and little respect for authority. That may be a defect : but, on the other hand, he cannot help believing that the reader will give him greater thanks for a living description of the players he has seen than for any extracts, however informing, from the Italian works that he has had between his hands. His chief purpose is to give effect to actual experience ; recourse is only had to authorities to supplement this, and is chiefly in the nature of that hearsay evidence which is admitted for certain purposes even in court of law. The reader is warned that the stage is taken seriously, as one of the great moving influences in human life ; is promised a laugh and a tear, as occasion shall serve. The aim of the commentary on the translations is to remove any strangeness of associations ; that of the descriptions, to place the reader in the writer's place—make him see with his eyes and hear with his ears. If it be said that the result must be a biased account, the reply is that all accounts by a single man are in that sense biased—even that which a man gives to himself.

If want of variety is objected, then it may be answered, again, that the reader has as much advantage as if he were present at the performance himself. If he detects, or thinks he detects, in the account laid before him, a note of prejudice or a touch of carelessness, and if these doubts and suspicions lead him to equip himself to go forth to investigate the matter at first-hand, then all concerned will be content—the brave player, the worthy managers, and, last and least, the author himself.

Before that little which is to be said on stage history has been set down, it is a little difficult to define the scope of the work intelligibly and without repetition. The range of the Italian theatre is exceedingly wide, and to treat of it all, historically and descriptively, would need volumes. There is a small and outlying class of play which is in every sense a popular one—that is to say, in which the people (with a big ' P ') arrange the spectacle themselves, and in which actors and audience are of the same class. These plays are only briefly referred to in the text, but a few notes will be found on the subject in an appendix. Then there is the theatre in our ordinary English sense, which divides into three parts. But the difficulty of keeping the distinctions are considerable: firstly, because one part is far and away the greater; and secondly, because the other two—from a student's point of view at the opposite extremes—are historically linked together. We have, then, firstly, the theatre of conventional types, in which certain personages—such as Arlecchino, Brighella, Stenterello, &c.—whose clothes, manners, and part in the drama remain always the same, or nearly so ; thirdly,

the dialect theatre which, in theory at least, absolutely
rejects all convention, and studies life—and, most of all,
external life—in its characteristic local forms ; secondly,
in between these two, and far more extensive than either,
lies the ordinary prose theatre.[1]   This is to be the
subject before us. But as the dialect theatre is
much discussed, and several distinguished actors belong
to it, a chapter has been given to that subject as well.
The matter throughout is drawn almost entirely from
the writer's personal experience, which extends—so
far as witnessing plays is concerned—over some twelve
years altogether, though the principal part of it lies
in the last four or five, and comprises something like
two hundred performances of various kinds. It is not
exhaustive, but is that of the ordinary playgoer of the
day ; and includes almost every player of first-rate
powers. The limitation of a work confined to things
seen and heard are obvious. It is hoped that they
may be compensated by sincerity in observation and
freshness in description.

The present moment is an auspicious one for the
attempt. For while things concerning the theatre
are in a state of flux and change, the present state has
endured long enough for distinct tendencies to have
developed : yet not so long but that criticism may be
of interest, and, perhaps, even of value. The time is
critical, in the true sense of the word—that is to say, it is
a moment at which, in more than one question of moment,
a decision must be taken.   It is therefore interesting
and picturesque.   There is even, perhaps, a slight danger
that it is too critical : that momentary and pressing
questions may obscure larger and more vital ones ; and

---

[1] The words 'Teatro di prosa' and ' Scena di prosa' are commonly used
to denote what we should call the ordinary, or 'legitimate,' drama.
They do not exclude verse plays.

that the writer, who sets to work to describe the theatre at this point, may give as misleading an idea of its real nature as an artist who sits down to paint a waterfall would, of the general nature of the river valley.

To understand how the theatre reached its present position, we must give a glance back and see it on the road. This is, on the whole, like that taken in other countries and at other times. The Church gave its first home to the Italian drama. When its leanings became too secular for it any longer to be an accompaniment or aid to religious observance, it found its way into the public square. But it did not, and could not, survive on popular support alone. Losing the ecclesiastical patron it sought a substitute, and found it in the tyrant prince of the day. It was under his care and for his advantage that the drama, as we know it, was born ; and the first Italian comedy of importance that has come down to us was written by the author of ' Il Principe.'[1] It was towards the end of the fifteenth century that theatres, as we understand them, began to grow up. In Ferrara, Florence, Mantova, and elsewhere, the rulers encouraged and made use of the stage which thus throve in various localities, supported by various centres. Each one had its writers, players, and singers, who were attracted and maintained by the court, that was at once their beacon and their camp fire. Medieval Italy has given way to Modern, and the many little courts have become fused in the one great government at Rome. The intellect of the country is fast gravitating thither ; the elegant life of higher society, less serious, but yet more faithful, is like a persistent current of water still swirling round its old sunken stones ; yet for all that it, too, is slowly following. But the theatre is still left behind ; clinging—partly by habit, partly by reason of

[1] Machiavelli.

false encouragement—to its old empty homes. It has lost the support of the local courts; it is losing that of the local societies. We have the proof of the past, we have the evidence of the present, that it cannot rely on popular support alone: far less be sustained on the thin decoction of intellectual approbation which is supplied by the critical press. Let these facts be remembered while we attack perhaps the most important theatrical question of the day : namely, whether the stage shall continue to find its chief interest in local colour and local association, or follow its patrons, the court and society, to the seat and centre of national life.

Owing to the changing state of the country, the state of things as regards the stage is even worse than might have been first supposed ; for the unity of government has done more than leave the artistic centres in isolation ; it has made locality more local still. When Venice, Milan, Naples, were political powers, all their subject cities knew and recognised their headship ; but now, these bonds being dissolved, it is as if a number of parcels had been thrown on one great heap, breaking their wrappings and setting the contents loose. ' It is too far for you to go up and worship in . . . Rome,' and so men set up the golden calf of art in Brescia, in Rovato, in Pesaro, in Pistoia. Local jealousies are infinite ; city striving against city. Worthless productions are brought out—often the more numerous in proportion to the insignificance of the venue. With men of power, a production in their own native place counts for nothing : ' But that was at Pesaro,' a Pesarese musician has said to me, with an expressive shrug, when I was asking him as to the production of his works.

Then the local centre has a local press at its service, the art criticism of which is often supplied by ardent young men without experience or literary style ; and the only common denominator of criticism which can be found in Rome, Turin, Milan, or Venice is a purpose at all costs, and by any means, to exhalt and glorify the dear native place. Of this spirit of local patriotism, and the kind of language in which it is conveyed, let this example be quoted from the ' Gazzettino ' of Venice. Similar remarks might be found in a dozen journals every other day ; ' Venice, however,' added Sgr. Gorio, M.P., ' to the cult of Art, and *that primacy therein which no one disputes with her*, would fain add also that of Commerce, and win back her dominion of the seas.' Let her by all means employ herself thus usefully; but . . . oh, shadows of Michelangelo and Botticelli ! Primacy ! While in the very heart of their own city, the bronze rider of the Florentine sculptor stares down on them as he seems to ride proudly by.

It will be not found surprising that, with a spirit like this abroad, the reception of a play is always a doubtful thing. The touring companies—and all are touring companies save the few but important exceptions to be hereafter noted—go from place to place ; and at each one they must submit to a fresh ordeal of criticism.

In England or France there is a finality in the result which compensates, to a great extent, the difficulty and expense of production. When once Paris or London has pronounced, the road is open ; and no provincial judgment would venture to oppose. If the beginning is made in the provinces, there is always Cæsar whereunto to appeal. But in Italy, the cause may have to be tried many times over, and each time in accordance with a new set of principles—or, rather, a new mass of prejudices and caprices. Nor is the court always an orderly one. When the honour of the native city is at stake, manners, as well as reason and justice, sometimes go by the board : and the Italian, who, in his proper nature, is courtesy and chivalry itself, will receive with rude cries and jeering even the women who are labouring for his entertainment. Instances of what are really moods of this sort are of common occurrence, not made any the better by the fact that the local newspaper has always some rational and philosophical explanation to supply. I will take two, which, being picturesque, have remained in my memory. In Venice, we were offered a play whose title was 'L'ultimo Doge' (The Last Doge). It was said to have been a splendid success in Genova, and the papers spoke well of its performance in Milan. Surely in Venice the returned Doge should have a warm welcome! But, alas! there were other republics than that of the Lagoons, and this doge was the Doge of Genova! 'Go, then, friends, and take your vapouring elsewhere!'

'If you had found in the Piazzetta and on the Rialto your aspirations and ideals; if through St. Mark you had dreamed a larger and statelier kingdom over which St. Peter was to rule; if by our strivings, toils, and privations you had won your way to serenity beyond, then we would have listened to you. But your petty politics of Genova do not interest us. Take your vapourings elsewhere!'

Another instance, and a better one still. Venice is said, with some truth, not to furnish critical audiences. Let us go, then, to the mother of the Italian language —the city of Machiavelli, Dante, Guicciardini. Surely here we shall have judgment for reason's sake! One of the best plays (in his opinion) which the writer saw during his last residence in Italy was 'La Commedia della Peste' (The Comedy of the Plague), which will be described at length later.[1] The theme was a delicious, if improper, story; original in its motive, with characters

---

[1] Page 131.

that were original, too; yet the whole might have been bound up with 'The Decameron' without any contrast being perceived. It was the Florentine contada in its old dress; fresh, delightful, as if it had just been discovered beneath the sheltering ashes which the ever-active volcano of human progress slowly and heedlessly pours forth. Something that, perhaps, the Florentine of the present day might have viewed with at least an interest, one would have thought. But, alas! as before it was a case of 'you interest us too little'; now it is 'you interest us too much.' The author was not a Florentine, and he wrote of Florentine things. Can any good come out of Nazareth? Is it possible that a Ravennese can reproduce for us Florentines the time, the country, the atmosphere, of our own Boccaccio? It is unthinkable. This play must needs be absurd and ridiculous. Concittadini! Let us rise like one man and show this miserable outsider what it is to invade the ground of Florence, wander by the Arno's waters, or among the sacred Tuscan groves. Let us seize him, hustle him, hiss him, hoot him! Let him be 'fischiato'! And when we are 'fischiato' by a Florentine audience it is as well to retire in good time.[1]

I ask—as I am well aware I must ask—the reader's confidence that these are not cases carefully chosen for the making of an effect. They are instances which have remained in the memory, out of many, which might have been written down. Nor is the view put forward of that of the foreigner only. Thoughtful Italians will agree as to the fact that in regard to the theatre, as in regard to many other things, there is much local prejudice abroad. It is when we come to speak of the

---

[1] As further evidence of the excellence of this play it may be worth noting that it has since been produced by the Compagnia Argentina (see p. 19) with great success.

remedy that a difference of opinion arises : some, holding that the stage must be allowed to go its own way; maintain and even enlarge its divisions ; rely, as in times past, on native talent and family traditions for education and training : others, on the contrary, looking to unity of language, unity of training, and unity of position, to found and maintain a theatre of national traditions, which, while it amuses, shall augment and instruct young Italy's growing strength.

We are not suggesting that the touring system should be abolished in Italy—one would as soon think of abolishing the circulation of the blood ; but we are suggesting the formation of some great centre which should send out the blood of Art pure, and receive and renew it on its return.   It is the possibility of this that is now hanging in the balance.   Thoughtful men in Italy are discussing it from both sides, and, as the reader will see before this chapter is finished, there is now on its trial the latest of a series of attempts to found a permanent theatre, which seems—it may be only appearance, but it does seem—to be founded on a broader, a more rational basis ; and which has had, until now, a measure of success at least equal to any of its forerunners.

With the hopes and fears for a permanent theatrical centre is bound up, evidently, the question of the merits or demerits of the dialect play.   It is, of course, logically possible that a dialect and a national theatre should exist side by side ;[1] but we believe that it would be only on the terms that a cat and a dog could be kept in the same cage: those—that is, of taming the characteristic life out of both of them.   The purposes of the national theatre is to make for unity; those of the regional, to emphasise division ; and a perpetually recurring local

[1] See Boutet's speech, p. 19.

interest in Turin, Milan, Venice, Naples cannot consolidate a faith in Rome—mistress and foster-mother of all.

The writer had hoped to include his case against the dialect theatre here. But the subject grew to greater proportions : several noticeable actors, and even an important play or two, became part of it ; and it seemed better to give it a chapter to itself. The dialect theatre is, of course, the extreme left of the house. It is that which divides the forces of the stage to the utmost. But even apart from the efforts of its promoters to keep up a barrier of place and associations, there is still a division : that, namely, between those who would maintain the present system of companies, founded on divided centres, and those—idealists they are thought as yet—who look to the creation of a fixed and united theatre with permanent traditions, permanent schools, and constant canons of criticism.

It is to this latter party—the extreme right, they may be called—and the success or failure that has attended their various efforts, that the reader's attention is now asked, and to a few facts and dates briefly set forth just as those concerning the dialect theatre will be set forth later.

In response to very careful inquiries concerning the education of the actor in old days, the answers seemed to show—it is difficult, apparently, to have very precise information—that until quite recently, there were no schools of acting for the professional player. Actors were ' born on the stage ' (to translate the phrase that is constantly recurring), went round as children with their father or mother on tour, used a child's native talent for observation, and began acting when they were of an age.

Such among many others is ' La Duse.'

The only schools for recitation were certain ' società

filodrammatiche,' which were scattered broad-cast throughout the country for teaching of the amateur actor. These schools have existed for hundreds of years; and out of them have come good professional actors, among whom we may name La Reiter, every now and then. It is interesting, as confirming the fact that the stage owed its real nourishment to the interest shown to it by high social life, that for hundreds of years the amateur should have required and maintained, for his amusement and training, societies such as these.

During the past century several 'Capo Comici,'[1] as the heads of companies are called in Italy, are mentioned as having done much for the training of the actors and the production of the plays.

A certain Gustavo Modena, who was the master of Tommaso Salvini, dominated the stage of his time. He must have been an actor of great versatility and power, and a leader of real capacity. His monument, lately erected in Venice, shows a massive, if ungraceful, frame, and suggests a rugged and conquering personality. Moreover, he was really keen to bring and keep together young actors, and train them for their work. He does not, however, appear to have had the teacher's instinct, and his 'Faccia come me' (Do as I do) spoke the one idea that, soon or later, compelled his followers to imitate him or leave him. Besides such men of outstanding importance, others—such as L. Bellotti-Bon, and Virgillio Talli in our own day—have enjoyed the reputation of maintaining companies of which it was good fortune to be a member: although even of Talli's company, I have heard it said that its members act too much like the Capo Comico himself. Such

---

[1] The phrase is used indifferently of managers of all classes. Irving or Tree would be termed a Capo Comico.

companies, however, could not, wandering and single-handed, do the work that is to be done.

There are now two—and I believe only two—schools of acting in Italy. One is a government institution in Florence, dating from about sixty years ago, now presided over by Sigr. Luigi Rasi, himself both an actor in earlier, and a playwright in later, days. The other is in Rome, founded a few years ago, and of which the management is shared by Sigr. Edoardo Boutet with a well-known actress of former days. Sigr. Rasi is a man of middle age, and, as has been said, of practical experience. Sigr. Boutet is older and technically less well equipped, but full of vigour and enthusiasm, and the organiser, in great measure, of the attempt now being made to establish a permanent theatre in Rome. At the first place, I saw the school at work; and the lesson, while differing in no essential principle from similar instruction elsewhere, was useful to one who is keen on judging how much of the differences of the Italian's acting from ours is due to the different training which he undergoes. I had the advantage of being able to note some of my objections to the teacher, and of hearing his replies; and was struck with the fairness and consideration with which the English point of view was received. At the second, on the other hand, I soon found that the master's object was a larger and more ideal one, which, perhaps necessarily, involved giving less practical instruction. His purpose was to create the ideal actor; and the course he sketched out for this end seemed to me so interesting, that, neither to cut it short nor to interrupt the narrative at this point, I have put my notes into an appendix at the end.

But besides these schools for actors, there has been a persistent movement towards the unification of the stage in the shape of various attempts to found a permanent theatre. One was in Naples, in 1878. Another, the Compagnia Carignano of Turin, with which La Duse was connected, lasted from 1877 to 1885. More recently, there was another attempt in Turin, which was known as the Teatro d'Arte and only lasted for a short time. Then some time in the eighties, an attempt was made in Rome. There must have been some money available this time, for the syndicate built the Teatro Nazionale, in the street of that name. Then there was another attempt, by Ermete Novelli, at the Teatro Valle in Rome, which he named the Casa di Goldoni, in imitation of the Maison de Molière. If Novelli's success as a manager had been greater, the looseness of his language would have been forgiven him ; but this attempt went the way of the others, and all that is remembered of it is a grammatical blunder.

Finally, in Rome, within the last three years, as many permanent theatres have been founded, which have not yet been gathered to their predecessors.

Now, before we come to speak of these actually existing, a word of comment on the permanencies which have ceased to be. Naples, Turin, Rome ; why these, and nothing at Florence, the centre of the Tuscan speech, Venice, the city of Goldoni, or, most noticeable lack of all, at Milan ? This latter maintains the first opera-house in Italy. It has newspapers which—especially the ' Corriere ' —present larger and more reasoned criticisms than any other paper in Italy. I suppose the Teatro Manzoni would be considered by popular estimation the first prose theatre in Italy. At any rate, I am confident that, until a few years ago, a dramatic author with an absolutely free choice would have preferred a production there ; and would have found in the applause of the Milanese public, the approval of the Milanese press, the strongest encouragement to proceed. Why was this apparently ideal situation not taken up by any of the eight separate undertakings that have tried, and are trying, to establish themselves? I believe the answer is to be found in the close connection of court and theatre to which reference has already been made. The reader will note that Naples and Turin are, with Rome, the capitals of the three last existing kingdoms in Italy. The two former must have left their stamp on the habits of the people ; and the then national, but now regional, nobility must to a great extent keep the old habits and the old ideas. These attempts to form a permanent theatre have been made in cities which a court has lately inhabited, or in one to which it has newly moved. These things may be mere coincidences, but I cannot help thinking that they have their meaning.

I believe, too, that the passionate longing of the modern Italian to reach Rome was not born altogether by force of idealism or illusion; and that, if its mother was memory, it had a lusty father in expectation and hope.

Furthermore, I believe, that this hope and this expectation were wide and comprehensive. That they were not limited to founding a mere seat of government, but aimed at a centre of national life. Rome in the past had been as large in her works, as lofty in her ideals. Government, art, learning, architecture, almost every department of intellectual life, had flourished there, and gained power and freedom, without losing individuality.

Modern Rome was to do what ancient and medieval Rome had done : and when men cried with Garibaldi ' Rome or Death ! ' they meant death, not only for the Quirinal palace. They meant it for all the hopes in the future, typified by all the monuments of the past ;

greatest among which, towering head and shoulders above its fellows—in spite of its savage brutality and vain display, still the most splendid existing monument to the desire of man for the spectacle—the Colosseum of Rome.

And in the greatness and the unity of this national life for Italy in the future, I hopefully and profoundly believe. 'Credo in una Roma. Credo, Credo!'

To deal now with the existing Compagnie Stabili: as that of the Argentina is the most interesting fact connected with the stage which the writer encountered on his last visit, it will be reserved till the last; and the other and less important enterprises first described.

That of the Manzoni theatre, then, presents no special peculiarities from and above the ordinary touring companies. It is just an attempt to give what might be one of these a permanent home, and at popular prices.

It is impossible, of course, to judge an enterprise like this as to its financial condition by one or two visits; but the view the house presented when the writer visited it was not very encouraging. It is just one more instance of the failure of a popular theatre to draw, in Italy where the stage is supposed to be more popular than in any other country. The company at the Manzoni boasts, in Febo Maria, one actor of really great powers, and the rank and file of it are quite up to the average; but with seats, which are little more than half-price of those at the Valle, the theatre was certainly a little less than half as full. It may be that there is some explanation of these facts which does not appear on the surface. Phœbus with his rays is certainly a powerful luminary, and, when he deigned let his god-like effulgence serve as a background to the figure of the eaglet, uplifting his dark and struggling wings in one last flutter towards the heights of majesty—in other words, when he played a well-known part created by Madame Bernhardt—the effect was thrilling and inspiring.[1] Nevertheless, it is proverbially hard to awake empty seats to any great show of enthusiasm : still less to draw from them any substantial pecuniary return. The enterprise at the Manzoni may succeed. It has our good wishes, though not our confident hopes.

The second is an undertaking of a very different kind, destined—again, if appearances may be trusted—to a far better success. Its home is the Teatro Metastasio, a smaller house, between the Corso and the river ; and its title is the ' Compagnia Drammatica Stabile del Teatro Minimo a Sezioni' (Fixed Dramatic Company of the 'Little Theatre' in Sections).[2] On an ordinary night there are played five sections—that is to say, five one-act pieces of about three-quarters of an hour each— with intervals just long enough for the changes of scene and make up; the first beginning at 6.30 ; half an hour's interval from 8.30 to 9, and the last at 11. One actor will play as many as four different parts in the course of the evening. There seems to be good supply of one-act pieces in Italy; for, besides an occasional translation from the French, there are plays available by Goldoni, and also by Felice Cavalotti, Giacosa, Rovetta : in fact, nearly all the modern brigade have devoted some—and these not the worst—of their energies to writing short pieces ; certain of them, especially Roberto Bracco, with marked success. The *mise en scène* is not distinguished ; but the acting is thoroughly adequate, if not always brilliant, and some of the actors have been trained in first-class companies. All this,

---

[1] This is not meant ironically. It was really a great performance.
[2] This is explained by what follows. The phrase is not an elegant one in the original.

reader, at the modest price of fifty centesimi per section for the most expensive seats. Two hours' entertainment for a franc. Now, to the unattached Italian male, after his day's work and his dinner, there is no place like this for recreation—and freely he makes use of it. No one takes tickets beforehand ; but ten minutes before the hour the entrance hall is full of men and smoke. At the rising of the curtain, the audience is perceived (for knowledge comes through more than one sense) to consist of the same ingredients—men, we may say, speaking generally, though there are a few ladies present ; as their hats, the only thing about them visible, testify. But the audience is wholly respectable, and the attention they give to the play at least equal to that with which acting is received at the more fashionable theatres ; the smoke, indeed, with its invasive powers, tending rather, perhaps, to close up the mouth—a quality which would go far to compensate its disadvantages, considerable though the latter are ; for the Roman cigar is neither Nectar nor Ambrosia to him who is not to the manner born.

In the result, however, the arrangement is so good, so satisfactory the assurance of at least one good piece in the course of the evening, such a relief the freedom from the harassing cares of booking beforehand ;—all this makes amusement such an easy thing that one wonders whether a similar institution could not be run in England for the benefit of those who find the music-halls unsatisfactory and the theatres laborious. Much, however, may depend on the personality of the actor ; and it is to be doubted whether they are to be found in England who would play four different parts in succession, without weariness and without monotony.

We come now to what is probably the most striking attempt for many years to found a permanent theatre. Here again it is a little difficult to deal with the topic satisfactorily in an introduction. Points have to be discussed and references made which can only be understood after a certain amount of detail is in the reader's possession. It seems better, therefore, to confine ourselves here to a few leading facts and some general remarks taken from those who represent different views of the enterprise and its results.

The 'Compagnia Stabile Argentina,' then, is something near four years old now.[1] Therefore, as things go in Italy, it has stood the test of time. It has made and survived its first mistakes ; it has preached its sermons and eaten its words. It is still the subject of controversy in the press : controversy adorned now with sneers, now with an affectation of contemptuous pity. But the main facts about it are: firstly, that it is an institution apparently of solid base and rising prosperity ; secondly, that it has succeeded in producing a kind of relation among its actors dimly resembling that among those of the Comédie Française ; and thirdly, that it has been the means of bringing to light the leading playwright of the day—one Sigr. Sem Benelli, with whose works the reader will have, later on, the opportunity of making himself better acquainted.

Having given the results of independent observation in these short terms, it will be interesting to set down the purposes of its founders, as described in a speech given by the leader, Sigr. Edoardo Boutet, at the foyer of the theatre in May 1908. It is too long and too roundabout in its expression for direct quotation, but a very fair idea of it can be gained from a judicious ' boiling down.

The speaker, then, in reviewing the past, holds that abuses have crept in owing to theatres being managed by the leading actor. Plays are put on for no other

[1] June 1910.

c

reason than that they furnish him with an effective part. Everything is neglected which does not contribute to his advancement and glorification; while, on the other hand, it is contended that want of general education and of breadth of views, among other defects, renders him unfitted for the direction of a large enterprise. Wherefore, in the first place, the Argentina proposed to create a directing board of semi-lay members, who should overlook and control the movements of the actor-manager, much as a commander-in-chief is supervised by a Board of Strategy, or Council of National Defence.

As a corollary of this principle of reducing the leading actor to his place, the aim was to be to produce good all-round acting, not to give individuals the opportunity for distinguishing themselves. All parts are to be regarded as being of equal importance and demanding, in their kind, equal ability in the acting; and requiring to be filled by actors recommended by their suitability rather than their reputation.

Again, the inequalities of the relation between actor and author are to be remedied; for if the former is, in a measure, to be debased, certainly the latter is to be exalted. He is to be no longer the servant of the actor, writing for him, altering scenes and situations at his bidding, but his fellow and equal worker in the cause of art.

No department of the stage is beyond the reach of the speaker's reforming idealism. As the actor-manager is to be in his place, the playwright brought out, so the director is to be given a new view of his duties in the light of moral, social, and political well-being. He is to 'recognise the hitherto existing trammels of the stage and pant to be free of them.' He is to have 'the generous ambition of the strong man towards his destiny, which is vegetating on the stage as it now is,' and to be therefore, ' a young man with potential forces adapted and educated towards this fortune, so far beyond our hopes.' Sigr. Boutet would have the programme of the theatre comprise ' solemn festivals, recalling the greater glories of the stage ; spectacles showing the steps in the march of universal art in its constituent elements ; illustrative lectures to accompany the special festivals and spectacles; programmes of poetry for our instruction and delight, and presentations showing the history of the stage in its material aspect also.'

The author of these grandiose schemes is an idealist and he knows it ! He knows, too, that many of us are laughing, sneering, pitying—yet he holds on. ' Bitterness, disillusioning—the nausea that certain unlooked-for and hateful forms of the human animal create—will never make me renounce that ideality, that faith of mine.' Go on, brave spirit ! For my own poor self, I am as far from contempt of such an ambition as I am from belief in its realisation ; but if it will not be realised, it will not be wasted. Such purposes of man resemble the great forces of nature rather in their essence than in their results. They are like the calling into existence of a whole breeze to waft one boat on its way : some gets hold of the tiny sail ; the rest blows round it, over it, past it, and all goes three times as fast as the little craft ; and yet nothing less would have served.

Finally, I quote the ' candid friend,' from the letter of a writer whose position is a fair guarantee of as much impartiality as can be expected from any Italian in a matter of art. After describing the *personale* of the directorate, he says : ' But how much money has been spent, and how much might have been done with that money ! To-day there has been the great and unexpected good fortune of the " Cena delle Beffe," for which, if Sigr. Benelli is much indebted to the Argentina the Argentina, in turn, is much indebted to Sigr. Benelli. But if that had not happened? Then staging—gorgeous if you like, but nothing more than staging—and demanding an impossible amount of effort, like that of the " Midsummer Night's Dream " of your Shakespeare. What interest for us do you suppose there can be in an entire translation of that poem, which I should call simply a piece of imaginative extravagance? I saw it in London at Daly's Theatre, but, then, that was another thing. No attempt at grand comedy, it was purely and simply the fairy play, which was performed with vigorous life in so fine a theatre, in so large a metropolis—which was, moreover, the legitimate mother of the work!' The criticisms of the Teatro Argentina have a sound common-sense ring. Those of Shakespeare's play are so characteristic, illustrating the Italian's point of view, that I did not go out of my way to exclude them.

The undertaking of the Teatro Argentina can hardly fail to be a pleasant subject for the critic, whatever his views may be as to its actual success. The same cannot, unfortunately, be said of the next topic to come under discussion.

A serious split has arisen between the actor-managers. The dispute seems at first sight a trumpery one, but it is touched upon here at some length because it affects the very important and, just now, much canvassed question of the relative merits of a national and an imported drama.

First, then, the facts which are beyond dispute. There is an old existing society of actor-managers— ' Unione dei Capo Comici ' is its title—which was founded in 1808 ; for the Italian actors have long been a thriving and more or less united body. It is only in recent years, however, that a band of writers for the stage has collected together and formed themselves a society for the protection of their interests, under the title of ' La Società degli Autori Italiani,' with their headquarters in Milan. Now, about six months since,[1] they made approaches to the ' Unione dei Capo Comici,' with the result that the latter agreed to enter into the now notorious ' Patto d'Alleanza,' under which the members of the ' Unione ' bound themselves to represent only works which formed the repertory of the ' Società '—they receiving specially reduced terms as a consideration. Now, there exist in Italy certain agents for the sale and production of plays, chiefly foreign. Of these agents there is one who deals chiefly in German works, one for English, and some few French; one, I believe, for Scandinavian, &c. But the most prominent, and, for our present purpose the one important one, is a certain Re Riccardi, who holds the copyright of the bulk of the French works.

Now, the ' pact of alliance ' was a sweeping affair. Foreign plays—French especially—are very popular on the Italian stage. Many companies—Dina Galli's and Sichel's, for instance—draw from them the main part of their repertory. The leaders of such companies naturally became anxious, and they seceded from the old ' Unione,' which thereby lost a large part of its active members.

Thus the matter stands with regard to the facts; but each side naturally gives a different description of the motives which animate the partisans, and the probable result of the encounter. We are told, on the one hand, that the whole affair has its origin in the personal animosity between two men, Re Riccardi aforesaid, and Marco Praga, president[2] of the ' Società degli Autori,' who hate each other like Italians; and that their motive is—professionally speaking—to cut each other's throats.

[1] June 1910. [2] Now resigned.

And that the 'Società' really wants to stop the performance of French plays altogether ; in which, if they could succeed, they would be not without the sympathy of a large part of the Italian theatre-goers—the more thoughtful of whom are both personally irritated by, and patriotically incensed against, the light-armed French invader.

On the other side, nothing is said about personalities ; and the movement of the 'Società' is represented as merely a desire to make the agents, including the said Riccardi, come in and submit to their rules : in fact, generally to make themselves, for good or evil, arbiters of the situation.

Two comments very naturally suggest themselves. Firstly, as it is quite clear that the submission of these outsiders must necessarily have been a matter of months at the least, certain companies whose whole repertory, practically, was in the hands of Sigr. Riccardi, would have to give up acting for the time, or suddenly learn a new set of plays, whose character might not have suited them or their public so well. It is not surprising that these companies chose resignation as an alternative. The split among the 'Capo Comici' is a thing therefore that the leaders of the 'Società' could have, and ought to have, foreseen. Secondly, if their object was not to prohibit, or at any rate to reduce, the production of French plays, it is not very clear what advantage the Italian author (for whose sake action was taken) would gain. And the offer of the society, of reduced terms to the 'Capo Comici,' was clearly a bribe, not given without the hope of a corresponding material advantage.

However it be, the quarrel is a very pretty quarrel as it stands. The papers make the most of it. Once a week, if we may trust the glib lucubrations of the illustrious penny-a-liner, some fresh 'Capo Comico ' gives

in his resignation and adheres to the other camp.
Once a week, some revered author, dashing actor, or
weather-wise critic, expands into a column and a half
of commonplace reflections. The spacious cloudlands of
philosophy are exhausted to produce that jet of steam
which shall drive one of the rival's pistons a thought the
faster; and yet, like the Queen in ' Alice in Wonderland,'
with all their running, they seem just to keep abreast,
and no more. To the press, then, it gives copy; to
the public, conversation. Even the actors—though the
statement sounds rather like that of the huntsman,
to the effect that ' the fox enjoyed it '—draw some
fun, not to say profit, out of the affair. Picturesque
disputes like these relieve the serene monotony of a
professional existence: give them a fresh interest beyond
that of the too persistent ' rule of three '; and the
continued statement that two people are quarrelling is,
like the fluttering of flags in the piazza, likely to attract
a crowd; while the intelligent public goes, as it is at
liberty to go, to inspect each combatant in turn; to
judge whose powers they rate most highly; whose style
they like best; on whose chance of success they will,
with the most confidence, put down their uttermost
centesimo.

The object of this introduction has been to show
how the state of social and political Italy of to-day
affects the state of her stage. I have dealt first with
the effect on the actors and acting, and the result
has been a criticism, which may seem ungracious, of
small and often paltry details. But there is another
side to the theatre—the plays. And here the relation
of life to art is larger and more gracious, making art
in her turn ' lovelier in lordship of things.' I do not
mean that in the present day the writers of plays are
greater than the actors of them. Far from it: they are

fewer and less able. But I do mean that the effect upon them of the surrounding life is more beneficial, more inspiring, more hopeful for future success.

A slight glance at almost any page of history will show us that the great periods of art—far from developing, as we might have imagined in times of general tranquillity—have accompanied, or immediately followed, years of warfare and stress. Attic sculpture and drama, medieval art, the Elizabethan stage, were not only cradled, but grew up and matured, in hearing of the surges of great international struggles.

Art or literature might, in truth, just as well expect to triumph by retiring into the cloister, as man, by this means, to train himself for feats of endurance and strength.

Art, to be mighty, must be able to dictate to the world. True ! But she must first understand the world. We cannot win battles, or paint pictures, by sitting in silence, however complete, in the midst of surroundings, however fair.

And this impulse is all the more vivid, immediate, and pure, in proportion as the great events are recent and near home. Lengthen the line either way, and its slackness is wonderfully increased. It is the old problem of the Mandarin which we find in Balzac. Let anyone balance the emotions he feels on reading of an accident which caused the death of twenty persons at a distance, with that which he feels from seeing one man lying in the road gravely hurt. It is the near, the immediate, which, out of all proportion, tells.

Now, I suppose, in spite of all the talk we exercise our imaginations with on the subject of invasion, there is no life more easy and certain, and therefore more uninspiring, than life in an English country house. Our walks, our meals, our pleasures, our engagements, may

be mapped out with certain freedom from interference
by any other tyrants than bad weather and ill-health.
The butcher or fishmonger may forget to call; but that
is the worst act—Is it of God or the King's enemies?—
that can affect us.[1] Then, further, consider that this
state has been developing to its present perfection for
hundreds of years; that to the origin of our court, our
Parliament, our system of justice, no living man's
grandfather is any nearer than we are; that the last
exchange of musketry by banded armies on English
soil was in the year 1685 : and I suppose your
resultant is a state of things unequalled among all
that is peaceable, easy-going, complaisant; unmatched
as narcotic to all great emotion, and therefore to
all great art.

Turn then to Italy, and back some sixty or seventy
years. If one picture is rose colour, the other is
sanguine or sable. Do you think—you who walk, guide-
book in hand, through the streets of Milan, or of Brescia—
of the bloody work that was done there in 1848 ? Of
the barricades across the streets, the half-armed, half-
naked crowd ; the whistling bullets of the soldiers ? Of
the butcheries of the Austrian marshal; of the tears of
the Italian mother; of the empty places in the desolated
rooms ? No ; you are among the mild smiles of Luini's
angels or by the faded dream of God on earth, supping
with His chosen. When you walk the Calli of Venice or
bask on the Lido's opal shore, do you think of the months
during which desperate, hopeless men, with the door
of support shut behind them, with the might of one of
the greatest nations of Europe at their gates, wrought
on that smooth sand, before that azure sea, whose waves

---

[1] Since this was written the coal strike has revealed a new danger :
freezing as well as starvation; but I fear that Demos Britannicus will
have forgotten it in six months' time.

seem to lisp of ease and tranquillity, the bloody and toilsome business of war ? When the dull sound of the cannon without, the slow progress of starvation within, awoke the morning with terror and shut in the evening with despair ? Do you think of that hero, with his strangely commercial face and bearing, who incited, maintained, comforted, disposed ; and when the end came—practical as he was heroic—went into exile without a word ? No ; you have been standing before the Bridge of Sighs thinking old sentimental tales of Foscari or Faliero, or feeding pigeons in the Piazza, thinking of nothing at all. If you touch modern Italian politics at all, it is to comment on the innumerable Piazze Vittorio Emanuele, or grumble at the formalities of the Dogana.

Yet these are things that represent and typify the life of the Italian to-day. He is flattered that you should visit his country, inspect her movements, read the stories of her past great men. He will talk to you of such with intelligent interest and literary appreciation. But do not suppose that they represent his national life any more than yours is shut up in the Tower. His heart and his eyes are elsewhere ; and if you talk practical problems to him with intelligence you will get answers of a very different sort.

The bearing of all this keen memory of the immediate past, and this keen hope for the immediate future, upon the art of the playwright, does not, perhaps, at first sight show very clearly.

It does not seem to us a sound reason for a man writing good plays that his father was executed, or his mother flogged at the stake. But the suggestion; in reality; is not so ridiculous as it sounds. Great events awake noble impulses, and once aroused they irradiate all round. And the poet writes better verse, the en-

gineer builds better bridges, the orator makes better
speeches, the draftsman draws better laws; because
their fathers won their way to freedom up a dark and
stormy path.

There is another side to the question, too; and one
that, though not so wide, is perhaps more evident.

There may not be—if there is it will not hurt the argument—any kind of office or employment in use in Italy
now which is not known in England as well. But there
are some, if not many, that produce a very different
effect from their novelty. The officials of this country;
the merchants, bankers, tradesmen—even street rogues—
have been established institutions for years back, and;
though they enter on our stage as characters, the effect
they make is produced not by their mere presence, but
by the part they take in the drama. In Italy, on the
other hand, the introduction of characters which are
types of new offices, professions, callings, sets the audience
on the alert at once and often redeems an otherwise
insipid play. The movements of the ' onorevole,'[1] to take
one instance alone: the indication of his various types
and characteristics, are watched with an interest which
certainly would not be accorded in England to an M.P.,
simply as such, upon the stage.

I think we are coming to the end of our general
observations. I have tried to clear the ground so that
we can go straight on. If in so doing, I have used words
and brought in considerations which seem to some of
my readers out of proportion to the subject, I can only
plead that though the importance of the theatre as a
visible fact is obvious, there are many ways of regarding
it. Some I know there are still, who, regardless of the
fact that it took its origin in the Church, look upon it

---

[1] ' Honourable ': the ordinary way of describing a member of the
lower house in Italy.

as an invention of the devil. There are those also who, on the other hand, regard it as a place where sermons and moral lessons may be delivered, and the race of mankind improved—this class, oddly enough, comprising certain distinguished actors ; [1] and a third class regard it simply as a place where they may be relieved, without serious effort, from the tediousness of their own selves. I can fall in with none of these. I find the theatre—it will perhaps help to clear the ground if the author states his point of view—a place where one can indulge in the pleasures of vicarious action, and in such action have all the delight, and none of the disadvantages, attending similar action in real life. There are many fruits delightful in the eating which leave a bitter taste in the mouth ; there are many things which wear the braveries of romance and excitement in the doing, which delay and reflection strip bare to a brutal reality beneath. But in the course of a stage play, we can have all the excitement of action without the subsequent remorse. Our imaginations will credit us with the honours of others, our consciences will never accuse us of their crimes.

It is a theme which seems simple enough ; but which, like a simple phrase in a musical symphony, may be expanded to almost infinite variations. ' What is the theatre ? ' demand the double basses, in a growling rhythm ; and the thrilling and flashing of the violins, leaping from point to point, now advancing, now retreating, now circling round, make answer.

It is to sit in darkness and look on light ; to be isolated in one of a thousand cells, and yet in sympathetic company ; to look out thence undisturbed and watch the

---

[1] Our own Henry Irving is a typical instance ; another, Tommaso Salvini (Chap. III.) But the attitude of mind is not peculiar to the leaders of the stage.

life of the world with all its manifold interests, with
its depths and its heights, its suffering and its success ;
its apathy, its failure, its despair. And to watch it
no longer confused, as it seems to our every-day eyes
and ears, but marvellously ordered and disposed, as
if we had passed from the wild forest into some sweet
woodland dale, where the flowers were defended and
cared for. To follow the great deeds of life, as it were
by the aid of some subtle commentator, who clears our
difficulties without letting his presence appear. To
enter into the mind of the legislator, bridge the thought
of the engineer, mount with the aspirations of the poet ;
aye, and crawl too with crime, disgust, degradation ;
totter with enervation and despair. To strive with the
toiler and not grow weary ; scheme with the criminal
and not be stained. To stand before the King awed
by his majesty, and then enter his private study and
see what is behind that outward show of pomp. To
be met by the siren ; to feel her burning eyes fixed in
yours, her breath warm upon your cheek, her hair sweet
with the perfume as a summer eve ; to come close, almost
lip to lip until . . . and then a moment after, to
see her wearily laying aside the paraphernalia of charm,
undoing the strings that held the idol beauty in its place ;
patiently, methodically, listlessly, shutting the doors
and setting in order for the next day.

And the clumsy may enjoy, there and there only,
the delights of the dance, the infinite delicacies of motion ;
he to whom beauty never gave aught but a contemptuous
side-glance may come out from his shadow and bask
in her noonday radiance ; and he whom society found
too uncouth or strange, for want either of frock-coat
or an air to wear it, may pass at his ease among dukes
and countesses ; and he whose tongue is hobbled may
engage in repartee with the wits of the age.   Where he

who has vainly tried to soar on the poor wings of his own ambition may mount bird-like in the air ; command armies, direct kingdoms; flaunt the grandeur of priesthood; rule by his words the angry crowd; win by his smiles the most delightful sympathy : and his thoughts may refine, expand, sweep upward with irresistible beauty and force, till the gates of pearl open before him to the sounding of cymbals and the thrilling of lutes. Or if he fall, it shall be like Lucifer : to fall with terrible uproar, driven forward by the hand of well nigh almighty Gabriel himself : but, unlike Lucifer, to rise again next day, fresh and unhurt, to attain other successes by following out new paths.

This is the theatre as I know it. That great institution whose officers have as trying and toilsome a duty as any known to man ; and to whom, if my thoughts could affect the great balance of doom, I would mightily pray the Maker of man—man with all his frailties and his aspirations—to pardon the weaknesses they may be guilty of, for the sake of the bounties they bestow.

At any rate, is it not worth perhaps a half-hour of study, some warm words, and the taking in vain of a name of dignity here and there, before we come to analyse, divide, and describe ?

CHAPTER II

ITALIAN PLAYS AND PLAYWRIGHTS

ITALIAN plays of to-day are like Italian wine. No great art or education goes to the making of them. They will not keep or carry well. But, consumed on the spot, they have a wonderfully real and sound flavour. We rarely or never find in them signs of obvious means or convention. We are nearly always convinced of the reality of the personages who occupy the scene, of the facts of the situations, difficulties, problems, through which these personages have to pass. But we do not always find them, nor the times at which we are allowed to see them in their dealing with those difficulties or problems, well or wisely chosen.

To put it into technical language: the life of an Italian play is generally good and real ; the construction often very bad. There is an obvious tendency to study real life, instead of models for writing: the Italian having a perpetual fear that he may spoil the spontaneity of his art. That is all very well, provided you have first an art to spoil. And in writing the plays, as in acting them, if a little more attention was given to form, the work of the Italian writers— sufficient in abundance and variety—would acquire permanence, for which it can never hope as things

33   D

are. But if it were only a question of permanence, perhaps the Italian might pass the criticism with a shrug, or reply to it with Goethe's,

> If I should choose to preach posterity,
> Where would you get contemporary fun ?

His business, he might say, is to get home now. He must let the future raise her monuments as she will. But it is evident that to-day also suffers ; that effects are missed because of want of study on the author's part. For the dramatic writer has two things to consider : he has his characters, themes, situations to choose ; and he has also to find the best means for conveying them to his audience. And to do this he must not only study mankind in general life as the subject—which the Italian writer does well—but he must study them in a special department of life, namely, a theatrical audience, as his object ; which he does far less well. Often there are instances of a failure to bring out and distinguish the real issues ; with a result that things often end in a confusion on the stage, and sometimes perhaps in the mind of the dramatist himself.

Perhaps this is a convenient point to pause and explain the different classes into which Italian plays are divided and the terms used to describe them. There is no generic term for a play in Italian. You must speak of it under one of the heads : *farsa, commedia, dramma, tragedia*. *Farsa*, I think, exactly corresponds to our farce. *Commedia* is any play which does not depend upon buffoonery and physically ridiculous situations for its humour (on the one side), and does not end with a death (on the other). No matter how serious the issues, no matter how sad the result, it is a *commedia* if it ends without loss of life. The *dramma* and *tragedia* alike end in death ; but the former is concerned with personal and domestic issues ; the latter with larger and more heroic

ones.   The line is hard to draw in words, but in practice
there is not likely to be any confusion.[1]

The farce proper has rather less importance on the
Italian stage than it has upon ours, and may be dismissed in a few words.   Boisterous knock-about humour
does not, on the whole, commend itself to the Italian.
His nature is fed by two main streams of passion and
intellect.   It has not, like ours, a Mesopotamia, fertile
with the sentimental, the picturesque, the merry.   His
sense of humour must perforce dwell on one of these
two ; and it has naturally chosen intellect.   This, then,
is apt to be the character of the Italian's laughter.
Frivolous they certainly are at times and in places, but
with a more intellectual frivolity than ours.

The farces that one is constantly meeting are few
in number and may be rather summarily dealt with.
I am not sure how many of the few are native Italian.
Some are obviously translated from the French ; and
sometimes even from the English.   I have met our old
friend ' Whitebait at Greenwich,' disguised as a translation from the French into Milanese dialect.   At Venice,
especially after a dialect play, I have seen farces, the
humour of which consisted in having a Venetian soldier
among a lot of non-Venetians; and hearing his comments
on the stupidity and strange speech of those about him :
an easy way of getting a laugh, which no doubt is practised in other cities besides.   We come now to a class
of play more peculiar to Italy—light comedies in one act
—which we should be inclined, but mistakenly, to set
down as farces.   In England they would be such ; for
the situations, and often the characters, are grotesque ;
but their treatment by the Italian writer is in the style of
pure comedy, and from this the plays justly take rank.
Many good dramatic authors of to-day spend their energies

A *dramma* is never written in verse ; a *tragedia* often is, though
not always.

in producing plays such as these ; of which perhaps the best known among those which I saw, ' Un' Avventura in Viaggio ' (A Travelling Adventure), and the most comical, ' Non Fare ad Altri ' (Do not do to Others !) are both by Roberto Bracco.

In the first, a husband, separated from his wife, is approached by a friend, who begs the loan of his chambers (where he carries on ' business ' on his own account) for the reception of a lady whom he has met on the journey. This proves to be the separated wife, who was coy to the friend's approaches until he produced a card with her husband's address on it, whereon she became very naturally interested. The attempts of the friend at love-making, and his discomfiture on the reconciliation of husband and wife, are very diverting and quite legitimate comedy.

In the other, the police magistrate is interrogating a man caught in the act of escaping over his (the magistrate's) garden wall. The delinquent confesses to burglary: but, on his being searched, his portfolio is found to contain a portrait of the magistrate's wife, with an inscription. Furious, the magistrate assumes possession of it, summons his spouse ; and, with the air of a Rhadamanthus, takes from his pocket a photograph which he presents to her. But, alas ! it is not ' the ' photograph ; but one of their maid-servant, and also bears an inscription ! The end is very characteristic of Italian fun-making. The police-sergeant is beguiled by the burglar, as a last score, to confess to being Teresina's young man. Still more furious, the magistrate orders his arrest. On the highly ceremonious dismissal of the burglar, the wife remarks : ' When you are seriously in love, good Mr. Magistrate, you are vindictive towards your rivals. You punish the sergeant for your servant, but haven't felt the need of punishing the robber of your wife.' And on the splutterings of the husband towards a satisfactory reply, the curtain falls.

Such comedy as this, though amusing, is limited in scope, being simply an attempt to develop certain whimsical situations. There follows the play which is to interpret life itself. We have under this description technically four, but really three, classes of plays to deal with: light comedies, serious comedies and *drammi*, and tragedies. The latter are, on the whole, written on a distinct plan; often in verse, and of a more lyrical nature than the others; dealing with situations, and making use of phrases, which do not occur in ordinary life. The more serious of the *commedie* and the *drammi* have certain points in common, but they have also points which are particular to each: and it will be best to deal with these first.

For reasons that we have already suggested, comedy has rather tended to enter the preserves of farce, than farce to invade the castle of comedy. It is a fact that will again have to be referred to in writing of Italian acting. The drama in Italy is far more a purely intellectual affair than it is with us: it is less dependent on external associations; it goes more directly from brain to brain. There are many little devices which go to make an English comedy picturesque, the want of which makes an Italian comedy (to an Englishman at least) seem barren; and which, though not farcical in themselves, are of such a nature that they can be used in farce. And therefore in England light comedy (as light comedy-acting) tends to degenerate into farce; whereas in Italy, in plays as well as acting, farce tends to rise into the manner of comedy. In certain plays, Italian writers have attempted to copy the French light pieces: not with any great success—at least, in those that the writer has seen. They are often ludicrous enough, but,

when an Italian author begins to deal with actions and
results, like a class of children with a new master, they
are apt to get out of hand, to riot to and fro, to jump
on each other's back in quick succession ; without their
play having any of those grace notes, witticisms, or
divagations which excuse, if they do not make reasonable,
the Frenchman's absurdities.

As most of what remains to be said concerns the
more serious type of play only, I think it will be more
convenient, and will lead to less repetition, if we go on
to speak of them, only adding a note where necessary
to say where the remarks made concern the subject of
light comedy as well.

We are struck at the outset by a fact that Italian
plays,[1] with a very few exceptions, are occupied with
the relations of husband and wife. The two single-act
pieces mentioned answer this description. These are the
principal characters in some longer ones :—

> *La Crisi.* Husband, wife, wife's lover.
> *Il Malefico Anello.* The same.
> *Fra due Guanciali.* Wife, husband, husband's mistress.
> *La Modella.* Husband, wife, and two lovers.
> *Tristi Amori.* Husband, wife, wife's lover.
> *La Moglie del Dottore.* Husband, wife, wife's former lover.
> *Papà Eccellenza.* Husband, wife, wife's father, and wife's
> flirt.'

Even when you do not see one of the parties on the
stage—as in the case of the wife in 'Ne Paese della Fortuna '—the play turns on their existence. And very rarely
is it (as it is in the dialect play of 'Acqua Cheta ') that
the plots hang on the innocent loves of two young
people. So, whether in laughter or tears there is a
monotony ; the silent monotony of autumn which has

---

[1] These observations apply to light comedy as well.

ousted the playful variety of spring. Whether in laughter
or tears, we are brought into the company of those who
have drawn their nourishment from the sun and the
rain of experience, and who, in thought or action, are
ripe for fruit-bearing. There is a power, a reason, which
impresses, but no impulsiveness or heedlessness, which
delights, in surprising. Hermione would find other
sad and tried matrons to bear her company ; but the
charming confidence of Perdita would be out of place.
We must not, however, pass away with the idea of a
too great sameness. There are plays on patriotic themes
—such as ' Romanticismo '—absolutely startling in its
real intensity ; or ' La Regina,' inferior, but instinct
with the pathos of Italian country life ; or ' Come le
Foglie,' which searches the heart of a middle-class family ;
or that delightful ' Commedia della Peste,' where we
play with the fires of immorality, but so gentle are
they that our fingers are but comfortably warmed.
These, and such as these, relieve the monotony, while
adding to the power. And to travel outside the ' Scena
di prosa,' we may make an occasional visit to the dialect
theatre for this, if for no other reason, that there we may
scrape acquaintance with Innocence, if we meet with
few adventures; and may wipe out the stain of illicit
longings with fresh loves and flaxen hair.

With regard to the manner of the Italian playwright
there is perhaps more criticism, and less praise to be
bestowed. His plays are open to the charge of being
wanting in art. The charge is partly true ; nevertheless,
it is easy to be misled in pressing it home. Art is a
means to attain an end. When the end the foreign
writer proposes to himself is the same as our own, it is
easy to judge him : but when it is a different one, it
is easy to be misled into supposing that he means
the same thing as ourselves, and that by clumsiness he

has missed his aim.   With that reservation we will begin our remarks.

The use of the stage conventions is different in England and in France.   We, on our part, wish to realise —to dispense with them altogether.   They, on the other hand, wish to accept them frankly.   It is with them, to take a simple instance, quite enough when a person means to be hidden, for a fern or a fire-screen to conceal him from the most penetrating eyes.   Both these points of view are logical, though the English one is hard to realise in practice.   The Italian, on the other hand, has followed a kind of hesitating middle course : not being bold enough to dispense with convention altogether, yet not using it with freedom or confidence.

There are on the Italian ' Scena di prosa ' none of the conventional characters of the French ; the beneficial grandmother, the confidante, and so forth.   On the other hand, we do find conventions used for getting the characters on or off, explaining facts which the audience need to know, and so forth ; yet they are used not with the frank avowal of the French writer, but with a kind of hesitating attempt to make them appear real.

The following openings of plays, used to introduce the principal characters to the audience and to indicate the scope of the action, are chosen as showing the characteristics of the different ways.   The first is from ' Le Marquis de Priola,' by Henri Lavedan.   Scene : ante-chamber to a ball-room : Marquis de Priola and ' Jeune homme ' in the background : in front, at the side, two gentlemen.

1st Gent. Tell me, who is the gentleman sitting at . . . with the young man ?
2nd Gent. The Marquis de Priola.
1st Gent. The modern Don Juan, the ladies' man ?
2nd Gent. The same.

1st *Gent.* I have often heard speak of him. It is the first time that I have seen him. I don't like him.

2nd *Gent.* Men never do like him.

1st *Gent.* Where does he come from ?

2nd *Gent.* His father is an Italian, his mother an English woman.

1st *Gent.* Not French, then ?

2nd *Gent.* Yes, naturalised.

1st *Gent.* And the young man with him ?

2nd *Gent.* I heard his name just now. A very common one. Pierre Morain.

1st *Gent.* Don't know him. Let's go back to the ball-room. Here it is mortally . . .   [*Exeunt.*

Compare with the foregoing scene, the one following the opening to ' Il Cucculo ' (The Cuckoo) of E. A. Butti. The scene is a public room in an hotel at some bathing resort. There are on the stage two groups, of which the nearest to the foot-lights consists of the Countess Ortensia and her mother. Between these two pass Calpurina and Lucrezia, two girls (sisters). Lucrezia has entered.

(*Voice of Calpurina outside.*) Lucrezia, Lucrezia !

Luc. Hurry up, Tortoise. What do you want ?

Calp. (*appearing*). Let's wait for mother here. You know she particularly told us to . . .

Luc. I don't care a button. If she wants to mount guard over us, she ought to get up earlier, or sacrifice the time she spends dyeing her hair. We're late already. All the young men will be leaving the beach soon. If we don't go and get ready, we might just as well not bathe at all. (*Seeing Ortensia, with a short sarcastic laugh*) Oh ! The Countess Sibari, in deshabille.

Calp. How pretty she is !

Luc. Pretty ! She is fair. All fair women look pretty at a distance. Funny that she's alone.

Calp. She's not alone. There's the old lady with her.

Luc. The old lady doesn't count. It's just like saying

that a dog's not alone because he's got his tail. I meant funny that she hasn't got any of her butterflies round her.

Calp. A great deal run after, isn't she ?

Luc. I believe you ! Coquettish, rich, a widow. You are too young, Calpurina, you can't understand what good luck it is to be a widow. And to think that I shall never be one !

Calp. And why not ?

Luc. Because it is a long and difficult affair. To become a widow, it isn't enough to find a husband, you've got to lose him. See what a business it is. . . . Puff ! A beastly life an unmarried girl. . . . (*Changing tone*) Quick, let's go and jump into the water. It is still the best thing that remains to do on the earth. (*They move towards the exit between the two groups—to the Countess Ortensia in an insinuating voice*) Good day, Countess. Good day, Sigra Nobelli.

Ort. (*with cold courtesy*). Good day.

Luc. Have you had your bath already ?

Ort. No, I don't feel quite the thing this morning.

Luc. Take care of yourself. Your health is very precious. (*They move towards the door and stop again to speak to the other group.*) Oh, Signora Lasio ! and our good doctor, caught ' in flagrante.'

Sigra Nobelli (*low, to Ortensia*). Two young monkeys, I can't stand them.

Ort. Poor girls. You must be indulgent to them. They wear two such very reassuring names, and they can't find a husband.

Luc. (*to Sigra Lasio.*) If so, good-bye till lunch time.

Sigra L. I hope you'll enjoy yourselves.

Calp. Thanks.

Luc. (*to Calp. as they go out*). How thick they are, those two. They are simply nauseating. [*Exeunt.*

Now, at first glance these two scenes might seem much alike ; but a second will reveal several important differences. In the first scene the ' deux messieurs ' are unnamed characters and do not take any further

part in the play. They might just as well be designated
' Prologue.' The two girls in the second play re-appear
and take part in the action. But even more striking is
the way in which the ' prologue ' delivers its information
and goes out, with hardly a pretence that its disappearance
has any other reason than to make room for the main
characters. We do not therefore seek to call their
remarks in or out of character, natural or unnatural.
We are simply grateful for the information given. The
two girls, on the other hand, come on in a violent hurry
to be off to their bath ; and then delay, successively,
to discuss a woman that they might have discussed
any other day or time : and to sneer at a couple across
which they (on their own showing) must have been
running constantly. The first scene is a frank disregard
of nature ; the second an attempt to seem natural
without success. The last extract given is, of course,
not the universal mode of opening an Italian play. But
there is often a want of crispness and conciseness about
the beginning ; so that it is some time before you
understand who the characters are, and in what relation
they stand towards one another. Sometimes, again, but
more rarely, the cardinal situation is flung at your head
with an almost brutal suddenness; as in ' Tristi Amori,'
when the curtain draws up and discloses the lovers in
each other's arms. It is like a douche of cold water on
the body, which makes it difficult for the mind at that
moment to register any sensations. But the tendency
on the whole is to begin in an easy, undeliberated way,
with no very conscious effort to explain to the spectator what he wants to know at any particular place or
by any particular time.

With regard to the ending, either of the separate
acts or of the whole play, the light comedies are much
more apt to end with a pointed situation, or a definite

cadence of words than plays wherein the themes are great and weighty ones.   It would rather seem as if the writer felt that point would be pertness ; that the great and serious emotions of life have no need to be cut and finished off neatly, like the end of an embroidered band ; one method resembling (indeed, to compare small things with great) the musical exactness of Mozart, the other the less elegant but more mastering flow of Wagner. In one point at least, I cannot help thinking that the Italian writer would improve the composition of his play by a little study.   Nothing is clearer than that you must not comment on a situation until you have explained it to the audience.   Yet it is easy to point to cases where this principle is transgressed.   In 'La Crisi' (The Crisis), by Marco Praga, the theme is the return of a retired colonel to his brother's house, and his discovery that the latter's wife, newly married, has a lover.   The scene opens after lunch ; the lover is on the stage for a few minutes only.   He says little during this time (which is a matter for no surprise, for nothing passes to tell you what he is) ; and when the wife comes and says to him ' Drop it,' meaning his taciturnity, it is difficult from these hasty words to grasp the fact that he has been moody and silent all through a meal at which the favour of your company has not been requested.   It is hard, also, to realise in a flash how out of place is this man's presence at the meeting of two brothers for ten years separated.   And so the suspicions of the soldier brother seem rather too pene-trating instead of being perfectly natural as they really are.   In fact this lover, who only appears for a few moments, and is talked of all through the play, is rather like Queen Elizabeth in ' The Critic.'   Perhaps it would have been better had the resemblance been complete ; or at any rate that he should either not have been introduced at all, or have been on the stage long enough for his nature and relations with the other characters to have been made clear.

Yet another, and perhaps a more convincing, instance of the same thing. In ' Il Malefico Anello ' (The Baneful Ring), the scene to which you are introduced is the wife of a man of high position, who hates and lives apart from her husband, and has an ardent, though not yet an accepted, lover. The latter, puzzled by what to the audience, if they noticed anything at all, might equally well be her coldness, her shyness, or the inability of the actress personating the character to express any definite emotion, keeps saying, ' There is a mystery about you that I don't understand.' The hearer cannot make out the bent of all these searching remarks : but it proves later on, that there *is* a mystery; for the lady has had a former lover. This, however, is not revealed until late in the play ; and meantime the mystery remains to the audience why the lover persists in making these remarks without any apparent cause ; the actor, in this case, divining more than the audience can, when exactly the reverse ought to be the case.

Serious Italian plays have, however, one advantage over their counterparts in England. In Italy, plays of the problem class—plays, that is, which state the characters and the situation, and leave the working out of the latter to the three or four acts that are provided—are in demand, as much as, if not more than, amongst ourselves. Such plays necessarily produce long dissertations, interminable arguments, weighty reasonings. But with the Italian such reasonings and dissertations are natural to the people in their real life ; with us, they are not. With them the meeting of a circle of men is commonly the signal for the formation of an impromptu debating society ; wherein themes, propounded on the spur of the moment, are taken to pieces and put together again by men who do it as a kind of mental exercise, and forget it a moment afterwards. Such discussions spring from no principle and generate no heat. But if a play depends largely on discussions which the characters hold about themselves and their intimate interests, it is easy to see how this habit of academic discussion clears the ground. It renders natural the brilliance that must be displayed to make these conversations interesting on the stage, while furnishing to the speaker what the parallel bars and the vaulting-horse are to the athlete who is preparing for the serious contest. But—and perhaps depending on this—there is another quality which distinguishes the Italian play from the English. In the latter, the conversations are always abundant and often interesting, but they are not in themselves the action of the drama. They are the flesh which covers the dry bones and tense sinews of the body ; and, though without them its existence would be grotesque, they do not direct or control it. It is still an event which precipitates the crisis. To take ' The Second Mrs. Tanqueray ' as an example; the catastrophe is caused by the reappearance of one of the lady's former lovers, and his attempt to marry her step-daughter. In an Italian play, on the other hand, it is not uncommon to find the result brought about without any external happenings, such as biography could chronicle. We are led past the obvious material world. We are bidden to enter into a world where ideas, to us as invisible as spectres, are precipitated into reality ; where these, armed with a force nearly as definite and far more terrible than our own muscular powers, drag, push and hunt us invading mortals to destruction. The reader, perhaps, thinks this an exaggerated picture. I will quote from one play, ' Diritti dell' Anima ' (The Soul's Rights), by

Giacosa. I shall be surprised if he keeps his opinion till the end of the quotation.

The play is a comedy in one act. The characters—a man, his wife, a friend, a servant. The lover (the wife's) is dead—a suicide. Hear how it happened. She has written the lover a letter which the husband has found. ' Ah ! ' We picture, perhaps a passionate declaration, perhaps a desperate leave-taking ? Listen, then. ' You write me that if I don't answer, you will come back at once. I love my husband, that is my answer. This, this alone, always this. I beg of you not to torment me any more.' Simple and effective, apparently. What should be the end of it but confidence renewed and a quiet breakfast-table ? What is the end of it ? A passionate and hopeless parting. By what steps is this inconceivable straying from a turnpike road effected ? Listen again ; longer, and more patiently this time. There have been other letters found, it seems, all of the same nature, except one which was written when Luciano (the lover) had an accident ; which the husband describes as a splendid letter, noble, high-toned, and offers to his friend to read.

Mario. No, no, no.

Paolo. Only hear . . .

Ma. No, I'd rather not.

Pa. It only speaks of me, of a youth of friendliness. It speaks of you, too . . . it says . . .

Ma. No, please. I know what sort of woman my relative is, and I don't need proofs of her honesty. Why do you go back to those unfortunate [?] letters. Is it so grievous that you should have known of them ?

Pa. Grievous ! It's grievous that you won't be at the pains to deplore a false relative who tried to rob me . . .

Ma. Let be. He's dead, and he has robbed you of nothing, and if he had lived, he wouldn't have robbed you of anything either. Anna knew . . .

Pa. And this, and this! You think it little. Is this grievous? I never have had the shadow of a doubt on Anna's account. Never; there never even passed through my mind the thought . . . but it is one thing not to doubt and not to have thought, and another to possess the palpable proof of her faith and her love—I love my husband. It's the refrain of all her letters. [He sees the turnpike road before him at the start, at least!]

Ma. Was it really necessary that she should say it to you!

Pa. She didn't say it to me. She said it to him, to him she said it, you understand? Luciano had all the qualities which would go to beguile a woman. He was a younger and handsomer man than I am, he spoke well and was full of ardour and courage. [He begins to look aside.]

Ma. You take a pleasure in praising him now, eh?

Pa. Grievous! [how a word has set him going!] When you had burnt those papers as you wanted to: if I had come to know of that love one fine day who could have got out of my head . . .

Ma. Certainty makes you suspicious.

Pa. What do you mean?

Ma. It's true. If you had had warning a year ago, perhaps all this would never have happened. I ought to have opened your eyes. Separated from you perhaps, Luciano would not have killed himself.

Pa. And I should have had no proof.

Ma. Your ease of mind is dearly bought—for others.

Pa. I don't pretend to be sentimental over Luciano's fate.

Ma. I'm not speaking of him.

Pa. Of whom, then?

Ma. Of your wife. Think what her state of mind must be!

Pa. Do you think she attributes . . .

Ma. I'm sure of it.

Pa. I have seen her in great grief, but not in agitation.

Ma. You see things in their continuity; I, every now and then. Besides, Anna is mistress of herself.

Pa. And has done her duty . .

Ma. Not for the first time.

Pa. I shall be able to bring her tranquillity back; yes, I shall be able to console her.   See, Mario, I seem to be back again in the early days of our married life, to possess her to-day for the first time.

So ends the first stave.   It seems that he has come back to the straight road.   Yet the spirit of wandering and suspicion has entered in.   There follows a scene between husband and wife, wherein she shrinks from his embrace, saying in explanation : ' I have killed a man and you kiss me for it': deplores the fact that he has read the letters and unsettled his mind, and wants to put off their departure into the country.   Another follows, between Paolo and the servant, in which he discovers for the first time that Luciano had once been to the house, just after his departure with his wife for the country.   He returns to the letter and gloats over it ; and then again he comes, together with the friend, whose presence apparently acts as the web whereon to work out the woof of his suspicions.

Mario. I've persuaded her [to go on their expedition to the country].
Paolo. Lucky to have so able an advocate.
Ma. You see, it didn't take much.
Pa. Will you bet I don't guess how you got her over ?
Ma. Oh ! Very simple. I . . .
Pa. No, let me say it. I, too, want my little triumph. [Poor, poor creature !] You gave up your business and made up your mind to come away with us.
Ma. Yes, just that.
Pa. Eh, didn't I know ? And when you went to her, I was on the point of telling you, and then I wanted to see. And then Anna was at once ready . . .
Ma. Why not ?
Pa. Just think ! the more we are . . . and aren't we going to amuse ourselves ? The places, the travelling, the hotels ; quite delightful. But the company ! And for

E

flight, you want to be few. . . . [He travels fastest who travels alone—as Kipling has it.]

Ma. What !

Pa. (*putting his two hands on Mario's shoulders and speaking to him face to face*). For flight, you understand ; that you must be few. For flight, as Anna and I fled last year.

Ma. I don't understand.

Pa. You never told me that Luciano had been here last year. Nor the day he came.

Ma. I don't know. . . . I don't remember.

Pa. Go on with you! You knew it. And you knew that Anna made me take her away to escape him. [' Small harm there,' says common sense. ' If she had put off a journey to receive him ? ' . . .] and went off with her, so happy. You watch this husband who takes the train and—off he goes just before the other comes.

Ma. Suppose it's true ; this tells you neither more nor less than the letters did.

Pa. No, a little more. It all says a little more. Grain on grain will make a millstone which will crush you. [Take care then, O collector of deadly molecules!] It says a little more. It is one thing to keep a man at a distance, another to fly from him. You banish a troublesome man, and without supplications. But you fly from fear.

Ma. Ugh !

Pa. And look, look, look ! let's examine a little just for the sake of doing it. Let us see. It's improbable that he should have written her word that he was coming. Nay, it's certain that he didn't, else she would have written. ' You write that you are coming. I love my husband. I beg you not to come.'

Ma. Oh !

Pa. Then it was she, . . . foreseeing his intentions, . . . felt his coming . . . by that divination.

Ma. You are the first husband who ever tortured himself because his wife did her duty. [Bravo !]

Pa. H'm ! Duty ! Beastly word. [Yet he used it himself not so long ago.]

Ma. If there is in the world a more honest woman . . .

Pa. Woman or wife ?

Ma. It is the same.

Pa. No, no. Woman for all, wife for me only. Do you think one marries a woman because she is honest ? Not much! I marry her because I love her and I believe she loves me. There are a thousand honest women. There's but one whom I love and who loves me ; if there is that one.

Ma. Paolo!

Pa. And if she did love him. Good God! If she did love him. If she rejected him for virtue, for duty's sake. What becomes of me ? If he were alive I could resist him, conquer him . . . but he's dead—he's killed himself for love of her. If she loved him no force can ever tear him from her heart . . .

Ma. Do you think . . .

Pa. I don't know . . . That's just it—I don't know. [How far has he strayed from the point where he said ' I have never had a moment's doubt on Anna's account.' This is the half-way house on the by-way of suspicion which leads to despair], and I want to know. I want to hear myself cry it out in her face and to hear her answer. . . . Oh! I had an idea of it directly I read her first letter [Did he really think so then, or is he only now persuading himself that he did ?] I did not understand then. I even believed. ' I love my husband,' but I felt suddenly a hammer below here, which hurt, hurt deeply. And I did not know the reason. Oh, it wants time for certain fears to take shape . . . first they bite deeply . . . you don't know what it is . . . I was happy . . . I told you that I was happy. I wanted to be persuaded that I was. [Note the double retirement before the onslaught of doubt. I was, . . . I said I was, . . . I wanted to think I was—the next to follow, I was not.] But you saw that fear was biting me all the time. And if she loved him. Oh! Yes. So much more admirable, and all the world would admire her. A noble satisfaction. I, too, should admire her on bended knees if she were the wife of another man. But she's mine. I am not the judge of my wife, I am a party to the dispute ; I cannot judge. I am the owner. I ought to admire her because, when she might have cheated me of the whole, she has cheated me of a part only. . . . I look at what she has taken away, not what remains.

E 2

Ma. Pah! You are mad.

Pa. But don't see that I am hateful to her?

Ma. Good God!

Pa. Hateful! You weren't here a moment ago. [He has a shade of justification here, however.] Perhaps you'll deny that she can't bear my presence without you.

Ma. To-day, perhaps, because she knows that you have read . . . I told you myself. It's embarrassing for her.

Pa. It's not to-day only. You never go away from her, never at all. In fifteen years that you've been a country mouse, you haven't been a week away. And a fortnight ago you took a sudden fancy to make a tour of the world. She begged you to . .

Ma. I swear to you . . .

Pa. I don't believe you. Anna will tell me. [Anna is called. Anna denies all pre-arrangement, but admits that after what had happened she would have felt it awkward for a while to be alone with her husband and was glad when Mario suggested coming. This is enough for the mad inquisitor who imperiously demands to see Luciano's letters to her. There is a delightful touch here. She is going away to get them. ' All,' he cries after her. She comes back and gives him the key. He comes back with the packet. His mood has changed. He goes to the desk where hers lie, takes them all together, throws them into the fire and himself at her feet, demanding pardon. And that is the end? Oh, no. We are in Italy not in England. What genius of mischief can turn this happy ending into a tragedy? We are very near. Only a few pages left. You must be quick, evil spirit! Some sudden darkening of the skies, some sudden annihilation of the vital power.] (*They are sitting together.*)

Paolo. You see that fit of violence has soon passed. It was just because Mario was here. He's a good fellow and a tactful man, but his presence irritated me. Yes, yes. You were right. But you ought to have understood my state of mind. (*He gets up and begins to walk about.*) Adding it all up, what does this storm come to?—This—that I am devoted to you; and that's the essential, it seems to me. Go to the bottom of things. We have been husband and wife five years and you know if I have ever given you the slightest cause of complaint. I don't believe I have, and five years are five years. I have gained a good position by my work. You have always figured in society. Pleasure is pleasure. I have had friends. The Club . . . other married men, after a year, in the evening . . . I have given up every other thing. I don't want to make a merit of it, but . . .

Anna. Oh! Please don't walk about so.

Pa. I'm sorry. May I sit here beside you? (*Long silence.*) When shall I see you smile again, Anna? No, don't get up. You have forgiven me, haven't you? [Be quick, spirit of mischief. The sands are running.]

An. What do you want, Paolo, eh? What do you want of me? Tell me quickly.

Pa. You made me promise that I would never speak to you . .

An. And I told you at once that you would break it. But you are wrong. Trust me. Don't ask me anything. When there's no more danger I promise you, and I'll keep my word. I promise you that I'll tell you everything without you asking me. It will do us good, both of us. But just now I want to be judge of what is wise.

Pa. Very well. Tell me nothing, but come away with me alone. I'll persuade Mario. He was coming to please you, and he'll be much better pleased to see us go off together as a sign that we are as one. I understand how painful it may be to you to awake old memories; I won't awake them, on the contrary I'll make you forget them. I swear it to you . . . I swear it to you that I will never speak of it again, but come with me; come away with me and you shall see how much love . . .

An. Don't demand that of me, Paolo. If you demand it I will follow you, but . . .

Pa. No, no, I demand nothing. You see that I am here as a suppliant. I will not possess you by force, but hear this— just this much more. I recognise, you know, what you have done. Oh! I shall be rewarding you for it all our days. I recognise that there is not a more righteous woman in all the world than you. But you ought to enter into my mind and have pity on me, too.

An. Ah! Ah! (*Laughs bitterly.*)

Pa. Why do you wish to prolong this torment? [She is right, he cannot keep his promise.] When there is no more danger, you say. What danger is there? What does this danger depend on?—You or me? What can time change in us? I have always loved you—I love you; and see! at this moment, I love you as I have never loved you before. Give me your hand, only your hand. Good God, Anna! how lovely you are, and you are mine, my wife! And the oath you took at our wedding was not only one of faith, it was of love as well. Come with me, Anna, come!

An. Oh no, no!

Pa. No? You are afraid, eh? Afraid of being unfaithful to him?

An. Paolo! Paolo!

Pa. And if I want you?

An. And you cannot wish it?

Pa. And if I do wish it?

An. Paolo!

Pa. And if I command it? [Oh, suppliant, how quickly risen from thy knees!]

An. You would destroy in a moment all my work. But learn that your violence is my liberation.

Pa. Oh, come! Speak, speak!

An. Will you have it so? Have we got there at last? I have done what I could . . .

Pa. Go on, . . . speak.

An. I loved Luciano and I love him still! [Man, you have worked your own undoing! If ever mortals can command success it is towards misery. He who demands unhappiness will have it. It is the one certain gift that fortune has for men

We have come now to the end of a rather lengthy analysis of a not very conspicuous play. A needless task, some may think; but as national types are not to be sought for in beautiful faces, so interest and nobility are not always found in company. As an acting

play, ' Diritti dell' Anima ' has not proved a favourite ;
but, as a prologue to the theatre, it could hardly be
improved.

We have now, I think, clearly before us the three
cardinal points of an Italian serious play : a somewhat clumsy—at any rate, a deliberate—beginning ; a
tendency in the body of the play for the catastrophe
to be produced by reason and argument, rather than
by events ; and, in the end, a perpetual hauling in of
the sheet to fetch sail past the Islands of the Blest, out
into the wide Sea of Misery.

We are not here using metaphor without a purpose.
It is not only the unhappiness, but the aimlessness, of
the end which strikes an English theatre-goer so forcibly.
We ourselves can bear with a terrible ending, if it is
striking, picturesque, forceful. If it seems to concentrate the agony or the terror of years into one moment ;
illustrate in one action the upheaval of many souls ;
if it stands clear and distinct, like some dark ruin against
the sanguine sheets of the sunset ;—then we can shudder
for a moment and endure. But the Italian likes his
drama, when it is serious at all, to bring him out into
a wide expanse where misery can be, cumulatively or
successively, picked as a flower or felt as a wave. ' So
the drama ends on the stage, but continues in life.' [1]
That is what is demanded of the Italian serious playwright : not that with a crisp, tremendous catastrophe
he should put an end to all, but rather that the
apparent end should form the gate to a Paradise, where
sadness can be indulged in unchecked.

I had intended, in my account of the Italian writers,
to omit the outstanding figure of D'Annunzio ; partly
as being already well known, partly as standing rather

---

[1] Said by a critic, in some leading Italian paper, of some *dramma* that he
was describing. He did not perceive how universal its application was.

outside the class of which I want to speak. But little by little, a change has seemed inevitable: both by reason of the fact that the omission of so characteristic a personality would have detracted from the values of other forms in the picture; and because, reacting against a reaction, I was ready to appreciate that which everyone who has a voice, but perhaps not eyes or ears, is already engaged in crying down.

D'Annunzio, with all his faults and limitations, is undoubtedly the best known Italian literary figure of to-day, whether in Italy or out of it. To say that he will not in the future be one of the great men of the past, that he is a bubble that will be pricked, is to indulge in prophecy. The end is not yet come. Time, if he means business, is still grinding the point wherewith to pierce the bubble's skin. It was said years ago that D'Annunzio owed his position to his association with Eleonora Duse. Well, that association has ceased; but his position is as sound as ever. His last great play, ' La Nave,' which was produced with La Paoli in the leading part, was made an event of national importance and commanded prices which could only be equalled by famous foreign plays such as ' Chantecler.' He is therefore a phenomenon which needs explanation. If his works are altogether as thin and flashy as the critics pretend, it redounds very little to the credit of the Italian theatre-goer that he has been raised to his present high position.

As usual, the truth lies half-way between two extremes. It is commonly said that D'Annunzio does not understand character; that the merit of his plays lies in a clever and meretricious ornamentation. It occurs to me, when I hear such remarks, that I have heard the same thing said of Mozart. But, comparisons apart, D'Annunzio's critics have overstated their case.

It is true that he does not shew an all-round appreciation of character ; but one kind he does understand
as few understand it : namely, that known as the artistic
temperament.   The highly strung, the sensitive, the
intellectual; that which, overstepping the limits of convention in search of the beautiful, disregards order always,
and morality too often ; that which, like some weird
instrument, will vibrate to so many themes that it alone
seems enough to fill the hall with melody and the heart
with joy—such characters as these he chooses for his
principals, and on their beautiful and sensitive souls
plays with a master's art.   We are now speaking of
his prose pieces.   The themes are simple, the characters
few ;   the speeches long, but worked up with an almost
oratorical art ;   and   the   action   proceeds   towards   its
tragic end with the gait of a queen towards the scaffold,
who disdains to soil her robes upon the ground.   Every
thing is lifted into an atmosphere of its own.   The
ordinary landscape of life seems replaced by a world
wherein thoughts take the place of persons, emotion
supplants light and shade, and where, thinking to enter
earthly caverns underground, we find ourselves wandering   through   the   coils   of   the   brain,   where   strange
lights and weird shadows delight and delude us.   Where
poverty and riches cease to be felt, where the common
fruits, either of the earth or the mind, do not ripen,
where reality is represented by things which to our
everyday eyes seem transcendental and absurd ;   but
which here become as actual and visible facts as the
vapour of the sky precipitated into clouds, or held in
a solid if momentary miracle on the point of a blade
of grass.

In ' La Gioconda,' to take one instance out of many,
the principal characters are Lucio Settala (the sculptor)
his wife Silvia, and Gioconda Dianti, (the model,) who

charms the artist from his allegiance to the woman whom, as a man, he really loves.   All the rest are merely chorus.

In the extract following, we have Lucio discussing the siren with the chorus-leader, old Cosimo Dalbo. The latter has just said, referring to the statue of her that Lucio has made : ' You have perpetuated in a type ideal and incomparable, an ephemera of its kind. Are you not, then, satisfied ? ' and Lucio breaks out: ' A thousand statues, not one!   She is always different, as a cloud which appears to you changed from second to second without your seeing it change.   Every movement of her body destroys one harmony and creates another more beautiful.   You ask her to stop, to remain moveless ;   and across her immobility passes a torrent of shadowy emotions, as thoughts that pass across the eyes.   Do you understand ?   Do you understand ? The life of the eyes is in the look : that indescribable thing   more   expressive   than   any   word,   or   any sound ;   infinitely deep, and yet as momentary as the lightning—nay, swifter than the lightning ;   innumerable, omnipotent—in a word, the look.   Do you understand ? One beat of the eyelids transfigures a human face, and expresses an immensity of joy or sorrow.   The brows of the creature you love are lowered, and their shade enfolds you as a river an island ;   they are raised, and the power of summer heat burns up your world. One beat more, your soul is dissolved as a water-drop ; one more, and you seem to be king of the universe. Imagine   this   mystery   through   her   whole   body ! Imagine through all her members, from forehead to heel, this fulminating life made visible !   Could you carve the look in stone ?   The ancients made their statues blind !   Now, . . . just imagine . . . all her body is just like one look. (*A pause : he looks round suspiciously—fearful of being heard.   He comes still nearer to his friend, who hears him with growing emotion.*) A thousand statues, not one, I told you! Her beauty lives in all marble. This I became aware of, with an anxiety made up of pain and fervour, one day at Carrara, while we were watching some of those great oxen which drag the waggons of marble down from the Alps. One aspect of her perfection was shut up, for me, in each of these formless blocks. It seemed that there went out from her towards the senseless mineral thousands of life-giving sparks as from a brandished torch. We were to choose a block, I remember; it was a cloudless sky; the marble blocks were set down in the sunshine and shone like the everlasting snows. From time to time we heard the boom of the mines which rent the entrails of the voiceless mountain. I should not forget that moment, were I to die a second time. She went among that collection of white cubes, pausing in front of each. She bent down, noted the grain attentively, seemed to explore the veins within, hesitated, smiled, passed on. To my eyes, her clothes no longer hid her. There was a kind of divine affinity between her flesh and the marble, which she seemed to animate with her breath as she bent over it. A confused aspiration seemed to rise towards her from that indefinable whiteness. The breeze, the sun, the grandeur of the mountain peaks, the long file of yoked oxen, the cloud rising from the sea, the lofty flight of an eagle, all visible things exalted my spirit in a boundless poem : made it drunk with a dream whose like I never knew. Ah! Cosimo, Cosimo! have I dared to throw away a life on which the glory of such a remembrance shone? When she touched with her hand the piece she had chosen and turned to me saying "This one," the whole mountain, from summit to base, became alive with loveliness.' (*An extraordinary fervour*

animates his voice and informs his gestures. The listener is
taken with it, and shows as much.)

'Ah ! now you understand ! Never again will you
ask me if I am satisfied.'

We may not ask for such things as these, but, if
we are to have them at all, can they be better done ?
What word added or taken away could intensify the
picture of the fair woman, the formless stone, the
exalted yet hesitating man ?

Our own poet Browning, much praised for his
insight into matters of art, has a somewhat similar
theme to handle in 'Pippa Passes.' This is the
result :—

> But you must say a 'well' to that—say 'well !'
> Because you gaze—am I fantastic, sweet ?
> Gaze like my very life's-stuff, marble—marbly,
> Even to the silence ! Why, before I found
> The real flesh Phene, I inured myself
> To see, throughout all nature, varied stuff
> For better Nature's birth by means of art :
> With me, each substance tended to one form
> Of beauty—to the human archetype.
> On every side occurred suggestive germs
> Of that—the tree, the flower—or take the fruit,—
> Some rosy shape, continuing the peach,
> Curved beewise o'er its bough ; as rosy limbs,
> Depending, nestled in the leaves ; and just
> From a cleft rose-peach the whole Dryad sprang.
> But of the stuffs one can be master of,
> How I divined their capabilities !
> From the soft-rinded smoothening facile chalk
> That yields your outline to the air's embrace,
> Half-softened by a halo's pearly gloom ;
> Down to the crisp imperious steel, so sure
> To cut its one confided thought clean out
> Of all the world.   But marble !—'neath my tools
> More pliable than jelly—as it were

Some clear primordial creature dug from depths
In the earth's heart, where itself breeds itself,
And whence all baser substance may be worked ;
Refine it off to air, you may,—condense it
Down to the diamond ;—is not metal there,
When o'er the sudden speck my chisel trips ?
—Not flesh, as flake off flake I scale, approach,
Lay bare those bluish veins of blood asleep ?
Lurks flame in no strange windings where, surprised
By the swift implement sent home at once,
Flushes and glowings radiate and hover
About its track ?

The two pieces do not, of course, cover the same
ground, but they are in the same demesne. I confess
that the effect of the second, to me, is merely to act
as foil to the first.   I confess that, when after
D'Annunzio's beautiful image of the brandished torch
and the scattered sparks—the masterly picture that
mountain, woman, eagle, and oxen compose, I read
how Jules ' divined their capabilities,' how ' suggestive
germs ' occurred to him, or how his ' swift implement ' was
' sent home,' I ask myself very seriously whether poetry
and prose are not masquerading in each other's dresses.
In the first passage, surely, we have feeling; in the
second, reasoning ; in the first, the sculptor, in the second,
the philosopher, speaks.

Nevertheless, in all such pieces of D'Annunzio, the
elegance of the method is not a little discounted by the
brutality of the fact. It is like a base metal made
the subject of a decorative artist's delicate curves. And
however elevated and imaginative the descriptions may
be, nothing can disguise the fact that, like flower-
bordered walks which adorn a graveyard, they lead
us back finally to our own perishable body. The
ideas which they arouse in us are purely physical ones ;
and the author shrinks from no display of realism to

excite our emotions or harrow our feelings. In one play, a woman is blind : in another, she has her hands crushed before us on the stage ; and the last act is nothing but the playing on the one note—the maimed woman. We are in the atmosphere of ' Titus Andronicus.'

It is the lowering of art, as it is the brutalising of the eye. Without saying that a dramatist must be debarred from such effects, it is clear that he must not make a whole act depend on them, as D'Annunzio has done. We northerners are, no doubt, apt to look upon such things with peculiar disgust. ' Titus Andronicus ' is infamous among the productions of our great writers. But among the peoples of the south, the physical is much more constantly felt and freely expressed than by ourselves ; and perhaps D'Annunzio, in using it as he has done, is only exaggerating, not contradicting, the spirit of his race.

But the practical dramatic critic will notice another thing about the speech of his that has just been quoted : namely, its inordinate length. Except in the works of Mr. Bernard Shaw, characters on the English stage are not allowed to develop their views so extensively. Here, again, though D'Annunzio is excessive, he is not unnatural. An instinct of the Italian is to be analytical and rhetorical : long discourses of this sort would not be out of the question with him in real life ; and, on the stage, it is merely a question of the time for which an audience can be held. With D'Annunzio, his work may be bubbles, but they are bubbles at which the public will go on gazing for a considerable time.

The foregoing remarks, however, apply to his prose works alone. When we come to his plays in verse, the whole centre of gravity is shifted. The stories are still simple, but the main characters have diminished in importance ; and to fill the space from which they have receded, subsidiary beings are introduced. The former no longer discuss and analyse their feelings with such free elaboration, but, instead, the latter, in words which are almost pattern-work, make a peaceful border, which contains and contrasts the tragedy within.

One especially, of which I shall speak presently, is like nothing more exactly than a series of stained-glass windows, in which the central figures are distinguishable only by some conventional attributes which pursue them throughout their wanderings. The pale bride in whose honour the maidens sing ' Tutta di verde mi voglio vestire,' in her pale-green robe, is like a thing diaphanous—some willow, pierced by the sunlight ; the young shepherd, with his lean body and his crook, recalls many a quaint-drawn figure that we have seen standing under a gilded canopy; the tangled locks of the witch shew up wildly dark against the might of the setting sun. The pictures—whether baby-like, as in the opening scene of the wedding ceremony ; or moving, as in that of the hunted thing crouching for protection at the hearth, while the fierce faces of the reapers glower at her from the window-bars ; or mystic, as that in the silence of the forest of the guilty pair alone ; or fateful, as in the awful return of the once innocent boy ;— each and all give birth to emotions else only to be had, when, in some old arched building, whose white columns are spotted with stains of which the falling darkness will quickly wipe them clean, we lose ourselves in the labyrinth of the glass-maker, or glide up a stream of light into a place of wonder and peace.

The story can be briefly told. Aligi, the shepherd, is to marry Vienda, and it is the wedding morning. The harmony of the bridal party, and the picturesque ceremonies of offering and receiving gifts, are rudely broken by the inrush of a woman pursued by a threatening crowd. This is Mila di Coda, the ' figlia di Jorio,' who is accused by the reapers of casting spells over their harvesting. Aligi is about to deliver her up to them ; he has his hands on her to drag her forth, when, behold ! he sees behind her an angel, weeping. He goes up to the door and opens it, true : but he stands in the doorway holding up the Cross, and the reapers shrink back in superstitious awe. Act II. finds Aligi and Mila together in the mountains. He is engaged in carving out of the trunk of a tree the angel whom he saw behind her on the first memorable day. Then there are episodes of a holy man, with whom Aligi discusses the situation ; and an old woman, who carries charms in her sack—who teases Mila, and gets robbed for her pains. The stage-management of this part of the play was very good ; and although it must be nearly ten years since I saw it, the old woman's—

' Non ne ho ; non ne ho più nella sacca '

(There's nothing more, there's nothing more left in the bundle)

rings in my ear as if it were yesterday. Then Aligi is followed : first by his sister, Ornella—the only one who raised a hand on Mila's behalf—and then by his father, Lazzaro. The latter offers violence to Mila ; and Aligi, furious, seizes the hatchet sticking in the block—which is still half-angel and half-formless wood—and dashes his father to the ground. In Act III. Aligi is brought back, bound and doomed to the most awful of deaths, by fire, for that most awful of crimes, parricide. Amid the wailing of the women, the pale, silent figure passes before us. Suddenly, a wild, breathless creature rushes in. It is Mila. In spite of Aligi's protestations, she takes the blame on herself. They have accused her of being a witch ;—well, she is a witch. By her spells she compassed Lazzaro's death. The angel that Aligi saw was wrought by a demon's power. Of the blow that struck his father down, the shepherd is not guilty, but she—the sorceress, the witch. Interest and prejudice alike bid the judges to receive this evidence. Mila is torn from before the fainting Aligi, triumphant at having saved him ; and from the midst of the fire is heard her voice : ' How fair is the flame ! how fair is the flame ! '

Drama such as this is clearly not to be judged by the standards of real life. We must transport ourselves into a new world where the inhabitants have other customs and other beliefs; and, if the perpetual antithesis of Christianity and witchcraft is more picturesque than pleasing, at least we may be consoled by the thought that desertion and parricide find a better and more wholesome excuse in incantation than in any that is offered to us by the modern stage.

Of all the pictures that the play presents, some of the best come in the first act. The opening scene is charming, with the three laughing sisters over the chest packed full of beautiful things for the bride. The very names of the sisters—Splendore, Favetta, Ornella—are like jewels on a marble wall. They bend over the hoard, toss its treasures about, threading their white arms among the stuffs, whose many colours match the graceful fantasy of their words.

> *Splendore.* What wouldst thou, Vienda, our darling ?
> *Favetta.* What wouldst thou, beloved sister ?
> *Sp.* Wouldst thou wear this woollen garment,
> Or this silken one, besprinkled
> With flowers of rose and yellow ?
> *Ornella (singing).* All in a green, green robe I'll grace me,
> All green, to keep St. John's day holy,
> Who in midst of the green came down to plight me.
> Oili, oili, oilà.
> *Sp.* Here a doublet of delicate broidery

F

Made bright with a facing of silver,
The gown of twelve stuffs interwoven,
The necklace, an hundred of coral,
The gift of thy newly gained mother.
    Or. (*singing*). All in green the robes and the chamber,
Oila, oili, oilà !
    Fav. What wouldst thou, Vienda, our darling ?
    Sp. What wouldst thou, beloved sister ?
    Or. The pendants are here, the collar
That hangs from a crimson ribband.
Hark ! now the bell is tolling,
They are ringing the midday bell.
    Sp. See, see ! the folk are gathering,
They are bearing hither the baskets,
The baskets with grain are laden ;
And thou, thou art not ready !
    Or. Sluggard, and thrice a sluggard !
The sheep high up in the mountain,
The wolf in the wide plain wanders,
Seeking, men say, the filbert ;
The filbert much to be longed for.
Truly this bride is early,
Early, just as the mole is,
Who, at screech of dawn, is stirring,
As the badger and as the dormouse.
Hark, hark ! the bell is ringing !

But perhaps the prettiest scene of all is the entrance of
the women with the wedding gifts. It has all the freshness
of children at play ; all the grace, stateliness, and colour of a
Byzantine mosaic. The pale bride is reclining in throned
state. The door is open, but across it is stretched a ribband,
held in place by a hay-fork and spindle ; while at either
side, to watch the passage, stand Favetta and Ornella.
The women bearing the baskets on their heads approach
the opening ; then follows this dialogue. It is something
between a child's game and the interchanges between a
Greek actor and the chorus.

Teodula di Cinzio. Hail! Who at the bridge with-
stands us ?

Fav. and *Or.* Love and blind love are keepers.

Teo. Hear, I would fain pass over.

Fav. Learn, then, that fain is not finished !

Teo. And yet I have passed the mountain,
The plain I have passed over.

Or. The bridge is rent by the waters,
And the flood streams onward wildly.

Teo. Come out to me with the ferry.

Fav. The boat is making water.

Teo. Then pitch and twine I'll give thee.

Or. There are seven holes in her bottom.

Teo. Seven pennies I will give thee.
Wade out and wet thy shoulder.

Fav. Nay, nay, that little likes me !
I had ever fear of the water.

Teo. Wade out and wet thy girdle,
I'll give thee a silver shilling.

Or. 'Tis little enow ; eight gilders
Would scarce suffice to heal me.

Teo. Out with thee ! Bare thy knee, then,
I'll give thee a golden ducat !

Or. and *Fav.* Now leave to pass we give thee.
Let thy company pass with thee.

Teo. (*entering*). Peace unto Candida della Leonessa !
Peace to the son of Lazzaro di Roio !
Peace to the bride that Christ hath given him !

(*She sets down her basket at the bride's feet ; takes a handful
of grain and sprinkles it over her head ; another, and sprinkles
it over the head of the young man.*)

This is the peace that heaven hath sent upon you,
And may your heads upon the selfsame pillow
Ripen to age, even to a snowy whiteness ;
And may no strife nor vengeance come between you :
No cross to bear, no waste and no deceiving
Day after day ; even till the hour of passing.[1]

[1] These two scenes are translated as nearly as possible into the exact
rhythm of the original.

She stands, bending her graceful arms over the reclining bride, who remains as inactive as a graven image. Aligi and Candia are in the background; and the others, their baskets still on their heads, their draperies falling as straight as the garments in a Greek relief, in long diminishing file, await their turn; when, into this picture, shattering it like a stone flung by some apache into a beautiful window, rushes the hunted sorceress, whose magic and whose wiles are to make all the tragedy that is to follow. Truly, if there have been catastrophes more overwhelming, few have been led up to by a more delightful and more perfect contrast.

Though D'Annunzio's ornaments of rhyme are usually of a lighter kind, he sometimes falls into phrases that are more seriously worthy of quotation.

> Ah! questa casa, chi la fabricò [1]
> Tanto grande? E perche con tante porte?
> A quanti mali ei volle dare albergo!

> Why was this house built with so many doors?
> But to give entrance to so many woes.

is surely pregnant with meaning; and of two lovers in their meeting :—

> Disse 'Aligi,
> Mi riconosci?' Io dissi, 'Tu sei Mila,'
> E non parlammo più, che non più fummo
> Due.

> She said 'Aligi,
> Do you not know me?' and I said 'Thou'rt Mila,'
> And no word more we spake, for we no more
> Were twain.

if reminiscent of Dante, is surely worthy of its great original.

Next in importance after D'Annunzio as a popular figure, and far ahead of him as a real student of life,

---

[1] From 'La Fiaccola sotto il Moggio.'

comes Giuseppe Giacosa. He is one from whom the average Italian playwright would learn much if he would consent to study as well as to praise. For Giacosa, while he was not much above several, though a little above all his contemporaries in the delineation of character, gained his pre-eminence by his knowledge of how a play should live and move. I have read plays of his, which, though commonplace in their themes, gave, nevertheless, the impression of being eminently actable. Giacosa's work was unequal, and he has left none of those brilliant light comedy pieces which we have from others. But three of his pieces have an outstanding reputation and will probably outlive the vicissitudes of the day.

These are ' Tristi Amori ' (Sad Loves), ' Come le Foglie' (As the Leaves), and ' Il Più Forte ' (The Strongest). The last I have not seen acted, and it is a play to which the action of the stage means everything. The other two are most striking, certainly; and, with the exception of ' Romanticismo,' the most telling prose plays on the modern Italian stage.[1]

When Giacosa died,—and his death is hardly yet passed out of reach of the mourner's cry,—his memory received justice in an article in one of the great English reviews. The substance of it has slipped from my memory, but I do recall that the reviewer, as was natural, reserved his blessing for the first two of the above-named plays, but opined that ' Come le Foglie ' was too purely and intimately Italian to arouse the sympathies of an English audience. From that opinion I beg respectfully to dissent. In the first place, since the review in question was printed, the play has been translated into French and acted in Paris with great success ; and I do not think that the Parisians are in a better—if, indeed, they

[1] See p. 93.

are in an equally good—position for understanding the inner life of an Italian family. In the second place, I do not know whether the reviewer in question had seen the play acted or had only read it. To me it is one of the most deceptive I have ever come across. Read it, and you will say to yourself ' Absorbing, but it is not drama ' ; see it acted, and you will say ' Splendid, but it cannot be literature : ' the fact being that its qualities on either side are so high, and so well balanced, that the one towards you conceals the other ; you are so entirely satisfied with what is nearest to you, that you cannot believe that there is anything else.

I am inclined, then, to believe that ' Come le Foglie ' is Giacosa's greatest play : his most profound and original ; his most worthy to be remembered. It is particularly Italian, true ; and without universality there can be no real greatness. But some men have a way of gaining this by a sort of direct attack, by themes which are, in their nature, of world-wide application : such were Shakespeare and Molière. Others make the windows of particularity frame for us broad stretches of the open world : such was Jane Austen ; such also, Giacosa. He looked out of the window of the commonplace. He burrowed down, down into the trivial, the every-day that lay about him. And from these recesses, as a man at the bottom of a well can see the stars of heaven, he gained for himself and perpetuated for us, a vision of things beyond : of things which, though simple in themselves, and proceeding from simple hearts and hands, are transcendental in their pathos, noble in their impulse, profound in their truth.

All this is revealed to us in ' Come le Foglie '; but the play reveals a good deal more. It may seem fantastic to compare such a play as this with the awful tragedy of ' Macbeth   the one treating of kings and queens, wild creatures prophesying in storm and wind, murders done for the sake of sovereignty ; madness, remorse, retribution : the other, of a gentleman whose money fails him, who goes into business abroad, who cannot manage his household, and whose affairs consequently get into a mess. Yet the plays, while in their themes they are as the poles asunder, have at least this much in common : namely, the remorseless persistency with which the inevitable comes on. As by Shakespeare, so in his humbler way by Giacosa, the end is never lost to view. Touch after touch, word after word, event after event—trivial, almost imperceptible, by itself—build up a misery that debases many lives and wellnigh leads to a poor girl's suicide. As of ' Macbeth,' so of Giovanni Rosani, Fate, to whom his own weakness unlocked the door, takes possession with a calmness which is as natural as it is irresistible. And the difference is only that Rosani, being in truth a lesser sinner, has a door of escape opened, and a guardian angel—if a somewhat unromantic one—sent him, who shall retrieve his fortunes and marry his child.

At the risk of giving an exaggerated impression of the play, I will add that, if Giacosa has approached Shakespeare in its construction, so he has Molière in the goodness of the things said. Like, after all, does not mean equal. Even an Italian would laugh if it were suggested that Giacosa was a rival for either of these giants : but that need not prevent us from illustrating, by reference to them, things which otherwise might be but imperfectly grasped by the reader.

The aphorisms, but for the differences made by translation, might be left to speak for themselves. They come chiefly from the mouth of Massimo, the angel above referred to. This, for example, in reply to the young fellow, who, removed from his elegant circle in

Milan, cannot settle to work, and declares himself an apostle of beauty :—

'But the beauty of things is in us, and there is more of it in me than in you, and it's more perfect and more frank. To me, that lake gives a sensation of beauty at any time, and in whatever state I may be. For you to enjoy it, you must have slept in a good bed, be well clothed, sitting in an armchair, with a cigar in your mouth. To you, then, beauty [and this is the aphorism] is an affair of the upholsterer, the tailor, the tobacconist !' To how many idle young men might not the same thing be said with equal truth ? Again, Tommy says, referring to his relations with regard to a certain Signora, 'You are going the very way to drive me into her arms.' 'Of course,' says Massimo, 'that is the refuge of all conscious cowards ; they want to be able to say that the evil they do is done because of pique !'

Again, in the same, Tommy says to him that 'he cannot make himself dictator by reason of the 250 ffcs. a month that he pays to the speaker's father. Massimo replies, 'I am giving your father what I should have given to any other. I am not a benefactor. Therefore, I am free to speak.' The idea that the tongue is tied by benefits given as well as benefits received, is a new, and, I believe, a very true one. Obligations disturb the scales of justice, equally for purchaser and vendor.

Again, 'by what right do you interfere ?' says Tommy. Again [and surely this is like Molière ?] Massimo replies, 'By the right of two stronger arms at the service of a saner brain. If I saw you in the act of pointing a revolver at your head, anyone would recognise my right to snatch the pistol from your hand, even if blows should be the result. Your relations with that woman are worse for you and for others than a revolver-shot. So I disarm you !'

But what is the story, and wherein does the tragedy consist? For it is so nearly a tragedy that the safety of the poor sufferers seems almost like that of Lazarus returned from the grave.

Reader, have you even lain, on a seemingly fair summer's day, upon an eminence with a landscape spread before you of great rounded woods, deep valleys into which the shadows run like water, pale, clear distances: and, somewhere,—far off, but most prominent point of all to the eye,—a jagged mountain range, whose central point is tipped with snow? And have you, dissolved in the sunshine of your own happy thoughts, failed to notice how the clouds began to gather, the sky to darken, and the clear contrast of sunlight and shadow change to woven medley of purples and greys; the while one part of the sky remained clear, through which the light still bathed the mountain range which you noticed before you began to dream: and slowly, without seeming to move, the clouds grew denser, as pure water into which some darker liquid is poured, and nearer and nearer the shadow crept, until the only light in earth or sky was that fair white peak to which, the more closely it was invested, the eye more desperately clung? There was a moment when it seemed to shine with an unearthly intensity, and then . . . Let us not push the simile too far. The white peak is a young girl, the heroine of the story. The one, the only one, of the family who has done absolutely nothing to deserve her fate. She seems the centre of misfortune because of her goodness and sense. It is around her that we watch the clouds gather, because her whiteness alone makes a contrast to them. And, as she is driven by blows that are imperceptible as units, irresistible in the mass, towards the bitter refuge of self-destruction, we watch her with an absorbed interest which we never feel but in the presence of great natural things.

The effect of these innumerable, minute touches cannot, of course, be given in a *résumé* ; but the whole story can be briefly told. The Rosani family, consisting of Giovanni the father, his second wife Giulia, and two children Tommaso and Irene—familiarly called Tommy and Nennele—has been ruined by a financial crisis. Its members are leaving Milan rather than support poverty in the face of people by whom they are well known. Massimo, a nephew of the old man, who has not been in communication with the family in the days of their prosperity, comes to their aid at this crisis. He offers the father employment at (in our money) ten pounds a month, and makes what provision he can for their housing and service. The packing up and departure of the family makes the end of the first act.

Act II. finds them in Switzerland. Giovanni is at work in his office all day. What are the others doing ? Giulia, who believes herself to be gifted with a genius for art, is casting her bread upon the waters in the form of subscriptions to art circles, bribes to editors, &c., and Tommy is ' making his fortune ' by gambling at the house of a lady of doubtful reputation ; having refused, after a very cursory trial, Massimo's offers of employment. And Nennele ? Nennele is doing the housekeeping, and giving lessons in English, by Massimo's advice and introduction, to the son of a neighbouring house. She has missed money of her father's and possessions of her own, but dares not voice her suspicions. From being Tommy's confidante, she has the mortification of seeing herself supplanted by her step-mother, whose whispered colloquies with Tommy bode anything but good to the family honour. But, piqued by some fancied slight, Giulia betrays Tommy's confidence as to the Signora Orloff, and Tommy accepts the post of secretary, which Massimo offers him for the second time, in the house of one of his friends.

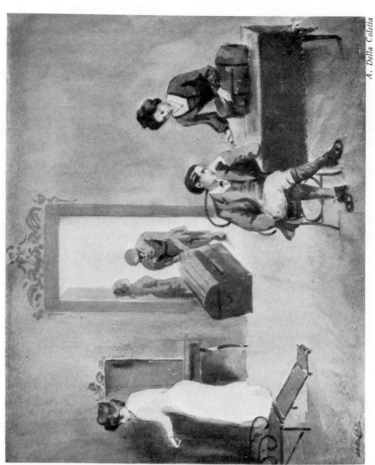

A. Della Coletta

'COME LE FOGLIE,' ACT I, SC. 4

In Act III. Giulia, now jealous of Nennele, insists on
having the reins of government handed over to her,
which Giovanni does ' for peace sake ' with many asides
of his daughter. Nennele, in handing over the keys
to her step-mother, hints that she has found them an
imperfect protection.

Then Giulia, trying to combine the offices of Aphrodite
and Athena, flirts with sundry painters; on one of whom
she bestows her portrait in an elegant silver frame. This
unluckily falls to the ground, is picked up by Massimo,
and the frame recognised as her own by Nennele, who
breaks into a bitter laugh. Her soul is in despair within
her for all this miserable deceit. Massimo has spoken
of a flooded river, and some one who lost his footing
and fell. ' Dead ? ' says Nennele. ' Oh ! any one that
falls in . . .,' says Massimo, with a shrug. ' Not even
time to drown. Smashed by the great tree-trunks,'
and a picture rises in the girl's mind of a wild night,
one leap, the hammer-blows of the great trees, and
then . . . peace, perhaps ! The humiliation goes on.
Giulia forces the girl to accuse her; Nennele turns for
support to Tommy, who has seen the step-mother coming
from his sister's room; but Tommy is now bound by
treaty to the enemy, and . . . his memory fails him !
' I am a liar,' says poor Nennele; but to her brother,
after Giulia has gone out, ' Poor Tommy ! what it
must have cost you,' is all she says. The blows fall
thick. Next Massimo comes in with a telegram in his
hand; it is from his friend, the ' wood-breaker.' Tommy,
who all this while has been posing as the busy secretary,
has only been to the office once ! Where has he been ?
Obviously to the Orloff's. He owes the Orloff money.
He must pay her. He has no money. Nennele wildly
thinks of everything. Even an aunt, a broken reed
on which they leaned. ' She'll send me a tie-pin,' says

Tommy, with bitter wit. 'Better take the plunge!'
'The plunge?' says Nennele, terrified. Has Tommy
thought of the river, too? No, not suicide, marriage.
The lady has taken a fancy to him, and he must pay his
debts with his own beautiful person. Massimo tries
to console her. 'I didn't even try to dissuade him,'
says the poor girl, despairingly. 'Your brother is not
all.' 'Giulia, too,' says Nennele, 'by another road!'
and she fears for her father. No, no, the catastrophe
is imminent, the house is doomed. 'Will you be my
wife, Irene?' says Massimo, for the second or third time.
Nennele's feelings have changed since he last asked her,
but her pride remains. 'I don't accept charity.' Then
he leaves her. 'May I come down with you?' No,
Massimo wants to be alone. 'You are not going to
leave me in anger?' No, he is just going to walk up
and down in the garden below. Out he goes. Nennele
follows him with her eyes, but her lips can hardly frame
the phrase, 'He doesn't understand!'

The act changes, but not the scene: it is as if we
had slept for a few moments on board a boat that was
being swept silently towards the cataract. It is night;
Giovanni is working at his desk in the common-room
into which all doors open. Slowly a figure comes along
the wall. He stops and listens without turning. It
crouches close. Dead pause for a moment. Then
Giovanni goes on writing and the figure moves towards
the door. There is a second pause; then the latch
clicks; Giovanni looks round; in a moment he has his
daughter in his arms. 'I was only just going out . . .
it is so hot in the house: a moment's air.' He throws
the shutters open and the moonlight streams in. They
exchange a few idle words, and in a moment Nennele is
sobbing, as if her heart would break. 'Cry as much as
you like if it does you good, my dear,' says her father.

A. Della Coletta

'COME LE FOGLIE,' ACT IV

Then the father begins to speak of Tommy. But Nennele
is dreaming of some one else. ' Hasn't he come back ? '
' No.' ' Such a fine night.' ' I was at the window ;
I was looking for him.' ' You were looking for him ?
You wanted to speak to him ? ' ' No, I was watching
to see if he came. I was afraid to meet him.' ' Afraid
to meet him ? ' And Nennele is aware that she has
been thinking aloud. Presently, she says she will go
back to her room. He gets up to accompany her.
Then she suddenly declines to move. He becomes
suspicious. ' There is something there that I mustn't see.'
He goes in. Finds a letter on the table. Brings it to
her and reads it without opening it. ' You were going
to die ? Why should you die ? What is there that
I don't know ? ' ' Don't ask me,' says Nennele. He
insists. ' It is Tommy ? ' ' Lost irrevocably. He is
to marry a bad woman. And I was going to desert
you in your need.' ' They are lost,' says Giovanni to
himself, ' one by one they go their way. Come le foglie ! '
But there is one thing yet that Giovanni doesn't know—
nay, that Nennele hardly knows herself. They are still
watching from the window, and Giovanni thinks he sees
some one. ' Yes,' says Nennele, pleased. Then the figure
they are watching is lost to view. ' No,' says Nennele,
disappointed. ' You are sorry there is no one ? ' says
her father. ' But there is—there is ! ' she says, almost
petulantly. ' You'll see ; shall I call him ? He's there for
me.' And she goes to the window ; waves her handkerchief,
and calls, ' Massimo, come ! ' And in this moment of her
happiness and her hope, we see her for the last time.

We have dwelt so much on the frame-work of the
play that we have little time to spare for its details.
Yet we cannot help remarking both how varied and
how life-like the characters are. None are utterly
good or utterly bad. The one with the least light and

shade is the frivolous and easily led Giulia ; a most natural character for all that, as anyone who is familiar with Italian life will bear witness. The little speech in which her husband tells Massimo that she had brought an ' avvocato ' to him with a cut-and-dried scheme for cheating his creditors, is perhaps more suggestive of her character than anything that we actually see her do. Giovanni is, as he says, a working ox ; full of good intentions, but having this vice—for in a father it is a vice—that he does not rule in his own house. All the minor characters—the aunt, Helmer Strille the would-be wolf of Giulia's honour wrapped in the sheep's clothing of art, even the old painter Giulia's second string, who comes in, flustered, after her umbrella—all have just enough character to be a part of the picture. Tommy, hopelessly weak, conceited, and utterly selfish, has a real shrewdness through all his folly and a real affection for his sister, through all his misuse of her. Massimo, sound, honest, and helpful, has just that peculiarly Italian failing—the desire to give reasons for everything. And Nennele, even she, with all her goodness and her common sense, has just two blots on her maidenly perfection— her sadness and her pride : a sadness that clouds her own view of life ; a pride that hurts no one but herself. The one showing her herself stretched dead on the bed in the room she is quitting, and bidding her write on the window ' a curse on whosoever shall occupy this room after me ' ; the other letting Massimo go away disconsolate at the moment of his and her utmost need, and scarcely finding breath to whisper when he is gone that accusing, but self-accusing, ' He doesn't understand ! '

Of ' Tristi Amori ' we shall speak at some length in connection with its performance by Zacconi. Enough has been said for the present to give an idea of Giacosa's powers and limitations as a dramatist. Let us pass on.

Roberto Bracco is another dramatist whom one must at least take seriously, if one takes him at all. Many Italians decline the potion, shrugging their shoulders with a gesture about which, if it be not philosophic, there is at least no doubt. But it is impossible for a theatrical critic to pass him by. Have not his works been collected, nay, are they not still collecting in seven (and prophecy knows not how many more!) important volumes? And have not the reviewers meted out to him honour and praise?

Honour and praise should certainly be his; for he has made a serious effort to be pathetic and humorous. Moreover, his work has an intellectual character which demands and deserves attention. You know that it is not careless, or slipshod. That it is the work of a man whose observation is considerable, whose aims are high, and who has taken pains. But the true fact of the matter is, that you know too much: the intention is too palpable, the means used to attain that end, too evident. As in the case of our own George Meredith, the workings of the mind, the touches of the hand, are too easily seen. It is like the foreign-built engines which show their works externally, compared with our English ones, whose gear is concealed, and which appear, mysterious and majestic; the incarnation of speed. In mechanics, this is, perhaps, a too imaginative point of view to have value: but in literature or drama, the imaginative is the practical; the apparent, the real. And characters in a play lose their convincing reality if we divine the stages by which they came into being. Their gestation is an ideal one in the coils of a man's brain. They are as Athena, born out of the head of Zeus. And however much we may credit Athena as an affair of mythology, we are not easily convinced that her method of coming into the world could be made practically useful for the Mary Anns and Thomases of to-day !

The writer under discussion has another defect : that his spaces of the comic and the pathetic—the two dramatic regions that he chiefly occupies—are rather sharply defined. When comic, he is really comic ; when pathetic, he is deep and sincere. But he lacks the gradations wherewith to pass naturally and insensibly from one to the other. His work resembles a Rembrandt etching rather than a picture by Veronese. His light comedies in one act—they are so called, and they deserve the title—are well imagined and dexterously worked out. But they are all absurdity. His *drammi* are often powerful, moving—even terrible ; but they are pathos unrelieved. They sit on the soul as some legendary maiden, deserted by her lover, sits on a rock, looking over the river towards the sunset, giving out her continual cries. The sun sinks below the horizon, but the wailing goes on. So the theatre doors shut, but the heart is not relieved from the sorrows that have oppressed it.

Writers like this often attempt too much, and achieve too little. Reason is not always a sound judge of impressions and emotions. Their purpose satisfies them, and they work towards it with a complacent earnestness ; not perceiving that they are becoming guilty of the deadly æsthetic sins of tedium and unreality. They prolong situations whose only effect can consist in their passing like a flash. They try to spread out and examine things of so delicate a tissue that their specimens break in their hands. It has been said of Scott that in ' The Monastery ' he made an artistic mistake in exhibiting, at great length, the absurdities of a Euphuist ; and his treatment of Sir Piercie Shafton is compared with that of Osric by Shakespeare, to the great advantage of the latter. Exactly the same remark might be made

of Bracco, comparing his Teresa with Shakespeare's
Ophelia. I have already hinted that Bracco's seven
volumes are a substantial fact of the Italian theatre.
As such, they have naturally come into the dissecting
room of the reviewer, who has pronounced very learnedly
thereon. And, although it may be that a power of
perceiving subtleties begets a disposition to engender
them, I give the remarks of the inquirer as I remember
them and for what they are worth.

In Italy, as the critic points out, the position of woman
is still, in society, a subordinate one. The unmarried
woman can go nowhere without her maid, nor the married
one without her husband. An Italian lady (in the large
middle class, at any rate) must not be guilty of any
original thought or independent action. So long as she
keeps within these conventions, the man is her cavalier
and her servant. He will wait on her, tend her, succour
her ; preserve her from every kind of mental fear or
physical harm. But should she move from the throne on
which he has seated her, stray from the moral harem in
which she has been confined ; should she in act, word, or
thought, show a disposition to put herself into competition
with him, he immediately becomes a tyrant if she
is his, an enemy if she is another's or her own. It is
against this attitude, if we may trust the reviewer, that
Bracco's whole work is a protest. He is the champion
of her right, not to be saved all trouble and preserved
from all injury, not to keep herself apart in silence and
scent ; but to descend into the world, with its fumes, its
strife, its noise ; to seek the pleasures of toil, and dare
the pangs of disappointment.

A writer with a theme like this is, no doubt, apt to
exaggerate, to distort, or magnify, the most commonplace
facts into striking evidence in its favour : nor is the
critic we are dealing with except from this failing. Scenes

G

that are merely inevitable developments, characters which are simply natural and appropriate, become the drums of his propaganda. Nevertheless, though he applies it too seriously, it cannot be said that there is nothing in his view; and little consideration of it illuminates the author's pages in the reading and the speaking of his lines on the stage.

The two plays the present writer has seen, if not the best of Bracco's work are fairly characteristic examples : one, light comedy throughout ; the other, rather more relieved by touches of comedy than his plays usually are which are tragic in their end. It contains, moreover, one of the best male characters that I have come across in his works, and was chosen by Maria Melato for her ' serata d'onore.'

' Infedele,' the lighter piece, I saw twice. The first time by Evelina Paoli, when it struck me as insufficient ; the second time, by Tina di Lorenzo, when it ran—nay, leaped—from start to finish. It is a play in three acts, and has only three characters—the wife, the husband, and a sort of modern and not wholly efficient Don Juan.

It is eminently a play that should be judged by its best, in the way of executants. The writer has relied on a certain brilliancy in the playing. It is like a costume that is designed to be worn by artificial light : its jades and its sequins will not sparkle, its laces and ribbands will look flat and tawdry, beneath the cold, clear light of day. Or it is as water-weed, whose growth looks strong and peaceful when sustained by its own native element, but, when taken out of it, flags and falls into impotence and straight lines.

The intrigue is as light as can be imagined : a husband and wife who really love each other, but in practice go their own ways : she, proud ; he, jealous. She is defied by the Don Juan of the piece to endure his fascinations ;

accepts the challenge, and agrees to meet him in his own rooms. She is discovered there by her husband, who, in spite of her protestations, persists in believing her guilty, but, in spite of his belief, persists in loving her. She forces him to confess his distrust; gives him proof, by means of letters, of her innocence; and then says : ' But for your distrust, I owe you a lover, and I will pay you. It will be all right. I have chosen him already.' And when he insists on knowing who it is, tells him, ' You yourself.' The point of the little play is really reached here. But it is sheathed in one of the neatest situations that ever adorned light comedy. She has told Ricciardi, who has begged to be allowed to say ' farewell,' that she will receive him. She does not, however, await the valiant suitor, but follows her husband into their bedroom. The *tertium quid*, in fine conceit with himself, appears ; straightens his tie and touches his hair before the glass ; and prepares for a last victorious onslaught. Suddenly, wife and husband are heard laughing and talking in the next room. The intruder's face falls—' crumbles,' would be the better word—and no schoolboy, caught stealing and trespassing ever stole more lightly, more crestfallen, away, than this noble warrior from the scene of his proposed triumph.

This is not the only neat situation in the play, but it will serve as a specimen. As a specimen, in like manner, of the good things said, this shall serve : The husband says that this Ricciardi is a danger for every woman— even an honest one. The wife replies, ' Even for me ? ' And he, ' A man is not a danger who is not dangerous to all women.' She answers, ' A woman is not honest who is not honest towards all men.' It is a play, to come back to the point wherefrom we started, of which much may be made ; but which needs much making : and the character of Clara, to repeat our old illustration, is like a flimsy and fashionable dress; its effect depends on the wearer. On the sombre and mysterious form of Evelina Paoli it was comparatively ineffective; but it suited the supple and brilliant person of Tina di Lorenzo to a marvel!

'La Piccola Fonte' is a play of a totally different character. What exactly 'The Little Spring' is, I am not quite clear. Certainly, not anything similar to the 'Petite Source' of Rostand's 'L'Aiglon.' But whether the source of poetry or love, is a small matter; and assuredly its waters have a bitter taste of woe if the pathos is not altogether that proper to drama. Stefano is a writer who aspires to enter society by force of intellect, after having first married a bourgeoise wife—for love, it is to be presumed—in sum, if a genius, a rather unpractical man. A certain princess, fascinated by his manners and trustful in his powers, is ready to lift the velvet curtain for him, but expects in return to receive that homage with which the hand-maidens of the Muses have too often been paid. And while the husband is toying with white fingers and treading soft carpets, the wife is keeping his house, surrounding him with silence, selling her poor little possessions to pay his debts, and receiving, like a moral Lazarus, the broken fragments of confidences and smiles, which fall from the banquet of Intellect! One day, she finds out the true nature of the Principessa's sympathy; and, poor lady, she goes mad. This is at the end of Act II., and through two long acts —is there not something heartless and indelicate about this exhibition of the poor soul?—we see her in her poor crazy incompetence, witless but not painless, until Death, the consoler, getting leave of Fate, cuts short our sympathy and puts an end to her woes.

Some legitimate pathos is got out of an old begging couple, who rhyme and dance; and of whom the woman disappears at the same time as Teresa's wits ; but they are rather forced to the front, to the detriment of more important themes. Stefano, the husband, is not an original creation ; and Teresa, if a pathetic figure, is too perfectly colourless and submissive to give life and distinction to the play. We never have a moment's suspicion that she will be aware of, far less resist, her rival from above ; and the events being too evidently fore-ordained, the development of the action has no thrill for us. But the most interesting character in the play—at least, so it seemed to the present writer—is, as often happens, one quite by the way. Valentino is a cousin of the husband, who is never allowed to make his relationship known, but is kept in the house as a sort of major-domo. Natural incompetence and a hump have soured his disposition on the surface ; but have left him with a heart which is inclined to place his penetrating eye and caustic tongue at the service of the submissive, rather than of the strong. He is charming with Teresa ; kindly and tactful : insignificant with Stefano until, towards the end of the story, a sense of intolerable injustice and the growth of an overmastering sympathy give him courage to speak and act. The following dialogue shows us something of this Valentino. Don Fausto, a furniture dealer, has come to dun the lofty poet ; and the first defender of the fortress that he meets is Valentino, who regrets Stefano's unbusinesslike habits.

Valentino (*putting his pipe in the pocket*). Don't let us mind him. He's a bit distracted.

Don Fausto (*angrily*). Distracted !

Val. It's a disease that poets are liable to.

Don F. (*raising his voice*). It's a disease that I'll very quickly cure.

Val. (*stroking his back as if he were a horse*). Gently, gently, then, Don Fausto.

Don F. Put your hands down, sir !

Val. One of these days, I'll speak to him !

Don F. I've obligations due to-day; must have the cash to honour my signature. By midday, at the latest, my bill must be paid.

Val. By midday ?—it's a little difficult. You see, this is the time that Stefano shuts himself up in his studio, and woe to anyone who disturbs him !

Don F. Shut up or not, if I don't have my money in an hour's time, I'll send your cousin and master an eye-opener, in the shape of a writ and I'll put . . .

Val. A notice in the paper ? [*This was a little habit of Don Fausto.*]

Don F. Neither more nor less. (*Firmly.*)

Val. Stefano will answer in verse.

[*Teresa comes in.*]

Val. (*to Don F.*). This is his wife. Behave like a gentleman to her. (*To her*) There's nothing the matter, Sigra. Teresa. Nothing serious: that is, only Sigr. Don Fausto Cartajello, here present, has a little bill of seventeen hundred francs that he wants paid. A picture frame and two chairs.

Don F. Two armchairs, genuine Henry IV.

Val. Must be those two great chairs with the shoulders. (*Descriptive gesture.*)

Don F. Exactly so. On those two chairs it is certain that Henry IV sat himself.

Val. By Jove ! you can see the marks of him there still.

Don F. Then the frame held the portrait of Napoleon I.

Val. I see. That's why Stefano put his own there.

Teresa (*on the right of Don F., who is deaf*). Yes, but I don't think my husband can put his hands on such a sum to-day. You must have the goodness to wait.

Don F. (*to Valentino*). I must have the goodness to what ?

Val. On the left, Sigra. Teresa.

Ter. The left ?

Val. He's deaf on the right side ; you must speak to him on the left.

Ter. I said that you must have the goodness to wait.

Don F. Ah !—no, madam ! I have already explained to your cousin in the third degree, the reason why I cannot wait.

Ter. (*apart to him*). Valentino !

Val. (*quickly and readily*). What is it ?

Ter. (*aside to him*). You know Stefano doesn't like you to be known as his cousin.

Val. True, but every now and then I forget.

Ter. (*dutifully*). He has his principles. We ought to respect them.

[*Don Fausto cuts in and asks for a decision, with threats to back his request.*]

Ter. Good God ! What's this you say ?

Don F. Besides, my dear madam, I argue like this : that a man who owns a villa at Posillipo, built besides, in a fine position, at the cost of tens of thousands of francs, and goes in a carriage instead of in tram or on foot, as I do . . .

Val. Poor chap ! With that stomach ?

Don F. Yes, sir, with this stomach, I go on foot and hold my head up. What astonishes me, is that Sigr. Stefano Baldi . . .

Val. . . . Goes in a carriage and hangs his down.

Don F. He ought to hang his head, seeing that he can't keep his engagements.

Ter. You are letting your tongue run away with you, sir.

Don F. I don't enjoy being rude to people, but if it's a question of what I've made with the sweat of my brow, I don't mince matters.

Val. Did you make Napoleon's frame with the sweat of your brow ?

Don F. Certainly.

The little dialogue thus taken from its place may not seem a very dramatic one, but it shows on the stage some of the power that Giacosa showed, in a higher degree, in ' Come le Foglie '—of making the thoughts and words of ordinary people interesting upon the stage. The simple wifeliness of Teresa, who can stop in the middle of more important matters to rebuke her husband's cousin for disobeying the former's not very admirable directions, and defend these, clearly in spite of herself ; and the shrewdness of Valentino, his roughness, and desire to use his tongue, which always yield to an almost chivalrous gentleness where Teresa is concerned : all this is surely excellently like life. Valentino does not prove, on further acquaintance, to be only a marionette with tricks to produce a certain effect. He pleases us, largely because he is ineffective. Here we have him with the servant (Act II. sc. 1).

Val. (*in shabby evening suit, calling and ringing*). Romolo ! Romolino ! Romolone ! Base servitor of an imperial name ! Sigra. Teresa ! Sigra. Teresa !

Rom. (*enters from the hall with an important and insolent air*). Sigra. Teresa doesn't answer and it's pretty clear she's not in.

Val. Impossible !

Rom. She is gone out, I tell you !

Val. When ?

Rom. About an hour after Sigr. Stefano went.

Val. That's very strange.

Rom. Why ? Ought she to have asked your leave ?

Val. Don't try and be witty, and don't call me ' thou.' [*Rom. has used the familiar form of speech.*] I forbid you to call me ' thou,' and I call on you to respect the secretary of the great poet !

Rom. Pooh !

Val. Go to your place.

Rom. All right.

Val. Adorn yourself in your yellow livery. Mameluke ! open the principal gate of the villa, light all the lamps in the park, and illuminate the house. These are your master's orders, who will shortly come back to the house with a personage of the highest importance.

Rom. And aren't you going to put your livery on ? [*He uses the ' thou ' again.*]

Val. Will you still say ' thou ' to me ?

Rom. (*turning his back on him*). Go and hang yourself !

Val. I can't promise you that, because I have a mortal terror of death. [*Exit* Romolo.

Our next and best view of him shall be when the princess has come and gone; Teresa has failed in the ordeal of the meeting; Meralda has laughed at her; and Stefano has been more than vexed.

Val. (*after the others have gone out, from within*). The goddess has gone, Sigra. Teresa. (*Enters rubbing his hands.*) But I am always losing the great man's wife. Sigra. Teresa!

Stef. (*entering*). Where are you off to in such a hurry?

Val. I saw from my observatory that you had accompanied the princess to her carriage, and I had come to chatter over the event with Sigra. Teresa. Not finding her, I was going to look for her.

Stef. If you think I want to be present at your conversation, undeceive yourself.

Val. We won't converse, then.

Stef. But what was there to discuss? I have no patience with all the tittle-tattle that goes on in my house.

Val. What tittle-tattle, please?

Stef. (*not answering him*). Oh! the joy of living alone!

Val. (*anxiously*). Look! here comes Sigra. Teresa; don't be too unkind to her. Her little body and her brain are ground to pieces with these continual shocks.

Stef. Your imagination exaggerates every trifle.

Val. If you knew what she had done this evening you would be as frightened as I am.

Stef. What has she done?

Val. Hush! here she comes.

(*Enter* Teresa *with red eyes. Silence then, with a frightened voice.*)

Ter. Did you send for me?

Stef. (*trying not to speak roughly*). No, Teresa.

Ter. Then do you want me to go back to my room?

Stef. That's a superfluous question, too. We have nothing to say to each other, Teresa; and your restlessness . . . gives me great distress. I had rather we did not meet.

Ter. My restlessness?

Stef. Yes, Valentino, too, remarked to me that you were not in a normal state. (*Annoyance on the part of Valentino.*)

Ter. I was so glad for your success.

Stef. What has happened to make you change ? Do you think you ought to have cried ? I ask you, if you think it's a nice thing to do to come and make me unhappy this very evening ?

Val. (*aside*). If I don't go, I shall break out. (*Goes and takes a turn in the park.*)

[*Stefano then scolds Teresa, and tells her to be cheerful. Teresa begins to laugh, but with a laugh that bodes ill. Valentino hears it in passing, and mistakes its nature at first.*]

Val. Ah ! So good humour comes back when I am gone ?

Ter. (*her laughter becoming convulsive*). If you knew—if you only knew—Valentino, what a silly I've been !

Val. By Jove ! that's not the right sort of laugh, though.

Stef. Do me the favour not to trouble me any more. Is it possible that you are not aware of the respect you owe me ?

(*Teresa's laughter stops suddenly ; a long silence.*)

Val. (*timidly*). I don't think I have ever been wanting in respect to you, Stefano.

Stef. It's not of you that I am complaining now.

Ter. Then . . . it's I who am wanting in respect ?

Stef. (*following his own train of thoughts*). To keep the spiritual food that I have need of, I must concentrate myself in my inspiration, in my work. I must avoid, without considering anyone, whatever is unfaithful to me, albeit, with motives of affection ; and every other life which would attach itself to mine. If the woman who would call herself my wife were not some little creature, she would be able to stand by my side—loving and watchful, yes—but living her own life. Such as she is, she has only one way of respecting me—on the whole a noble sense of the word : that of resigning herself to the smallest possible existence. [Surely egotism can go no further.]

Ter. (*trying to conceal the distress that is overpowering her*). If it is for your good I will try and disappear altogether.

Stef. Oh, fine ! And now for my greater consolation, you are threatening me with the tragedy of suicide.

Ter. No, no ! I didn't mean that. Suicide . . . is not for me. I only said that I might . . . might go away. [Can you see poor Valentino all this time watching the dialogue, trying to interfere, but nervous both on his own account and of making her case the worse?]

Stef. Where?

Ter. I don't know. A convent.

Stef. A convent? Nonsense!

Ter. Or to my aunt's. (*Short pause.*)

Stef. I . . . naturally . . . should stop you. Nevertheless, I agree that if you were ready to go to your aunt's, not permanently, of course, but for a little time . . . I should do wrong to interfere. She lives near . . . we could often meet. . . . Meanwhile, I could work in solitude to finish some work that is promised; and you, chastened by some months' absence, would come back more inclined to be what I wish you to be.

Ter. For ever! For ever, Stefano! I am a burden to you. I've seen it for some time, and I've tried to deny it to myself . . . I am your incubus. I had better go away for ever. (*Bursts into tears.*)

Stef. Teresa! for goodness' sake, don't torment me by crying too.

Val. (*bursting out finally*). But, gracious heavens, you are just going to send her away and you won't even let her cry.

Stef. Oh! (*Goes out and slams the door.*)

The opposition of the two characters suggests a reflection for real life. How often, in point of character, is success commonplace, and failure interesting? How often should we pass by the managing-director for a concern, and interest ourselves in his dismissed employés? How often get away from the major-general and talk to the private or N.C.O.? And this is not because of the interest attached to possibilities, as Kipling has shown us in his drunken failure, Private Mulvaney. Mont Blanc rules the Alps by right of altitude, but has not the terror of the Matterhorn, nor the charm of the Jungfrau. The lion is the king of beasts, but he had no place found for him in 'The Jungle Book.' So the author in setting these two characters in opposition, though one perhaps strikes us as unnatural and exaggerated, has shown us a really deep truth. And as real truths are not to be picked up every day, let us confess ourselves duly grateful.

There are some authors who seem driven by Nature the spontaneous, to put out, year by year, that which the judgment of man, year by year, methodically consigns to the rubbish heap. These rubbish heaps of literature are strange things. They exist almost everywhere where books abound. Nearly every private library has its rubbish corner of works, bound, like antiquated ideas, with military uniformity. The catalogue of the second-hand bookseller is often nothing else than such a corner glorified: rich with the titles of works that no one reads, having a value only because their worthlessness has contributed to their rarity. And the situation is all the more pathetic because, owing to the press and the national library, it is hard if any printed matter perish utterly. It is caught and embalmed into an unnatural existence; it cannot rot like the boots, or rust away like kettles, which make the principal parts of our roadside jetsam; but is cursed, even as Tithonus, with perpetual existence without perpetual youth.

There are, nevertheless, some writers whom Nature seems to have excited to the output aforesaid not without a sound purpose: whose humdrum work, persisted in over long years, seems to be but the wrappings of some great treasure, or the roots of some noble tree. Of such as these is, I believe, Sigr. Gerolamo Rovetta. Most of his work is, if I mistake not, ordinary enough. He is gifted with a considerable insight, but one that is constantly misapplied: a man with patience enough to write continually, but not enough to learn by study what is needed to make him write supremely well. Perhaps, as we have said, Nature, who prompted him, knew best what she was doing ; for one day he girt up his loins and wrote a play which will, I believe, thrill the hearts of men wherever, and as long as, Italian patriotism endures.

We may first give just a glance at one of his ordinary works. ' Papà Eccellenza ' (Father and Statesman) is a good study of an Italian man of affairs, who, adoring his daughter, ends by letting his fondness for her disable him from serving his country. The worthless and frivolous girl, the trivial and speculating lover, the husband, faithful and affectionate, but proud and tact- less, are all good sketches grouped round the out- standing central figure. The play moves well enough at the beginning, but has the defect of an exceedingly weak third act. One's principal thought on seeing it is of what an exceedingly good drama might have been made from the materials.

Let us pass on to ' Romanticismo,' perhaps the most thrilling Italian prose play we have seen : one in which the spectator loses all sense of audience or theatre, and becomes as one who stands watching from a cliff some noble ship dashed on the rocks by contrary winds, breaking to pieces before his eyes ; hears the cry of the lost ; sees the fortitude of the sailors, and knows that there is hope and safety, the utmost that may be, for every traveller on an English ship, while English sailors can, with that tranquil courage, stand before the impregnable fortress of death. But what are we saying ? It is the Barque of State, the good ship Italia, which before our eyes is driving towards seeming annihil- ation ; waited by oppressors and pillagers, lured to destruc- tion by false friends. Is there, perhaps, some strange resemblance—if it were so it would throw light on the living sympathy of the time—between the British sailor and the Italian liberator—each daring a hopeless death to

give to others promise of life ?—each, cheerful and calm
in the face of danger, and, by a heroism, making his death
doubly heroic, concealing his own agony of mind, that
those who won to safety might not even have the bitter
mark of his trial stamped upon the surface of their joy ?

'Romance!' It is thus that the Austrian tyrant cyni-
cally characterised the longings of his Italian subjects
after the impossible ideal of freedom ; their wish to
rule in their own house, manage their own affairs,
dispose of their own revenue ; their hope that a time
would come when their brothers and sons would no
longer be shot for treason in resisting a power which they
hated : their mothers no longer flogged at the stake
for sympathy with those who were punished and put
to death : when only malefactors should be in prison,
only murderers brought to the block. Romance ! Romance ! The hope of liberty, of justice, of internal
peace, in the middle of the nineteenth century ; in
our great Victorian era of plenty and prosperity. When
our statesmen had nothing more vital to occupy them
than Catholic Emancipation, our gentlemen nothing
more serious than the sport of hunting, or the sirens
of Vauxhall. Romance ! So men thought then—nay,
so it was. But the wild dreams of yesterday have
become the solid fact of to-day. To-day, in Rome a
king rules and a parliament sits. To-day, at the passes
of the Alps, an Italian and an Austrian fort watch side
by side ; and the power that oppressed the 'geographical
expression' of sixty years ago seeks her hand in alliance
now. Truly she has risen ; and the wings that bore her
to her present heights, the weapons and the wisdom
which guard her present doors, were forged by a faith
that has indeed removed mountains, working in dark
recesses, which were only lit by the unquenchable flames
of the liberators' own great souls.

The play of ' Romanticismo ' opens in 1854, in the back-room of a chemist's shop in Como, kept by Giovanni Ansperti, whose son Tito is in the hands of the Austrians in Venice, and on his trial for conspiracy.   In this back-room, conspirators are meeting under the pretext of a harmless game of cards.   We see a mixed company to-night : a doctor, a publisher, a priest ; and a noble-man who has come to demand admission to the secret society, and who is distrusted because of his position and the known opinions of his mother.   We feel the sense of insecurity ; the hurried rush to the card-table, the heavier beat of the assistant's pestle (Demosthenes, Heaven save us !), signifying danger, the sinister faces of the gendarmes behind the glass door.   How much of our own emotions is due to what goes on upon the stage, it is difficult to decide.   It is a play that is not played by the actors only.   The whole audience become the ' supers ' who vivify and enlarge the action.   Consider that you are in Venice, where the patriot was actually put to death ; that you have men around you who remem-ber the despair that held the whole city—even, perhaps, saw the fatal blow fall ; that there is a stone not a mile from you, which the rains that have fallen have not yet washed clean of his blood, and then, remembering that it is the oath which he himself took, and for his faithfulness to which his life paid the penalty—listen to these words :—

In the name of God and of Italy.   In the name of all the martyrs of the sacred Italian cause, fallen under the blows of the tyrant, whether foreign or of our own race.   By the duties which bind me to the land where God has set me, and to the brothers whom God has given me. . . .   By the love, innate in every man, to the places where my father was born and where my children shall live. . . .   By the hatred, innate in every man, for evil, injustice, usurpation, oppression.

. . . By the blush that I wear before the citizens of other nations, for the lack of name, rights of citizenship, national flag, mother country. . . . By the fury of a mind created for liberty, powerless to exercise it ; created for an activity towards good and powerless to accomplish it, in the silence and isolation of slavery. By the memory of former power, by the consciousness of present abjection. . . . By the tears of the Italian mothers for their sons dead on the scaffold, in prison, in exile: I, Vitaliano Lamberti, Count of Agliate, believing in the power committed by God to Italy, and convinced that the people is the depository of that power—that in the guiding of it for the people, and by the people, lies the secret of victory . . . give my name to Young Italy, an association of men holding the same faith ; and swear to consecrate myself wholly and for ever to the task of raising Italy into a nation one, free, independent . . . Swear! Calling down on my head the wrath of God, the contempt of man, and the infamy of perjury, if I betray in whole or in part this my oath.

In fact, it is hard for any effort of mind to realise the scene in the house, the wrapped faces, the thunderclap of cheers at the end. No effort of the mind in absence can imagine how those words are received— nay, nor in presence enter into the feelings which ordain that silence and that cry—if they have not felt the oppressor's hand on them in their own home for many a long weary year. A Pole might feel it fully. An Englishman hardly can. The first act which contains this oath, which paints the life of the humbler conspirators in the agonising suspense which preceded Tito's execution, and which ends with the words, spoken to the gendarmes over the fainting body of his wife: ' Leave at least to our women the freedom to die of grief,' is undoubtedly the finest in the play. At this point it divides too absolutely into two parts; and henceforth the action revolves round a different centre and amid new surroundings. The fate of Tito Speri is our anxiety in the first part; that of Vitaliano Lamberti, in the second; and the death, or death-sentence, of each, ends the section which their lives had animated. Nevertheless, the last three acts of the play are good and full of force. And the end which the author proposes to himself—namely, to show how irresistible was the power of the movement all through its course in spite of the oppressors' apparent success—is never lost sight of. Scene after scene shows us the most improbable persons joining in the conspiracy; line after line, their utter self-devotion to the cause. In this respect there is a speech in the third act—short but wonderfully telling—which, philosophically speaking, is even more the hub of the drama than the oath which has been quoted above. The wife of Lamberti is being tempted to betray the names of other conspirators in order to save her husband's life. He comes on the scene in time to release her.

I will tell you—he breaks out to the inquisitors—and mind you remember them well. They are the names of all who have hearts and heads, of all who remember and hate. Go out into the streets and the squares. Go into the theatres, the churches : everywhere where people are pretending to amuse themselves or to pray; everywhere where people are suffering and hiding their torn coats. Name . . . the names ! (*He laughs aloud.*) Aha ! first enlarge your prisons, make them as big as our cities are, and take us there. . . . The name is the name of all. It is the hour—the hour has come ! We are all conspirators and rebellious.

This is the real keynote which holds the play together; and, when at the last we see erect the doomed figure of Lamberti, with his distracted wife clinging to his arm, we see, besides the destruction advancing towards their faces to crush them, the light of the new dawn, illuminating them from behind.

H

We come now to a writer of whom, if what we say seems to smack of damning with faint praise, let it be noted that from the mouth of the average Italian the damnation would be a great deal more definite, the praise still more faint. He is ' poveretto ' : label of all that is well-meaning and inefficient. And yet out of his inefficiency—not always, by any means, absolute—there is a continued outcrop of sound observation, pathetic power, and humorous suggestion. In a way, he is important, as being—if in exaggerated measure—a type, both of the virtues and vices, of the Italian writing in general. Beyond all others, he merits the title of sincere. His plays are earnest, his themes honourable, his efforts unceasing, his successes few. He has toiled all night— a night of strange dreams, wonderful lights, and spiritual visions—and when the cold, gray dawn comes upon him, its doubtful light distinguishes but a few small stiff and common fishes in his net. He is an idealist for the stage, and his idealism has landed him by his last strenuous effort in a castle of dreams.[1] And yet with all this, he, when he passes away to that place where, perchance, to-day's dreams shall become to-morrow's realities, will have left us good solid work; for which we shall be duly, if temperately, grateful. Nay, more : we may find among this dramatist's pot hooks and hangers something which will make us look on the cheerful side of life, and gather (perhaps from him alone among the Italian stage-writers) good honest mirth, without an after-thought and without a care.

The most recent of his serious plays that I have witnessed is ' Nel Paese della Fortuna ' (In the Land of Fortune). I cannot do better than transcribe,

---

[1] The title of an elaborate verse play : one never acted, I believe, but which the author was very assiduous in reading to appreciative audiences.

almost textually, the comments made the day following :—

A drama that very strikingly exhibits the characteristic of the serious modern Italian plays.

1. Unhappiness.
2. The use of physical means to attain it.
3. Uncertainty as to what the central thread of the story is to be.
4. Long preliminary divagations.

There is an Italian prince at Monaco, in impecunious circumstances, with a daughter aged about thirty, not in the best of health. There is also at the Casino a young German Jew, a millionaire ironmaster (Is the combination quite a natural one ?), who is desperately in love with the daughter. In the first scene of the play, which takes place at a public reception, Beatrice is indisposed, and the prince gets the ironmaster to see her home. She protests to her father, ' What you are doing is very wrong.' One would suppose from the prominence given to this incident that he was scheming a marriage which she was trying to resist. But the play does not develop on these lines. Enter next the confidential family solicitor, who tells the prince that all is lost, and wishes to resign. He is over-persuaded, and they are apparently getting back to friendly terms again, when the prince proposes to sell his daughter's patrimony to carry on his affairs. Crack goes the understanding ; exit notary, threatening to communicate with the prince's wife (who, it appears, has been either separated or divorced from him), and make common cause with her in the defence of Beatrice. Curtain falls on the prince letting off steam to a kind of Everybody's Confidential Friend.

In Act II. the Jew successfully makes love to Beatrice : his meeting with her being arranged by the E.C.F., on whose advice also, the prince her father borrows money from the lover. In Act III. Beatrice has to confess to her father the fact of her being in an interesting situation ; it having also appeared, since her act of folly, that the Jew is a married man. The prince now plays the Gran Signore for all it is worth. Pours contempt on Germany and Jerusalem, and scorn on the daughter who could have anything so personal to do with either. In the end, the father says ' You have gone the way of your mother.'

Beatrice. ' I had better leave you, and join her.' *The father.* ' You are not leaving me. I am turning you out.' But when Beatrice turns to go, the father in him becomes too strong, and he cries out ' You are all I have. I cannot part with you ; ' and the curtain comes down with them in each other's arms.

Act IV. finds the prince and the notary in discussion. The former wants to challenge the Jew (whose wife has appeared on the scene), but cannot in ' honour ' because of his debt. However, in real Adelphi fashion, the agent whips out notes for 75,000ffcs., derived from some economy or windfall, which he had not thought fit to mention before, and the prince proceeds to charge with the delicate commission the E.C.F., who has just dropped in. The latter, by ingenious, but as wholly disgusting casuistry, tries to persuade the prince to issue no challenge, and take the Jew's money as the price of his daughter's dishonour. He goes out, leaving the prince and his agent still in a doubtful discussion, when a ghastly figure rolls on to the stage. Beatrice has ended her own troubles and her father's doubts once for all.

Now the play has good moments in it, but is dreadfully wanting in stage-craft ; being now a kind of cynical comedy, now melodrama, and now tragedy, in a most bewildering sequence. The first act contains little or no action, and hardly succeeds even in indicating the scope of the plot. The success of the Jew in his love-making to Beatrice is both repellent and unnatural, and the way the former wholly drops out of the play, after having been its chief ornament in the first acts, leaves a rather sudden want in the mind, and can hardly be artistically justified by Sam Weller's prescription for letter-writers. The third act is the best : there is real, moving nature in it ; and the mixture of family pride and parental love, contending together, give that uncertainty of result which is the soul of dramatic interest. As regards the characters, we continually feel a want of nature in them : in the ironmaster, that he ever should have pleased a girl like Beatrice ; in Beatrice, that she should ever have been pleased ; and in the prince, her father, that he should ever have given an ear to a scandalous proposition such as that of the E.C.F. And yet, with all this, they interest us—interest us deeply. We seem to be moving in a world of dreams—to know that we are dreaming, and yet to lack the power to arouse ourselves and get back to real life.

In justice to Butti, I ought to make a short note of his ' Il Cuculo ' (The Cuckoo), which is an affair of real and pervading fun. It needs playing all through in a real comedy spirit, and the slightest touch would be enough to send the whole thing into farce. In fact (and this is typical of the author), at one or two points it does cross the boundary. But it was splendidly acted by Giovanini and the company ; and certainly sent us away—if I may speak for others besides myself—in the merriest frame of mind in which I have ever left an Italian theatre.

The theme is a simple one. A youthful-looking deputy of about fifty is trying, in one of those Spas so common in Italy, to pass as a young man and make love to a widow in every way desirable—young, lovely, charming, and rich. He is just beginning to flatter himself that his assiduities are being crowned by a discreet success, when, who should come down upon them but his lusty and bearded son of twenty-four? Fury of father, astonishment of widow. Gradual drawing together, first by the bonds of pure sympathy, then by a livelier and more tender interest, of the widow and son. The father orders his son to leave. The widow pleads for an extension of time, in order that the latter may lead the party on a long-planned mountain expedition : and the father, not liking the widow's advocacy, and yet not thinking it prudent to refuse her, lets him stay. The excursionists go. They are delayed. Some legitimate comedy is got out of the picture of the landlord, the deputy, and his secretary newly arrived from Rome, running out to watch, through the hotel telescope, the far-off mountain. While some one has his eye to the glass, the party, by some unexpected route, appear. But, alas ! the son, lamed by an accident, is borne on the back of a 'man of the mountains.' A doctor inspects his injury, and declares that instead of starting by the 9.50 for Milan, he cannot be moved for twenty days, so that the now desperate father, called to Rome by urgent public affairs, must resign himself to leaving behind his undutiful offspring, an object of sentimental interest to all the idle elegant of the Spa—'especially Ellen McJones Aberdeen,' in the person of the bewitching widow Ortensia.

Let us take leave of Sigr. Butti with this piece of straightforward innocent fun-making, and turn elsewhere. Marco Praga is a personage of importance in the politics of dramatic authorship, a president of the Society of Authors in Milan ;[1] but his plays hardly have the importance that this position would seem to suggest.

Of the two of them that I have seen, one, ' La Moglie Ideale ' (The Ideal Wife), seemed indifferent, and only

[1] Now resigned.

redeemed from failure by the excellent acting of Tina di Lorenzo, and of her husband, Armando Falconi. The other, ' La Crisi,' is referred to elsewhere.1 A good acting play, in spite of certain defects that have been touched upon, and one that, charged with not a few speeches of passionate self-expression and abandonment, is typical of the genuine character of the Italian drama—whole-souled, spontaneous, utterly removed from anything like tradition or the teaching of schools.

A short extract will suffice. Raimondo, an ex-colonel, returned from a ten-years' absence ; has fought a duel with a man whom he discovered to be his sister-in-law's lover, and he is lying about the reasons of the duel to keep his brother, Piero, in the dark. Finally, he is driven to confess.

Raimondo. The truth, . . . the truth is this. I saw, or I thought I saw, that Pucci was making love to your wife—was undermining your peace and your honour. Therefore, I chose the first pretext to give him a little lesson, and get him out of your way. That's all.

Piero. Which would have been unnecessary on your part if you had seen that my wife had rejected his advances : either because she was an honest woman or because she preferred her husband. Instead of that . . .

Rai. Instead—instead, . . . I never gave a thought to your wife and her sentiments. I am not one of those who are fond of reasonings or lengthy discussions. I see a danger, and I put it out of the way. To-day it was that one, to-morrow it might have been another. I thought it a good thing to make an example.

Pie. And since I didn't do it myself . . .

Rai. You, . . . you were in love—faithful and blind, like all lovers. Why give you a suspicion and open a wound ? To what end ? I act from caprice, as I have the right to do. I had not the matter for warning you—for attacking your peace of mind—in a suspicion : an impression which might be a mistaken one, and without a single proof in my hands.

---

1 Page 44.

Pie. And you are lying—lying still—out of pity. You have the proofs !

Rai. Of what ?

Pie. Of her betrayal and my shame. Hush ! hush ! Don't lie any more, my poor Raimondo. You're not a boy. You are a man of honour ; you wouldn't have acted as you have done without proofs. You have what I could have had myself—and very easily—if I had wanted it. I had only to intercept letters, or dismiss a maid to make her blab ; or follow up the indications, so precise and minute, which the anonymous letter-writers gave me !

Rai. But what are you saying ?

Pie. The truth—the truth—horrid and obscene ! The incredible truth !

Rai. (*stares at him for an instant*). No, indeed, I think my wits are wandering. You had suspicions ; you received denunciations and held your tongue ; never tried to verify the truth, and lived in a state of uncertainty and . . . went on loving and idolising your wife. Is it possible ?

Pie. It is the fact. I deceived myself for a while ; for a while I fidgeted and tortured myself ; but I ended by turning everything to my advantage—to the advantage, that is, of my love and my fear. Appearances are deceptive, I said to myself. Anonymous denunciations are so many ignoble grudges ; the venting of envy, or even the pastime of evil human nature, and the fear of discovering a miserable truth held me back, bound me, imprisoned me. I was near death at times, but death did not come. Search and inquiry might have led to it, and I did not want to die : I wanted to live for her kisses, for her caresses—desperately, abjectly.

The reader thinks, perhaps, that self-analysis cannot be more bitter, nor self-abandonment more complete ? What has gone before, in the presence of his strong and tactful brother ? What follows in that of his fickle and fascinating wife ?

Piero. You speak of proof, Nicoletta, and you don't see how, with a man like me, one warm, loving, affectionate word outweighs them all.   A kiss outweighs an oath; a caress, a proof; an embrace, a promise.

Nicoletta. Ah! how sentimental! That's not my way, you know. I had a very sad childhood, though it seemed gay enough. I had miserable experiences before my eyes and moving sights which have hardened me. Sentimentality was killed in me as a baby. As a child, I was like a woman with a soul full of bitterness. No, I love for love's sake, like you. In certain hours of our existence you have found in me the lover whom you wanted—who pleased you. But the sentimental was never in my life. At this moment it would be abject, because it would come from self-interest. Believe me, Piero, we had better part.

Pie. Be it so, then. You ask it yourself, so I ought to see that that amounts to a confession. (*Movement of contradiction in Nicoletta.*) Yes, because at the bottom, your character is sound and sincere. . . . Be it so, and since I love you, my statement will astonish you; but what would you have? It is so, and I, too, cannot lie nor hide my sentiments. So I have no vindictive feelings against you, and should never think of troubling him whom you had been able to love and prefer to me. I shall not harm you. Go where you will. I will provide for you with all the generosity of which I am capable. I shall need little myself. Losing you, I lose every reason and every desire towards life, and if I die . . . (*Movement of Nicoletta.*) Don't interrupt me. If I die, your existence shall be assured. I, too, have no more to say to you. I leave you mistress here, till the day it suits you to leave, and don't be afraid of annoyance on my brother's part. He has said nothing to me, not even that he saw you come out of that house. (*Nicoletta cannot repress a movement of surprise.*) I knew it from yourself. Raimondo has persisted till the last moment in trying to make me believe that he knew nothing and that his duel had another cause. Tell him that I already knew . . .

Nic. What?

Pier. All and nothing. See! you would not wish to live here suspected. Now that all is over between us, and it doesn't matter if I lower myself in your eyes, I can tell you that you have been living here unaware of it. (*Nic. looks at him amazed.*) For months and months some unknown person has been at work trying to wound me in my love, to strike at the root of my faith. I should hardly have had, perhaps, to move a finger, to take one step to find out. Perhaps I myself might have seen you coming out of that house. But I loved you so much, and so little wisely, that I would not. I preferred still to hide the danger and deceive myself. And the deception was not difficult, when all's said and done; because the only thing that I would have taken as proof—true, evident, absolute—was to be sought for in you . . . and . . . I didn't find it. You . . . (*with a sob*) you have said it . . . you love for love's sake. (*He covers his face with a sense of utter disgust.*) Ah! at this moment I despise myself, I swear, as I could not have conceived it possible for a man to despise himself. (*With a last effort*) Good-bye, Nicoletta! (*He rushes away.*)

Perhaps the most remarkable thing about the play is its end. I have already commented on the almost perverse tendency of Italian playwrights to twist a doubtful theme, even a theme in moving towards a prosperous issue, into misery and ruin. Here the materials for misery were abundant, but the dramatist has had character enough to take his own line, and find a happy issue out of all these afflictions.

It is short, and quite well written enough to pay for quotation. The husband, wife, and brother are together on the scene. She has already announced her intention of leaving him as we have seen. Raimondo is doing all he can to patch up a peace, but has himself determined that he must go and live in some other city, not being able to endure a continual intercourse with the false wife.

Raimondo. The truth! Yes! Oh, don't ask your wife! She's perverse to a degree. She hasn't denied her mistake. You may thank God she hasn't exaggerated it, for, . . . oh, deuce knows why! Accused and suspected, she disdained to defend herself. It sounds like the recollection of some romance or comedy. But she confessed the truth to me a month ago, when she was convinced that I knew the whole of it.

Piero (*breaking out*). The truth, the truth! What is it then, Nicoletta?

Rai. (*intervening*). That she has committed a silly blunder, and her pride prevents her confessing it. She's made that way. What could you have? A great sin she would have confessed, perhaps; a slight one, which wore a serious appearance, no. She went to see that man in his house, that is all.

Pie. (*sad and incredulous*). Oh!

Rai. When his wound was bound up, he might have gone on with the duel. He signified his wish to speak to me. I went up to him. ' I fought,' he said, ' and I am ready to go on. First, however, and now that it cannot have the appearance of cowardice, I want to give you my word of honour that I am not that lady's lover.' I repeated those words to your wife and she confessed that it is the truth. She cannot lie.

[*But Piero still is doubtful.*]

Rai. I cannot convince you and give you back your faith. Your wife must do that (*looking at Nicoletta*). And she will be able to do it, and it will be very easy. You will see. It's a question of time that peace and love shall reign again in your hearts, . . . and now I will leave you.

Pie. (*seizing his hand*). Ah, no, Raimondo! don't leave me at this moment. I implore you!

Rai. My dear fellow. My seconds are waiting for me; I've asked them to lunch—it's the least one can do under the circumstances. Then at four I start . . .

Pie. (*getting up*). You start . . .

Rai. Yes. Didn't I tell you? . . . Oh, confound it, with all this business on hand. . . . I'm going to Turin. I had a telegram from an English friend, in whose company I travelled in the Congo State. He's come from London, and he wants to see me on important business. It's a question of a project he had already spoken to me of out there: an enterprise that he wanted me to take part in. At London he had to get certain promises of support. The affair interested me a bit, and I want to go.

Pie. Will you be long?

Rai. I don't know. It depends; . . . three or four days, a week, perhaps. . . . Good-bye, Nicoletta! (*He goes off; Piero accompanies him to the door.*)

Nic. (*murmuring to herself*). What a life will it be! What a life! What a punishment! What a torment! (*They, too, hear her murmuring and turn. Nicoletta turns towards them, then breaks out.*) No, Raimondo, no! The truth, the truth!

Rai. (*runs up to stop her*). Nicoletta!

Nic. The truth—let me speak! It is not pride—no! It is the soul asserting its overpowering need. It is the desire for the right. Afterwards, let come what God will. But no more deception. Piero! Raimondo has lied—for your sake and for mine. I have been the mistress of that man, . . . but I did not love him: I did not love him, I swear to you. And yesterday was the end of it when Raimondo first saw me. And he has sent me my letters back. There they are! (*Piero makes a movement to take them, but Raimondo anticipates him and puts them in his pocket.*) I have told you all, now—all, the whole truth—because I had to tell you; because I saw that we had not the right to lie to you and deceive you. I mean well by you, as I have never meant to anyone else, and to-day more than ever, . . . and I shall always feel so towards you, and always be faithful to you, whatever you do to me and however you decide to punish me. I tell you, because I have lied to you for the first time in my life, and because I could not remain and live under a deception. . . . I was disillusioned, and I have repented. I would have been silent for your sake if I had believed that you knew nothing and believed in me; . . . but, since you doubted, I could not have lived so, suspected by you. . . . Now, do what you like. . . . Punish me as you will, . . . it will always be better than if Raimondo had had his way . . . (*She falls exhausted on the sofa. Piero covers his face. Raimondo goes up to him, takes away his hands from his face.*)

Rai. Piero, Piero! Look at me and listen to me. That woman is yours for the first time. Until now, you have had her body only, now you have her spirit and her heart as well.

To-day, for the first time, she is truly your wife. You will be noble and just. You will pardon and forget. See, Piero! (*He goes up to Nicoletta and lightly touches her hair with his lips. Then goes back to Piero, takes the latter's head between his hands and kisses it as a father might. Then he picks up his hat.*) And now I go away content. Not so before. I shall not leave you now. The Englishman and the Congo were a fib, too. Now I can stay. I shall be continually here with you two, and about you two. . . . We shall meet again soon. (*And he goes out and leaves the two together.*)

Surely, this is as powerful as it is wholesome, true, and natural! The dramatist has found his characters in disorder and woven in the threads of their life. He has found doubt and left confidence; found distrust and left peace and affection; and he has done it in simple and moving words. Were I a dramatic author, I think it is the praise that I should be best pleased to deserve.

I must note, finally, in the play one peculiarity, which I think I remember coming across in another Italian play of which I have no record: namely, that one act resumes the action at the point where the preceding one left it. It is not ineffective, in fact; but it would be rather a long matter to discuss whether it is artistically justifiable. One's feeling is that the repose between the acts should suggest a corresponding interval in the action: that the acts should resemble so many window peeps, which disclose to us just so wide a view of the events that our imaginations may supply the rest. However, if technically a mistake, it is one that is not very likely to be abused. For the dramatist is usually only too ready to make use of the interval during which —in England at least—we divert our palates with ices and whisky-and-sodas, for burdening our minds with all sorts of imaginary events, equally unnecessary and indigestible.

I cannot leave out from this list of dramatists—why,

indeed, should I desire it ?—the name of Alfredo Testoni. In truth, after Roberto Bracco, he has, most of all those who furnish matter for boards, the comedy-writing habit. Society pieces, in which countesses, barons, liveried servants—whether of present or past days—amiably figure passions no deeper than the paint on the marchesa's cheek ; plots held together by threads as light as the sewing of a silken blouse ;—these he has always on hand awaiting your esteemed orders. 'Managing his pen with the negligent ease of a man of quality,' wrote Scott of Byron. So can we see Sigr. Testoni, with carefully curled moustache, and flower in his button-hole, strutting along . . . the Pincio, the Cascine, the . . .—what does it matter which ?—receiving the bows of all the available contesse, marchese, baronesse, *e via dicendo* ; and noting down, in an elegant pocket-book too small to disturb the sit of his neat morning-coat, any peculiarities in their behaviour which were marked by his eagle eye.

'What nonsense is this ? ' says the perplexed reader. ' I'll wager a guinea the fellow has never seen him at all ! ' There you are out, gentle reader ; for we had the fortune, on the occasion of a celebration in honour of Giacosa, not only to see the said Testoni, but to hear him divide with the author whose discourse he read, and whom modesty or prudence kept in the background, the applause which greeted its delivery. And was he . . . Well, I give in, I cry ' Peccavi ! ' I admit, gentle reader, if you will, that this is not the way to criticise the serious drama.

But, then, is Testoni's work serious drama ? I doubt if either his worst friend or his best enemy could claim so much with a grave face. His comedies are good ones, then—they make you laugh ? Well, they do not wrench a laugh out of you against your will. Play one to a condemned convict, and he would probably take no more notice than of the buzzing of a blue-bottle. Go to the theatre with a headache, or a soul-racking grievance such as prompts a man to write to the 'Morning Post,' and you will probably think it a stupid enough show. You must be there in the theatre frame of mind. You must come to hear these society people, as a man goes into society—having carefully looked out a selection of his most appropriate repartees, and chosen tactfully from his stock of insignificant smiles. The applause must flow naturally from your finger-tips; the laughter crackle without an effort between your teeth ; and then lord, lady, and distinguished advocate will delight you with their graciousness, astonish you with their wit. Truly, Shakespeare's wise saw—

> A jest's prosperity lies in the ear
> Of him who hears it—

was never more aptly approved true. The success of these comedies lies in the mood of the audience—the willingness to be pleased. Take that away, and no demon of hell rebuked by angelic power, no flag flaunted by a momentary breeze, will fall more spiritless to the ground.

Their success must be intermittent and precarious, then? Not that, either, by any manner of means. Nothing is easier than to underrate the disposition which an audience shows—barring certain exceptional circumstances—to be satisfied. It is more enjoyable, on the whole, to laugh than to scowl, at the time; and afterwards, he who tells his friend of an evening pleasantly spent, is in the way of recounting a triumph ; while he who drones out an admission of hours wasted in monotony, is a good way towards bewailing defeat. And the individual goodwill—especially when it is an affair of laughter and not tears—is intensified in the mass. We come with open eyes and quivering lips, yearning (as Goethe says) to be astonished.

These gorgeous personages, then, these brilliant intellects, depend on us for countenance—nay, for very existence. If we withdraw our presence, our patronage—nay, even our smiles and our hand-claps—they wither into insignificance ; disappear utterly ; die, and are seen no more.

Nevertheless, the support, the advantages, are mutual. It is this that makes us tolerate such comedy on the one side, and dictates the choice of such personages on the other. A joke, which from the lips of the presiding judge produces a roar, would be received from the junior counsel, in stony—nay, indignant—silence. So on the stage. Put a kitchen witticism (having previously wiped off the grease) into the mouth of the marchioness, and it immediately scintillates : or, say, rather, that the flash which in both cases proceeds from it, in the latter denotes to our mind the true stone; in the former, an imitation. One of Testoni's conversations repeated in the servants' hall, would have no better flavour than the lukewarm remains of the feast which the parlour-maid has borne out with her; while any chance ebullition of kitchen wit would very easily take its place.

His plots consist generally of the same kind of intrigue with which we are familiar, only lighter and less persistent. This, in fact, is usually the salvation of the piece. Nothing is serious. Wit, wisdom, purpose, virtue, we feel that none of them would bear pausing on. Not even rank; for if we think of it, we have no real conviction that a sudden demand for their pedigrees would fall more pleasantly on the ears of these seemingly great folk than the voice of a policeman, demanding a motor-driver's licence, on those of a party of school-boys larking about with a car. But herein lies the safety of the whole case. We are all interested in preserving the illusion. No one wants to have his evening's entertainment disturbed. And so the fair progress of the show winds in and out; the elegant swords of speech play at thrust and parry; the masks are aptly and gracefully worn. And it is not till we lay aside our own masks in the solitude of our chamber, that the voice of the child within us cries out 'But the king is naked!' and even then, we hardly hear.

We have come to an end now, I fancy—at least, as regards the older writers—of those who utter drama by great swaths. We have, henceforth, to deal with a play here and there: to make no general reflections, draw no general conclusions; simply and briefly to describe. The drama which shall come first, is written by an author who has been guilty of not a few others; but, in spite of his own energy and the efforts of the critics, this appears to be the only one so far destined to permanent success. 'La Moglie del Dottore' (The Doctor's Wife) is a play for which I do not propose to offer apology or excuse. It treats of subjects which would not be admissible on our stage: but on our stage many degrading plays have appeared, and this is not a degrading play. It belongs to a broader, not to a lower, stage of morality. A young man or woman would hear, perhaps, things that were new to them: certainly, things which would shock and depress their minds. But though they might have to face facts that would lower their opinion of men and women as they are, they would in nowise have a lower motive set before them for their own lives. We find in the play certain facts alluded to with what seems to us horrible frankness. Herein we have an epitome of the two races. The frankness is the Italian's; the horror is our own.

I

Luisa, then, when quite a girl has been outraged and abandoned by a lover. She is found by a doctor, Carlo Conte, who succeeds in saving her life, but not her powers of maternity. The baby, prematurely born, dies ; and there is left no hope of others to come. Further—from what motives exactly, whether of love or pity, we are a little in doubt—he marries her. All this takes place before the beginning of the play. In the first scene, Luisa is before us, ignorant of her real condition, caressing the poor children who are brought to her husband's dispensary, and ardently desiring to have some of her own. And this desire is made plainer to us by various speeches, such as a wife might naturally make to her husband in the privacy of their own room. Then comes a motor-car accident, and a woman is brought in fainting. On examination, Dr. Conte finds her condition serious, and that she is expecting a baby. No remedy! She cannot be moved ; she must be nursed and cared for there. Then Luisa hears her name. She is the wife of her former lover ! End of the first act.

The play goes its way, after this, much as might be expected. Violent scene between Luisa and the lover, who begs her to moderate her just resentment for the sake of his innocent wife, and the still more innocent baby that is to come into the world. Pathetic scene wherein Luisa handles the baby-clothes, and wonders and weeps. Finally, some resemblance in the cases ; some chattering by a servant, gives Luisa a hint of her real condition. She questions her husband, who cannot find words with which to soften the blow. ' Never more ! ' breaks out the poor girl left alone ; and, her feelings mastering her, she raves at the former lover who has the misfortune to appear. In the midst of this scene, re-enter the doctor with the news that the baby is born. ' Ah !

there is no longer a God,' cries Luisa. The situation breaks on Conte in a flash ; and the curtain, falling on the two glowering men, with the helpless, raving woman between them, cuts short a picture that is wellnigh unendurably effective.

The third act is calm water after the other two—calm but not clear ! The happy mother, ignorant of all, and her babe, are taking their departure ; and Luisa's tortures will hardly allow her to return the grateful mother's caresses or accept her gifts. When they are gone, Carlo shows temper to his wife. He did not know who this husband of his patient was, and is angry that he was not told—angry and suspicious. He is going away in a huff—going away to Genova or Turin, it matters not which. Luisa is to be left behind while he decides ; and you feel that he will not hurry himself. They are to take a fine flat ; she is to wear smart dresses, and they are to live the life ! Luisa does not want to live any life of which her husband's love is not the inspiring influence. What has she done ? Why is he angry with her ? He explains to his own satisfaction—as most men can, when they are cruel and in the wrong—but not to hers. 'I judge by what I have seen,' he has said ; and she breaks out (and the speech is worth recording) :—

Oh, how little your science is ! What has it seen ? It has cut into my flesh without feeling its palpitation : that is your science. The facts . . . What are they ? I was silent, true, but for your sake : not to bring you face to face with an ugly reality. I was silent for fear of losing you. I betrayed myself, and I do lose you. When, for the death of my poor mother, for my little one reft from me, for my womb made sterile, I cried out madly—unnaturally—for revenge ! and you came in, the bright herald of a new life, Oh !

then, then, it seemed to me that you were proclaiming my shame, my inexorable sentence, and all the revolt and despair that I felt went into my cry ! Neither wife nor mother ! Neither wife nor mother ! What remains to me ? Why does not your science see upon what a rack it is stretching me ? Worse than that other—you are worse ; for you re-open the wound to grope pitilessly in it to find what ?—Carlo ! How can you doubt—you, who have given me every hope, who have made me live again the fairest dreams. You take away, resume, destroy—Wherefore ? What have you seen that was not love, adoration, veneration, for you ? What do you want more ?— that I should cut into my breast, take out my heart and hold it out to you in my hands ? You have possessed yourself of my spirit to make a plaything of it ; don't torture it ! don't degrade it ! It is already undone.

After this, they understand each other, and Carlo does not go away alone.

The play has, I think, taken a permanent place among works of its class. The main theme is certainly a moving one ; and, though the subsidiary characters are conventional, the chief personages are true enough to life to sustain aptly the emotions that the comedy calls on them to display. The critic, whose lucubrations are prefixed to the published edition, opines that the third act is the best of the three, and more subtle : in fact, it is the hub of the drama—that for the sake of which all the rest was written. It seemed to me, on the contrary, that the jealousy of Carlo, both in the acting and in the reading, was invented to make a third act. There is absolutely nothing done by Luisa to make him jealous, in the first place, and he has given no sign hitherto of anything more towards Luisa than of an affection which was founded on pity in the second. Jealousy is unreasonable ? Perhaps. But if it appear too evidently so in a drama it will never please. The jealousy of Leontes,

given the little cause for it, has always been held
a defect of the ' Winter's Tale.' The fact is that Sigr.
Zambaldi, like other Italian authors, occasionally has
put into a stage direction what ought to have been made
manifest in the text. This is almost immediately after
Luisa's speech quoted above.

*Carlo gathers her into his arms, bends back her head and
looks into her eyes. Jealousy has made the love break out
which he had hitherto confused with a sentiment of pity, of
tenderness, of fatherly affection.* There is everything in
the play to show that Carlo thought so : nothing to show
that he was wrong. All these things should have been
betrayed to us in the course of the action by the
characters themselves. It is not enough that the author
informs us of them in a foot-note at the end.

I come now to a play that has held the stage for longer ;
though, from one point of view, it belongs to a lower order.
' La Moglie del Dottore' verges on the melodramatic ; ' La
Morte Civile ' (Civil Death) is frank melodrama. Nevertheless, it has established itself ; is played by leading
actors (including Novelli) ; and is, I suppose, on the road
towards becoming a classic in its own class. And it is
so, in spite of its crudities of treatment, unnatural episodes,
clumsy speeches that have neither the elegance of the
essayist nor the point of the dramatist, because it has,—
as every now and then an Italian play will have—beyond
the particular story told us and the particular men
and women exhibited, a higher and a wider scope. It
is not only their fate that we feel is being decided, not
only the morality of their actions and thoughts which is
being judged, but the fate and the morality of a hundred
others whose situations may conform to theirs. If Italy
is not particularly rich in such questions, the Italian writer
is skilful in hunting them out.

' La Morte Civile,' then, turns on the attitude of

the Church towards divorce. Corrado, a hot-blooded southerner (as we are too often reminded) married a wife when both were young. One night, mistaking her brother, who was coming to the house, for a lover, he killed him; and for the deed was condemned to penal servitude for life. They had a daughter. Rosalia, the wife, in her wanderings with the child, comes across a philanthropic doctor, a widower, whose only daughter has just died at a time when they were away from their circle of friends. The convict's wife and her daughter, resourceless and friendless, appeal to his pity, and he allows the girl, who is of an age with his lost one, to come into her place, and the mother to take in his household the position of her governess; and they all go and live in a place where they believe that no one will find out the fraud. This is the situation at the beginning of the play—a situation which has endured for two years, and which seemed in no danger of being disturbed. But an old Abate, who is represented rather as a meddling busy-body than as a true father of Holy Church, has, little by little—partly by his own exertions, partly by inquiries of an old woman his *protégée*, whom he has placed in the house—been discovering facts which seem to cast a doubt on the family relations. He knows that Emma is not the doctor's legitimate daughter : he wants to know more. Finally, he has it from the doctor that the husband of Rosalia is an escaped convict. At this juncture, who should come on the scene, but Corrado, escaped from the convict prison at Naples. It is easy for the Abate to put two and two together, in more senses than one. The long-separated pair meet. Rosalia refuses to return to her husband. The fact that Emma is his daughter comes out after a little while, and Rosalia's return to her husband is purchased by his promise to leave the daughter in tranquillity with the only father whom she will ever love.

But the poor convict is, little by little, oppressed with the hopelessness of the task which he has set himself.   Little by little, the ties that formed themselves for others during his fourteen years' seclusion, become impassable realities to his dreaming eyes ; he sees that the rights of property, his by law, have passed to others by prescription.   That by no one is he loved, by none desired, save by a priest with whose tenets he is out of sympathy, and whose methods he abhors.   Seeing that his own, his only hope of happiness, has failed him in life, he takes the speediest way out of it : and while his child, his own flesh and blood, is saying a prayer in pity for the uncouth and terrifying stranger, he takes poison and falls dead behind her back.

The play was written with a purpose : to show the futility of the Church's attitude towards divorce.   It was also written in a spirit of hostility towards catholicism, which seems bitter to us, but shows mild beside the expressions of many Italians in real life.   These things the writer of the play has no wish—perhaps, no power—to conceal.   The Abate, with his insinuating ways, his artful meditations, his decisive and ruthless actions when it comes to the point ; and, again, the mixture of cunning and the devotee in the old servant, are drawn forcibly, heavily, as with a blunt pencil.   Nor is there more of the art concealed about Corrado, who is always telling us to beware of his hot southern blood; who is, apparently, mistaking every girl of the same age and colouring for his missing daughter.   Nor, again, about Palmieri, the atheist doctor ; nor in Rosalia the forlorn wife ; nor in the so-called Emma, whose love for her acquired, and terror of her real father, appear like two naughty children, each trying who can make the most noise.   It seems to be the fate of a play with a purpose that it makes use of means like this. We must take this one as it is.   And truly the actors do ;

they fall in with its tone and exaggerate its means until they out-Herod Herod; and, making more demands on our self-effacement than even the author does, often defeat their own ends. As an instance, during his interview with Corrado, the Abate hearing the bell sound for prayer, goes down on his knees; when he gets up, he brings out before his guest some more than usually superhuman piece of subtlety. The effect of this is admirable, but is entirely spoilt by his adding, aside, ' I thought of that just now while I was praying.'

I cannot find other space than here for the mention of a piece which resembles the foregoing in two respects : I mean in having become a classic, and being animated by hostility to the Church. In all else it is as different as lemon-sponge from roast-beef. It is in one act in verse, instead of five solid acts of prose. It sings like an arrow, instead of thumping like a battering-ram. It is full of elegance of wit, instead of spluttering out bitter facts. Its improbability lies in externals, its reality is behind— to be read by him who runs. It keeps its inner parts duly covered, instead of bearing its heart on its sleeve, suitably inscribed, while the other organs beneath the clothes perform as successfully as ever. Sigr. Felice Cavalotti was a patriot of the 'Risorgimento,' and a literary man ; and he left plays of which ' Il Cantico del Cantici ' is the best known, though others—of which the author had the good fortune to hear ' Lettre d'Amore ' (one act in prose), at the Teatro Metastasio in Rome— still hold the stage. The characters in the play with which we are dealing are only three : an uncle (a retired soldier), his niece ; and a nephew who has, to her great regret, gone (or is going) into the Church. And the steps by which the young enthusiast becomes convinced that the certainty of a bride on earth would outweigh the splendour of one in heaven; and that the state, equally with the Church militant, would welcome effusively, and reward amply, his tactical powers, fill many people with laughter, and none, I hope, with any shame or disgust.

From these old stagers, I come to plays of more modern origin. The proverb is an old one that 'one man's meat is another's poison.' It must not, therefore, be required of any critic that his digestion squares with that of the multitude, or that the dishes he praises shall have been permanently enrolled on the national menu. The two plays that follow have evidently failed to make their mark. Yet they made, in their different ways, such an impression on the present writer, at the time of their performance, that they are thought worthy of a mention here. ' Il Metodo,' which might be translated ' The Way It's Done,' is a light comedy of a purely frivolous type. It was said, by the newspapers at the time, to be derived from the French. That judgment, at the time, seemed to him a false one. It seemed to stand out so prominently from the French *pochade*, which was being played all round it, that he could not help believing that it had other blood in its veins.

The story is a slight one. Carlino, popular comedy-writer, and perfect ladies' man, is engaged on a new masterpiece. For its perfecting, he needs certain studies in love-making, and these he supplies by personal experiment. To one of the ladies (actresses, if I remember rightly), of whose services in the cause of art, he, unknown to them, avails himself, he is sincerely attached. The interviews lead to appointments; the appointments finally clash. And in the last act the three heretofore mortal enemies are discovered sitting on a sofa, together, awaiting the attack of the enemy. Enter Carlino. On seeing them, with a guilty start, he exclaims : ' The holy Trinity!' Led by Bice, one by one they denounce him, and go out with scorn. He sits dejected for a moment, his head between his hands. One by one they steal back, the last first. 'You are wicked and faithless, but I forgive you. Come to my rooms to-morrow at . . ., I shall be there!' and out she goes. Enter number two. 'Carlino, was there ever a man so false or woman so weak? Neither of the others would give way, but there . . . Come to my rooms at . . . ,' and out she goes. A slightly longer pause. Then enter Bice. Carlino, without looking up, 'I suppose you have come to make an appointment for this afternoon!' 'No,' she answers, 'I've come to stay.' He looks round and sees her taking off her hat and throwing it upon the table. Curtain.

Whether it was the genial plausibility of Baghetti, who played Carlino, the fascinating personality of La Rossi (of whom the reader will hear more anon), or really something special in the play itself, this deponent knoweth not; but it seemed as the quaint flavour of some old wine among the rude absinthes or vermouths of the common bar. My suspicions are that the bin was labelled ' Goldoni.'

With such a play as this however, so light and sketchy, it can never be a matter of surprise if its lines fade in a few years. It is otherwise with the play of which I must next speak. There, tragic issues—such as appeal especially to the Italian race—are managed in such a way as to give them force, intensity, and coherence. I do not think that the undoubtedly splendid acting of De Santis could altogether account for its success. It may be that it is his property, and that he is still playing it successfully. It certainly does not seem to have passed into the universal actor-manager's stock-in-trade.

The story is a simple one. Andrea Castans is a

maestro, with a studio full of pupils. Though no genius as an artist, he has won his way to success by hard work and knowledge of the world. Among his pupils is one, a boy and a genius, to whom Andrea, knowing his worth, has handed over the decoration of a cupola which has been entrusted to the master. The splendid creation, however, with which Domenigo is covering the plaster, raises the demon of envy in the mind of the elder man ; and when the former confides to him, as to a father, a desperate and timorous attachment to a married woman, he, with his mature experience, makes love to her and draws her away. In despair, the poor boy kills himself. In horror, at what has come about through her, the lady renounces her scheming lover, and a passionate scene between them is fought out under the vaults made splendid by the creations of the boy-lover, whose loss she now deplores. Fury leads Andrea to violence, and in his passion he crushes the life out of this frail and fashionable, yet withal human, thing : and the fall of the curtain finds him standing furious and baffled, between the paintings that he cannot complete, and the life that he cannot renew.

We have next two plays of still more recent date, of which it cannot yet be predicted whether they will live or die. I am far from attributing to them any unparalleled excellence. I will not prophesy for them an illimitable future. I will only say that here and now they are impressive ; and that, by reason of their having taken hold of a real phase of national life with the descriptive power that we have noticed before. The life of the Italian people seems, when fitly treated, to more easily furnish out of itself the proper themes for drama than life elsewhere. It is not that it is more profound or strenuous, that the events in the lives of individuals are more important, or the characters more interesting. It lies somehow in the fact that the Italian people are nearer to the beginnings of civilisation than we are, and that the really great pains and pleasures of life are less overlaid with a coat of semblances than with ourselves. Their life bears the aspect of a plant but newly shot from the ground, showing all its natural tendencies of growth unimpeded; ours, a large mature vine loaded with fruit, but confused, while it is sustained, by an artificial trellis of dead wood. Great matter for drama there is in our industrial and our social life, but it must first be disentangled. In Italy the disentanglement is easy: from the actual life of the day a comparatively un-skilful hand can set forth a play which is at once moving and real.

The one of which we are first to speak, ' La Regina ' (The Queen), sets forth one of the cardinal facts of a young nation : that in some parts of the land the resources in reserve are so scanty, that existence is a practical impossibility without patronage of some kind. A hail-storm will be enough to destroy the hopes of the year, perhaps : and the peasants have neither credit nor family chest. It is such communities as these that play the deuce with the calculations of the political economist, and often, as the play shows, of the moralist as well.

I transcribe, almost textually, my notes made on the day following the representation :—

The most striking of any Italian play I have seen since ' Romanticismo.' The population of a little hamlet in the south is gathered together, waiting the arrival of a certain Carmelita, its ' queen ' and benefactress, the daughter of the syndic. Her means of benefiting them, it appears however, come from the exercise of a usually condemned profession. Enter a group

of socialists, against queens and for morality ; led by a
certain Manfredo Spina. They disturb proceedings, and
when Carmelita arrives, insult her to such an extent that
she leaves, taking her parents with her ; while, raising
himself on the platform of a Cross which stands out in
the background, and clinging actually to the instruments
of the Passion which adorn its shaft, the leader of the
band of social reformers thunders out after the retreating
patroness a fiery and triumphant storm. The second
act opens in a miserably furnished café. It is winter,
and snow is falling. Manfredo is syndic ; has honestly
lived up to his convictions, but it does not appear, from
a long argument which he has with the doctor, that
they have landed him in a haven of peace. Reform has
been costly. He has—to give an example of his works—
built a wall to enclose a piece of waste ground. 'Why
did you do that?' asks the doctor. 'Look at what went on
there!' said Manfredo. 'The place was a perfect scandal.'
'It'll go on somewhere, all the same,' says the doctor.
He knew all about that. Such works cost money.
Carmelita's funds are no longer available. Misfortune
and bad weather have affected the commune. Every one
is either ill or starving, and they defy the rules of the
materialist government to the extent of having a procession in honour of the Madonna to induce her to change
the weather. Even his own friends are deserting him.
A parliament is held. It is a stormy one. Little by little
the opposition shifts across from his side to the other, and
more than one bitter repartee is exchanged. Even then
Manfredo's enthusiasm does not desert him. Difficulty
only arouses his courage and awakes his eloquence.
Back to the wall, he calls them cowards for their little
faith, and fools for their little persistence, and, as his own
warm faith is kindling a spark in his at first sullen hearers,
it grows lighter outside, and suddenly a gleam of sun breaks

through the falling snowflakes and touches with hope the forms of hill and dale. 'Look!' he says, 'neither bad fortune nor bad weather is everlasting. Have courage! Hold on a little longer! Reason will triumph, and there will be work and wages once again.' He is winning them, when . . . What are these cries from outside—peasants' and women's voices wellnigh delirious with joy? Grain, they tell us; bread, cigars—cartloads of them! Whence does it all come? Need you ask? The spell is broken. One by one his confederates slink out; Manfredo is left alone with an old ne'er-do-well ex-model, a *protégé* of La Carmelita. The latter offers him a cigar, which he takes and lights mechanically, and then 'old thirty-vices' throwing himself back in the only arm-chair, calls out to the hostess 'Maria, un buon caffè!' and the curtain slowly falls. Act III.; the return of Carmelita. The father is restored to his honours, while the deposed Manfredo is wandering about like a disembodied spirit. Once more Carmelita appears; this time with her prince, an Indian (not a speaking part); she being in local costume, and received—ah! with what effusion—by the peasantry, and even by Manfredo's late supporters. When the prince has gone to rest, the others have disappeared, the only true socialist wanders in and discusses things with Carmelita with a sad but not spiteful resignation. It seems that they have been old comrades. She picks him a flower. Where shall she put it? she takes the book he has been reading—'What's it about?' 'Karl Marx: Das Kapital'—and in between the leaves its freshness and fragrance is shut.

The others return; he tries to escape; she retains him. Enter his highness refreshed; he comes down the steps; profound bows (previously rehearsed) by the country folk, to the word of command by Carmelita. Curtain.

The first act plays well. The talk is interesting and characteristic. The groups seem to have been well rehearsed and work well one into another. The entrance by the socialists with their red flag is picturesquely managed. The dialogue between Carmelita and Manfredo is spirited in the extreme. The tableau at the end of the fiery rationalist pouring forth his diatribes, clinging to the shaft whereon is suspended the dead God, is a picture as poignant in contrast as the state of modern Italy herself.

If the first act is good, the second is better. There is less dependence on the rough-and-tumble, more on the comedy of suggestion. The dialogue between Manfredo and the doctor is good,—the former sustaining abstract right, the other opportunism of the kind wherewith Euripides used to delight his Athenians hundreds of years ago. And the debate between Manfredo and his doubting confederates ; the way they gradually turn against him ; the extraordinary effect produced by the blunt utterances of a lean, hawk-faced stammerer ; the speech of Manfredo ; the touch of sunlight ; his almost-won victory; and then the cries of the peasants over the food : all combine stage-craft and reality with exceptional success. For a long half-hour, the same question is in debate, the same issue doubtful, and yet it does not stand still, but adds and adds to itself, gaining fullness of interest as it sways to and fro, until the full climax comes —just soon enough to release the watchers from their suspense and the combatants from their toils. There is a certain falling-off in the third act. The author has no longer at his disposal his former picturesque means of getting an effect, and his powers of dialogue are hardly equal to filling the gap. Worse still, he seems to have lost his objective. After the actual return of Carmelita there is little left to happen; and they can only discuss

the philosophical aspect of events. Carmelita's dialogue
with Manfredo is too like that of the doctor with the same.
They remind one of the different sections of ' The Ring and
the Book.' The entrance of the prince is a pretty and
effective picture. But is it really the key-note on which
the play should end ? Perhaps it is, in the author's mind.
Perhaps he wishes us to go away with a reflection on how
much of the good things of life we owe to means which our
common sense cannot fail to be glad of, though our
consciences cannot strictly approve.

The next play has something of the same motive and
moral, although the surroundings amid which it is
worked out are entirely different. In Act I., in a Tuscan
village, we are introduced to a father and two daughters.
The eldest Cesarina, has a lover in the English sense :
the younger has been flirting with a married man. There
is talk between the father and Cesarina, both about her
sister's affairs and her own, and she rather prettily justifies
herself, and vouches for her lover's honesty. They go
out, and Enzo, the lover, then appears having arrived
in a motor-car of the ' Onorevole ' (M.P.), to whom he
is secretary. He is received by the second girl and
there is just a little scene between them—*gauche* and
awkward, especially on her part, before Cesarina comes
in. Then there is a scene between the lovers. It is
arranged that she is to go—as it appears that she has
done before—to Rome ; and the act ends with her
promising to take her sister with her.

The second act finds the sisters in Rome. But the
situated has changed. Cesarina has become the ' mantenuta' of Enzo's principal; while Enzo himself is making
love to the sister. The two are very well portrayed.
The elder, finely—at least, fashionably—dressed, holding
her own in conversation with the other deputies who
frequent the house, parrying with equal ease the light

attacks of the younger men, and the more serious pro-
posals of an elderly banker ; the younger sister, fresh and
charming, but with the awkward remains of the country
girl about her.   The latter resists for a while, but gives
in, finally, to the wooing of Enzo, who would appear to be
in earnest this time.

The third act is in the house of Enzo's parents, where
the old couple and an aunt are gathered together, playing
dominoes. Then Enzo bursts the bomb of his intended
marriage upon them.   In view of the relations which the
bride's sister maintains, the proposition is rejected with
fury. Enzo is turned out, and the three sit—if they do not
remind us of Æacus, Minos, and Rhadamanthus—in stern
judgment upon the sinner. Visit of Cesarina, who, with the
obvious intent to further the marriage, declares that never
under any possible combination of circumstances could
she be brought to give her consent.   Then she describes
the dowry that she has in store for the right man at
the right time, draws for them a very charming
portrait of her sister's excellence, and exit. Doubt
and dissension in the sheep-fold.   Rather sudden return
of Cesarina with the information that the pair are plotting
an elopement, and that if they carry out their scheme
not a penny shall they have from her.   To your
tents, O Israel ! Let those whom it may concern act
accordingly. The aunt still staunchly holds out, but
she is over-ruled and hustled into a corner ; the parents
preferring a proper marriage and a dowry, to beautiful
ideals and an elopement. The happy pair are duly
affianced and the dowry set down. Pressed to say
how she will raise so much money, Cesarina specifies
a certain sum which she has already, ' and the rest,'
she says, ' I will have from the banker Ferrante.' ' You
have the money on deposit then ? ' ' Yes.' And on this
the curtain falls.

K

The motive of the play, undoubtedly, is that a woman may fall sexually, and yet remain sisterly, generous : even heroic. Nothing could be more touching than the self-sacrifice of Cesarina, and the careful, motherly tact with which she works for the happiness of the girl who has taken her place. The chief merit of the play is the admirable way the acts are arranged to give an insight into peasant, political, and middle-class life, respectively : so doing, with some success, what it seems to me that the dialect play is so constantly striving to do and failing. Further, it touches on the eternal question of sexual relations lightly and without offence. Its weakness is the superimposition of one scene on another, with no very plausible link. The love-making between Enzo and Giulia at the end of the second act, good in itself, comes a little hard on other matters ; and, again, the three separate entrances of Cesarina in Act III. are awkward in the extreme. The play gained exceedingly from its acting. It might easily have been less effective in other hands.

And now, having paid first court to the writers of prose, let us lead forth the Muse who is lurking in the background. Which Muse exactly it is who presides over the production of an Italian verse play, I should be sorry to state definitely. The stage is somewhat ill-lighted, and she has a way of holding her mantle over her face, partly from a fear as to the nature of her reception, partly, I am afraid, from a sense of the somewhat doubtful quality of the matter to which she has given utterance. You need not be afraid, madam. Though we may pretend to be shocked, and wear gloomy faces, I warrant that we are laughing in our hearts. Assuredly, though your lord and master has ceased to have in name any substantial authority over the world, he who devised so many ingenious elopements must ever have a sympathetic following among those, who (if we may trust the storytellers) are occupied—like Penelope by night and Penelope by day,—the one half in setting up a set of family relations, the other half, in pulling them down again.

It is not a little curious, as typifying the vagaries of this Muse, that though we have undertaken to be ultra-modern, the first verse play of which we have to speak is a comedy which treats of the days and ways of nearly six hundred years ago : those days and ways—that is, for which we English folk have no other expression than the name of Boccaccio; no other means of acquaintance than a badly printed tome of unintelligible matter, and some ill-drawn plates ; reminding us of Hogarth without the colours and with little of the humour.   But, however we may come to know them, in ' La Commedia della Peste ' they live and move again.   Surely such a wonderful revival never was seen !   I have heard stories of galvanised mummies ; I have seen attempts at the revival of Byzantine architecture ;—and both leave the impression that the re-incarnate essence had slept away all trace of its original nature.   But Luigi Rasi has set before his countrymen what is acknowledged by all, save the Florentines, to be such a picture of Florentine life that it might have been taken exactly and textually from a manuscript of the day.   And not a bad manuscript either ; for, if the play is in parts prolix, and wants both adapting and cutting for performance, it is full of good situations and speeches ; and, at its best points, is worked up to such a dramatic intensity, in spite of the lightness of the subject-matter, such as could only have been given by a really practised hand.   Yet, have a care, gentle ladies !   Wrap your mantles carefully round your faces, and . . . carefully leave a loophole pervious to the arrowy glances of those hazel eyes.

I think I cannot do better than quote from my note-book again.   April 7.—' La Commedia della Peste.'

Luigi Rasi.—From the mud we are transported into fairy-land.[1] Boccaccio's country : maidens dancing and singing : artful ' donzelli,' amorous masters, white horses, gay trappings, refreshments in the noonday shade, love intrigues lightly passing under lustrous arcades or by the silence of clear waters ;—these are what the author has in thought revived ; what the players have in act presented. Brave Italian actors ! Excellent Talli ! How just the whole thing seems to be ! How thoughtlessly gay the garments ! How naturally gracious the movements ! Not the grace of education, but natural litheness, giving expression to innate gaiety of soul.

Plot ! It is like taking a dissecting-knife to a bumble-bee, to talk about a plot ! But an ye would hear, remember, good friends, that we are in an enchanted country, where the dull rules of this moral world are not ; where charm charms because it is charming ; where no man does but what is pleasant in his own eyes ; and where the only forbidden guest is the ugly, the witless, the bore.

Messere Amerigo, then, with an aunt still young and charming, is flying to her castle among the Apennines, as a refuge from the Florentine plague. He is greeted by graceful maidens, who, one after another, court his eye (to the obvious disapproval of the Sigra. Zia), until it becomes temporarily fixed on one, Fiammetta, a maid charming but innocent, and guarded by a widowed mother. He deputes his Donzello, Sennuccio, to carry out his plans. Their colloquy, however, has been partly overheard. The peasants gather in the fall of eve with a ladder outside the padrone's room ; lover, father, mother, each expecting to find his ewe-lamb in the clutches of the mighty one. They climb the ladder, one by one, and one by one explode with laughter and come down. Then

---

[1] The evening before had been spent in witnessing Sudermann's ' Honour '—a play not so agreeable as its title would imply.

A. Della Coletta

'LA COMMEDIA DELLA PESTE,' ACT II

there is an alarm. They withdraw hastily; and out on
the balcony, to whisper vows before a moon who has,
possibly, for this once put off something of her coldness and
fruitlessness, stroll the young gentleman and his aunt !

These events occupy the first two acts. Act III. sees
Sennuccio at work. He finds the damsel spinning : and,
by her mother's orders, before an open door. This he
shuts, and, with guile and with wile, by hook and by
crook, plies the forlorn maiden—the Serpent and Eve over
again.[1] Presently, the mother comes in, and Sennuccio
is hastily concealed under a chicken-basket. The mother
asks awkward questions. Why has she shut the door ?
Why does she look so agitated ? Poor Fiammetta does
her best in the way of answers, not aided in any way by
unexpected asides from Sennuccio. Finally, the mother,
in a fury, chases her out ; the tempter arises from his
hiding-place ; then enter the daughter hastily, still
pursued. Sennuccio admits the daughter, excludes
the mother ; and behind the barred door he prepares his
plan. They stand behind the door, which is suddenly
opened. Enter mother, exit daughter, in one breath.
Sennuccio bars the door again, and exercises his charms
with such effect on the raging mother that the curtain
falls on him striking an attitude over her vanquished
and prostrate form. Act IV. finds poor Fiammetta
in a doleful state : the cause of which is not far to
guess ; although her friends persist in attributing it to
improbable spiritual agencies ; to wit, one Satan, from
time immemorial the lovers' scape-goat. Something
must be done, as Messere knows. But what ? That
is more than he knows. ' But, by'r Lady and Iffakins !
wherefore do we harbour a worthless and do-nothing
donzello ! Sennuccio, find me a way out, or thou
perishest !' This being old comedy, and Sennuccio a

[1] This scene is illustrated and translated.

man of parts, it is not surprising that he chooses the former alternative. Brilliant idea! Fiammetta has the plague, and must be sent to some isolated spot. Excellent! But a father of a family is chosen as her escort, and the poor wife is in tears. The soft heart of my lady aunt is touched, and under a pledge of secrecy she confides to the wife the truth. The wife, of course, tells first her husband, then the maidens (all under a like pledge of secrecy). And the scene closes with the maidens singing after the departing Fiammetta, a little rhyme ' Gallina, Gallina, Gallinaccia,' which we have already heard, and which, by the custom of the country, is reserved for ladies in the like situation.

Now, is all this moral? Not for one moment! But is it immoral? An equally absolute ' No '! Lamb has dealt with the subject in one of his inimitable essays,[1] and shown lightly, but conclusively, that such plays are too far away from reality to influence us in actual life. There are no Sennuccios to-day, no dancing ' ancelle '; no more danger that we shall try to copy the amorous intrigues of the master than the picturesque attitudes of the man. Such a play is like a gentle dream, like a draught of the sweetness of old wine from which the lees have allowed to settle. Like the lovely puzzle-work of some tapestried wall, which may be watched and wandered in without leg-weariness. Like anything and everything wherein—the good and useful, but, at whiles, somewhat strident personalities of conscience and reason, being laid to a well-earned repose—Heart's-delight and Care-free, with a dozen satellites, a tip-toe and fingers on lips, creep out into the Garden of Pleasure; where the old plaster casts of weather-worn Morality unwillingly spout for them beside the sparkling waters which ' dance unchaperoned, and laugh unchecked.'

The play, no doubt, has technical faults. It is long

[1] ' On the artificial comedy of last century.'

for such a light story, and wants cutting and re-arranging.
Quite possibly the first two acts could be reduced to one.
Again, the fall of the curtain in the last act is delayed far
too long. But in the main it is not only easily written,
but it is dramatic besides. The dialogue is full of
point, albeit, written in exceedingly blank verse. It is
appropriate, too. The little fishes talk like little fishes, and
the great whales like great whales. Let us have a few
examples: Here are the mothers talking together. Can
one not hear the clack! clack! of the old women with their
marketing baskets, or see the solemn stroll through the
' podere' when the work is done ?

Lisa.   No, mistress Oretta !
Do what I will, I cannot from my head
Banish the coming of my lady, and
My lord Amerigo, her nephew, there.
So long it is since peril came anigh;
And in a trice, behold! he lets it loose
Upon us. Do you never think on death ?
  Oretta. You ! Mistress Lisa, many are the years.
And since we know that every mortal thing
By law immutable must have an end,
Either by pestilence or some other ill,
We hope for death as quickly as may be.
  Lisa. Many ! Many ! by my faith they are not so !
And here below exempt from crosses, I
Content with Bindo, my good spouse, would fain
Live out my life 'twixt song and laughter.
  Or.   You
Are happy, having Bindo ; happy, again,
Not feeling the years heavy. I, henceforth,
Am deep in widowhood, so that the months
Seem years to me, to curve my back withal.
To you the years appear not months, days rather ;
The more you have, the more they seem to you.
But as the seeds of springtide, you, indeed,
Are happy.
  Lisa.   Ah ! Yes, happy ! For you know
How full of wild-cat fancies, how distraught

Thinking upon the morrow, on this plague
Which sows death broadcast as it goes, and last
Upon the visit of my lady's nephew,
Why, mischief take me, every one of us,
Might get the hidden poison in ourselves ;
And pass along towards death.

Or.   Eh ! Mistress Lisa,
Believe me, these are the imaginings
Of fear. I told you but a moment since
That everything upon this world of ours
By law immutable, must have an end ;
Well, let it end just by its own sweet will.

Lisa. I am to let it end by its own sweet will ?
And think not on the morrow ! Never see
Dangers, nor guard against the woes to come !

Or. I say that when the hour which God has fixed
In His great book for every mortal man
Is reached, nor tears nor laughter shall avail
To stay the same. And death shall come therewith
To loose you, hale you by the hair, and bid [1]
You say farewell for ever to the world.

Lisa. Oh ! Virgin mother of the Seven Sorrows !
Marry ! What are you at me for, that I
Must needs say farewell to the world ?

Or.   Oh, Mistress
Lisa ! good ; are you, then, wholly content
With the world ?

Lisa.   'Tis thus. I cannot rightly say
If I'm content with this. The mystery
Of that beyond affrights me : that I know !

Or. She who knows ever how to hold the grace
Of chastity, and of the other virtues,
That make a woman wise, should never fear
To die.

Lisa. I know not verily if I
Have aught to do with that. I am very fearful
Yet am a good wife and a virtuous.
Just ask my Bindo if you don't believe me !

---

[1] I must ask the reader's confidence that I have not exceeded the original, either here or elsewhere, in my use of weak endings to the blank verse.

And this for the young people at play.   They are
undoing and arranging great masses of flowers in the upper
room.

Fiammetta. Ah, me ! what's here within ?

Ancella. Where, where ?

Fiam. I saw, I tell you, a great long thing ?

Ancel. Where is't ? Where is't ?

Fiam. There, there ; amid the flowers.

Agnoletta. A branch, I warrant, or a rose's stem.

Fiam. No, no, 'tis silver-white !

Violante (chaffing her). There, see ?

Ancel. (with a great cry). Oh, help !

Fiam. (shouting and crying). Oh, me ! poor coward.

Viol. (same play). Look ! 'Tis up your legs.

*Fiam. (rushes downstairs and hides herself behind her
mother's skirts).* Help, mother ! Oh, poor coward, me !
Help, help !

Ancel. Still do you feel the snake about your legs ?

Or. Look to your flowers, you mad things ! And let be
This ninny, lest she die of fright.

Bindo (also below speaking to Fiammetta). Oh ! oh !
Do you not see ? What babble is there ? And you,
Mistress Oretta, rouse her, it is time.

Giacomina (above in the room). Ah !

Ancel. What's the matter ?

Giacom. I have seen it !

Ancel. Where ?

Giacom. There 'tis !

Salvestra. Oh, beautiful ! Exact faith !
As Fiammetta said, a silver-white ;
But 'tis not venomous—just a garden snake.
Who'll take it up ?

Giacom. Not I.

Violan. Filomena.

Filom. Wherefore not you ?

Violan. Wherefore not Agnoletta ?

Salv. (taking it up). Fiammetta, have a care. Your
head's the mark.
Use it to make a garland when you marry.

*(She throws it at Fiammetta, who again runs to her mother
for protection.)*

But to give a better idea of the actual qualities of the play, I quote at length the scene of the temptation of Fiammetta by Sennuccio, in the third act. Without saying it is the best in the play, it is taken as being the one most easily rendered into English verse. It has, moreover, been admirably illustrated by our special artist, in the drawing opposite, which suggests the Serpent and Eve as fully as did the original. We begin at the rising of the curtain—Act II.

Sen. Happy Sennuccio! Straying through the woods
To find him on a sudden near to you.
　　Fiam. Away, I prithee! mother's neither here
Nor very far away. Good lack! and if
She suddenly returned and found you here?
　　Sen. She told you she was keeping near to you,
That you should still believe her watchful eye
About you . . . of a truth she is far away
At the castle . . .
　　Fiam. 　　　　　Ah! and pray, how know you that?
　　Sen. I met her but a moment since.
　　Fiam. 　　　　　　　　　You say
You met with her?
　　Sen. 　　　　　I did. Why do you keep
The door wide open?
　　Fiam. 　　　　Why? Because my mother
So bade me. Oh! In pity, Master Sennuccio.
Sit you not down. I am afraid.
　　Sen. 　　　　　　　Nay, tell me
If 'tis in truth the mother that you fear
Will catch you here, Fiammetta? Eh! or rather
Some other one?
　　Fiam. 　　　What other one?
　　Sen. 　　　　　　　　　Heigh-ho!
A lover?
　　Fiam. Find him first. The country side
Ne'er held but one. And him the good Filippa
Has angled.

A. Della Coletta

'LA COMMEDIA DELLA PESTE.' ACT III

Sen.   True i' faith one Tommassaccio . . .
(*aside*) So much the worse for you.   (*aloud*) Therefore, if none
Come from without to fix his dwelling here,
You, pretty wretch, will ever go bewailing
Like a fair flower, born in the forest grass
That cannot breathe its bounties to the sun.
   Fiam. I do not understand you.
   Sen.   Have you ne'er
A refuge sought with love ?
   Fiam.   Refuge with love ?
   Sen. It penetrates and enters bit by bit
Into the heart ; hides itself there and bites
Till the blood run ; and bitter grief ensue.
And therefore is your peace for ever dead.
Ever. And vainly shall you call on heaven
To help you. Restless shall you pass your days
In wishing and unwishing. And the nights
Lie wakeful biting at the coverlet
Like one possessed.
   Fiam.   Heaven keep me far removed
From such a malady !
   Sen.   Nor have you proved
The prickings, not so dire—nay, pleasant even—
Of the longing after love ?   For these shall lead you
To close the eyes, and you shall think you dream
The fairest dreams of gold, a pleasure feel
Sprouting upon your lips, and gentle shocks
Coursing your bones, and know in your sweet blood
The sea of some enchantment ebb and flow.
   Fiam. In faith I have not tried it. That should be
Delightful.
   Sen.   Will you smile now ?   Will you let
The eyelid down ?   Have you ever had a pain
Somewhat below the heart ?
   Fiam.   What do you mean ?
What will you do with me !   Alas, I ought not
To listen more. 'Twere mortal sin, perhaps
You are a man of wicked spells. Oh, me !

Sen. (aside). Uff! What a work!

Fiam. You are silent. Now,
what mischief
Stand you there meditating?

Sen. (watching her). Ah! How sweet
To look upon the flower that scarce has budded!
And sweeter still to see it open out
To the full sunshine. (*Approaching her.*) If I might.

Fiam. I'll call
For help. (*Sen. stops.*) How have I harmed you?
Leave me, sir!

Sen. Your terror likes me well. Your voice has just
That tremour, that it seems a silver tube
Vibrating. And your eyes are sweet and large
With some great woe. Oh! If I were my lord
Amerigo.[1]

Fiam. What have you said?

Sen. Oh! Nothing.

Fiam. I think you spoke of my lord Amerigo!

Sen. I only meant that were I, by some chance,
My lord Amerigo, and rich in coin—
Rich, too, in jewels, I would make you brave.
And I'd go buy samite and cloth of gold
To wrap you round. For, sooth, you have a body
Too sweet and delicate to clothe in frieze.

Fiam. (laughing). I am to have a gown woven with flowers
And golden broidery—as my lady has?

Sen. More gorgeous yet, and sprinkled all about
With wonderful clear pearls and precious stones.

Fiam. A goodly sight, indeed! Poor Fiammetta!
Clad like a queen. A goodly sight! Fiammetta
Washing the dishes, cleaning out the pans
In a gown slashed with golden broideries.

Sen. (aside). Uff! What a work! (*Aloud.*) Nay, look
you, when you stand
In your gown slashed with golden broideries,
You'll have, besides, to do the kitchen office,
Servants enow.

---

[1] The scansion of this name is doubtful in the original as well.

Fiam.   Servants, you say ! Whose, prithee ?
Sen. Your own.
Fiam.   Iffakins ! I should then become
My lady ! (*Playing the gran' dama.*) Eh ! Violante,
    bring me hither
The cup of Trebbian, and you, Salvestra,
Fetch me that vase of sweetmeats. So. And you,
Agnoletta, quick and link my collar to.
You, Chita, lift the train from off my feet.
Bah ! Are you mad, Sennuccio ?
    Sen. (*aside*).   What a work !
(*Goes to door and looks out.*)
    Fiam. What are you doing ?
    Sen.   Watching !
    Fiam.   Is there no one ?
    Sen. No one, but solitude and silence. So. (*Shuts and
        bolts the door.*)
    Fiam. Alas ! What do you ? If my mother come
And find the door barred ?
    Sen.   You will open it.
    Fiam. You have no fear to hunt you ; you are not
In bondage kept to anyone, except
My lord ; while I, oh ! I am twice a slave.
My mother's first, and afterwards my lady's.
    Sen. (*not heeding her*). What sort of living keeps you here
        i' the fields,
In this remote asylum far away
From the castle walls ?
    Fiam.   My mother, as a girl,
Went there as serving-woman, in the time
O' the mother of my lady ; who, when dying,
Left her in guerdon of her faithful service,
This cottage.
    Sen.   Do you ever look to draw
Your life out here ?
    Fiam.   What mean you ? We have folk
Often, not always, here. Alone, sometimes
At nights. My lady often loves to offer
My lord, her nephew, dances and delights—

They call us to the castle then.
          (*After a pause.*)   You liked
Last eve, Salvestra's dancing after supper ?
My lord, your master kept his eyes on her,
Methought, as they were fixed there.   Very lissome
Salvestra is : when move her feet i' the dance,
She is with every gracious gift adorned.
    Sen. That, saw you ?   Then you also had your eyes
Fixed on my lord ?
    Fiam.   I ?
    Sen.   You, you, you !   Nay, see
How the cheek kindles.   Do you like my lord,
Amerigo ?   Nay, tell me.   There is none
To hear you, save Sennuccio.   Speak !
    Fiam.   I know not,
Nor do I wish to know.   Away !   Much time
Has passed, and if my mother should return
And find you !   I am afraid.   I told you so.
    Sen. Eyes that are like to arrows !
    Fiam.   Whose eyes ?
    Sen.   Those
Of my lord Amerigo. . . .   Nay, now yours . . .
    Fiam. What have my eyes, I pray, to do with those
Of my lord Amerigo ?   You are pleasant.
    Sen. This, Fiammetta.   (*Taking a stool and sitting.*)   He
      is wont to say
' The eyes of yonder girl are like twain brands—
Ardent, which burn me if I look in them.'
(*Fiammetta gazes at him wonder-struck.*)
Thus, thus.   I never yet beheld them wide,
Wide open thus.   Methinks they are like the eye
Of a wild falcon.   Now, I understand
How, if a man opposed them in such mood,
He might dissolve in flame.   (*Fiammetta laughs.   He
      becomes more and more insinuating, almost whispering
      in her ear.*)
                              What I was saying
A moment since of brave habiliments
And jewels, were his very words.
    Fiam.   His words ?

Sen. ' Nay, by St. George,' he cried aloud, ' that girl
Has mazed me utterly, I seem to be
By her enchanted, even unto madness.
Of all the women I have ever seen,
The only one that thus has made me fond.
For a Salvestra who would fret himself,
When such a witch can cap her in the dance ?
Oh, me ! Sennuccio ! get you gone for pity
Unto my tyrant. Crave my guerdon of her.'

 Fiam. What guerdon ?

 Sen.   He shall tell you that himself.

 Fiam. Himself ! Impossible ! (*incredulous*). But when ?

 Sen.   Oh ! When
You like.

 Fiam.   And where ?

 Sen.   By side of yonder wood,
In the pavilion that the fowlers use.

 Fiam. And if my mother saw me ?

 Sen.   Think you not
It is high time that you were running free
Of mother's skirts ; and seeking other where
A refuge, where to screen your harassed soul
From all the needless threatenings, and reproofs
Needless, aye, and the needless rigours, too ?
Away from these dull solitary walls,
The fields are glowing, the birds carolling
Bright songs of love ; and love is full of light,
Fresh breezes, freedom, life itself. Go, then,
Fiammetta ! Go to the pavilion. There
With his sweet following, let him enter in ;
Do honour to him, bid him make his stay,
The wayward master of the universe.
Now do you understand me ?

 Fiam.   Yes.

 Sen.   Have you ever proved
The prickings, not so dire, nay, pleasant even,
Of the longing after love ?

 Fiam.   Yes.

 Sen.   When ?

 Fiam.   Even now !

And now let us take an unwilling farewell of Luigi Rasi and his comedy, to dwell for a moment on a more ambitious but certainly not more perfect production. Ettore Moschino is the author of sundry poems which I have never read; and also of an admirable version of ' Les Bouffons ' of Zamacois, which seems to have preserved all the acting qualities of the original, while adding to its verse a musical quality which is to be found in the Italian language alone. Emboldened by this success, he has ventured on a piece of work more original, without being perfectly independent: to wit—a stage version in blank verse of the old legend of ' Tristan and Isolda.' It has had a considerable success, well acted by Garavaglia and Gina Favre; although neither by their personalities seemed perfectly suited in their parts. It is a sound piece of work; even in quality, the incidents on the whole well balanced; but somehow it has not perfection of elegance, while attaining much of its superficiality; and in renouncing the sensual passion of Swinburne, and the elemental simplicity of Wagner, has failed to find any adequate substitute. The author has clearly an idea of respecting the integrity of the ancient legend, but he has failed somewhat to make it interesting to modern ears. It is as if a modern architect should try to build a temple which should be wind- and weather-tight, and yet resemble Stonehenge in its general style.

The first act opens after the arrival of Isolda, with certain nobles of the court discussing the situation; foremost among whom is a certain Andretto, who is to Tristan and King Mark what Modred is, in Tennyson's poems, to Lancelot and King Arthur. The king comes in, and Andretto, by subtleties, tries to set him against Tristan, who, it appears, is inclined to give up fighting for the life of the hunter and the ballad-singer. Isolda enters; and, stirred thereto by her, Tristan repeats the oath that all take on their knighthood. Tristan goes out. The king, after receiving from Isolda an assurance of her love, departs with his following, and Isolda is left alone with her handmaid, Brangiana.   It appears that the state of feeling between Tristan and Isolda has been brought about by a love-potion.   Tristan now comes back and Isolda proposes to him to dissolve their love by an antidote.   But the antidote is powerless and love triumphant.   Enter King Mark, suddenly.   Furious at the looks caught passing between the two, yet with a sore heart, he banishes Tristan.   But when Andretto comes, with evil triumph, on the scene, Mark demands his sword from him, and breaks it, saying that he has no use for the swords of betrayers now that that of his ablest and noblest knight must, perforce, be banished afar.

In the second act we have Isolda lamenting to Brangiana the absence of her lover, and rejecting the passionate advances of the king.   There is something displeasing, almost repulsive, in the exhibition of amorous old age, and we are glad to pass on to the scene wherein Tristan, disguised as a crazy mendicant, gets admission to the court; and is finally handed over to the queen that she may amuse herself with him—a proposal which she executes in a way not anticipated by the king or the courtiers.   Andretto comes on the scene, his suspicions being aroused, but pays the penalty of his precipitancy with his life ; leaving only behind him, Denoale, the ' cattivo donzello,' as he is called, to carry on the tireless purpose of revenge.

Act III. finds the lovers in the forest.   Soon Tristan departs on some errand, leaving his Isolda to the rather sententious rebukes of a hermit.   The knight returns ; the holy man departs, and the lovers lie down to repose together—the sword of Tristan being laid between them, guardian of Isolda's purity.   Enter King Mark, led in by the ' cattivo donzello,' whom he dismisses.   He has

L

come to execute dire vengeance, but, seeing the sword and understanding its import, his heart fails him; he substitutes his sword for Tristan's, and withdraws. The lovers wake. Tristan, seeing his liege-lord's sword, is smit with remorse, and runs to seek him to restore him his spouse. In the search, he finds Denoale, with whom he fights. The spy is slain, but Tristan receives a wound from a poisoned weapon, and he and Isolda die in each other's arms as the distant trumpets herald the arrival of the king and his train.

The story of Tristan is in some measure like that of ' Faust '—it cannot be touched without fire bursting forth. The names of the lovers seem almost enough. No man could mouth out the word ' Isolda ' without a gleam in his eyes or a glow at his heart. And at certain points our author has expressed the passion which all must feel. The arrangement, too, is good, and the purity of the victims' love is no doubt a real return to an ancient legend. But yet, on the other hand, as a drama, it loses something in renouncing that tremendous abandonment to an inevitable force. The sense we have of how utterly awful the simplest forces of Nature—be it love or gravitation—may become, is best realised in the abandonment—alike of a legendary knight or a river of water—to the force that carries them along.

As an illustration of the verse and poetic expression, this is given from the third act—Tristan's address to the hermit, whom he finds remonstrating with Isolda. It is characteristic, but neither better nor worse than many passages throughout the play :—

> Wise art thou, to what profit ? Wisdom is
> No heavy robe of terror which the Lord
> Hath laid upon thee. Austere it may be ;
> But linked withal to life. Thou knowest not that,
> Nor canst thou realise the might of love.

Amid thy silence thou are withered up,
Even as a shrub in desert place. Thy flesh
Is become fruitless as the seasoned planks
Whereon thou walkest. Do not dare to speak
Of love to one who feeds thereon alone !
Tell not the river it should climb the cliff ;
Nor check the falcon flying towards the stars.
Each one of us has his peculiar lot
Before him ; he shall patiently pursue it
Even into bitter death, the boundary-stone.
Ours is to seek the altar of sweet love !

This is good, apt, and convincing ; but sometimes, in
the more passionate speeches, one is less sure—doubting
whether it be not simply the voice of one who, with a
torrent of words, hides his want of vision. Thus Tristan
addresses his love, after the second potion has convinced
them both that their passion dwells really in themselves :—

Behold ! Exult ! From my heart's very blood
Shoots forth a growing tree, engarlanded
With flowers all about. Its mighty boughs
Twine them about thy heart, about thy thought,
About thy sweet desire.
   Isolda.   Ah ! Vain, vain, vain,
Every defence. The very potion fails :
Nay, strengthens love, even with a thundrous power.
Between the hair and forehead, see, a light
Opens, and winds me in a multitude
Of fiery sparks, and over all my body
A purple tunic clings, as it were woven
And dyed with blood divine.

Tristan may have seen it, but I must confess to
being blind. Finally, compare this oath with the
Giuramento of ' Romanticismo.'

I swear . . .
With justice and with valour to sustain

L 2

The name and yoke of chivalry. I swear
All other offices to lay aside,
Worldly advancement or investiture,
Save that of arms ; and if my lot it be
To fight the traitor or to bring to earth
The looter, or to crown the innocent,
My sword shall flash, whatever hour it be,
In my king's service or his progeny's !
And without shame shall in its scabbard rest
Till honourable death shall end my life !
This do I swear, and I invoke withal
The mighty name of God, of Jesus Christ,
And the Evangil of the Seven Laws.

All very proper and pertinent to a fighting-man of the day. But the reading of it leaves us cold ; and there is no thrill in the theatre when Tristan speaks it, like that which follows the oath of Lamberti.

I have dealt, perhaps, a little longer than absolutely needful over this play, because it forms such a piquant contrast to the poetic work of the dramatist who is to follow—the one with whom our examination of Italian plays will fitly conclude. A writer who, should he die to-morrow, would have earned a distinguished place in the literature of Italy, and I believe, of the world. Should he live—as God grant that he may—to use all the power that is in him, he will—not certainly, but possibly— leave a collection of dramas whose power and range will be exceeded only by the very greatest masters of dramatic verse.

It was told me by a lady friend that Sigr. Sem Benelli lost his beloved wife but a few years since ; that her word to him from her deathbed was a charge to try his powers on the task of writing for the stage ; and that it was the inspiration of the sacred memory of the message, breathing on powers already ripe, that produced the most striking Italian drama of modern times. The story was such a pretty one, that I have never wished to inquire whether or not it was true.

For the truth of such facts has no absolute importance. They serve to divert those whose interest in art lies wholly on the side of the picturesque : and they attach themselves permanently only to the lives of lesser men.

We do not think, while we look at the Sistine ceiling, whether the painter of it had or had not a wife to inspire him. In watching the tragedy of 'Macbeth,' all actual life becomes shadowy and immaterial before the mimic life that is before us on the scene. All the stories with which modern drawing-room chat has sprinkled the lives of Beethoven or Wagner are swept away by the chorus in the Ninth Symphony, or dissolved in the magic of the Good-Friday spell. Art is mighty as well as long, with regard to the little beings engaged in her pursuit. And, perhaps, there is no great artist who has ever lived or worked, to whom it would not be good fortune, if, while his works were preserved, he himself were consigned to oblivion.

That Sigr. Benelli will ever rank among the Titans aforesaid, he would be a bold man who would now assert. His work has many of the attributes of greatness. First among these, is the absence of any tendency to develop a manner. This is one essential point which distinguishes the great from the mediocre artist. The interest of the former lies in doing all he can; of the latter, in getting all he can. While Shakespeare, or a Turner, moves unweariedly from theme to theme, from this side to that of life, making new inquiries, trying new experiments, gaining new knowledge, a Robertson or a Marcus Stone settles down to some easy way of getting an effect, some simple means of working on the hearts of simpler mankind. One is like an Ariel, a living power, ever expanding and developing in flight : the other, like a railway engine, which, after a certain period of mechanical perfection, must be condemned to lose its strength and swiftness in its monotonous journey over the same measured road. Sigr. Benelli, then, is with the Ariels. His attack is vigorous; his confidence assured. Each work stands on its own base, and makes no claim on our memory for its success. He began with a play that had an extraordinary, though deserved, success; and which was for that very reason the more difficult to follow with anything else. The succeeding ones had an interest which fully maintained the author's reputation; but an interest, nevertheless, so different, that it would not take much to persuade one that they came from an entirely different hand. Not only that, but the author's style seems to vary with the nature of the subject he is attacking, as easily and as completely as a painter's palate changes with the nature of his picture. Each play exhibits new excellences, and in each they are properly and appropriately called forth by the matter in hand.

It is safer—indeed, the only safe course—to test a playwright's work by plays which have been both read and seen. But inasmuch as only two, and both verse plays, fulfil this condition for me, and both in verse, I propose to add a third—a prose play—which I only know from seeing it on the stage. The verse plays are ' La Cena delle Beffe ' (The Supper of the Pranks) ; ' L'Amore dei Tre Re ' (The Love of the Three Kings) ; and that in prose, ' La Tignola ' (The Bookworm).

The two first are so concisely different and present such picturesque and telling contrasts to each other, that it will be best to treat of them, as far as may be, in company. We will describe first, translate next, and keep comment till the end. In ' La Cena delle Beffe,' then, the scene is laid in Florence, in the time of Lorenzo the Magnificent. The play opens with the preparations for a supper in the home of an old nobleman named Tornaquinci, at which certain enemies are to be reconciled : to wit—two lusty brothers named Neri and Gabriello, on the one side ; and a certain young coward, Gianetto, whom they have had the constant habit of bullying, on the other. Neri, out of pure spite, had robbed him of his mistress, Ginevra ; and, on Gianetto's maintaining a less than usually submissive demeanour, had tied him in a sack, dipped him in the river, and, between the baths, hauled him up ; delicately pricking him in the fleshy parts with his good Lombard steel.

All this takes place before the opening of the play, and is recounted by Gianetto to Tornaquinci in one of the few long declamatory speeches in it. Gianetto has to make peace to please the Medici ; but he has his revenge ready to please himself. The thread of it is foreshadowed in the speech referred to, and in a few others that follow it. Ginevra, Gabriello, and Neri arrive, and the conversation for the moment takes a general turn. But Gabriello, it appears, has loved the girl as Neri never did ; Gianetto contrives in the course of conversation to give his weakness away. Gabriello, being neither able to deny it nor to master his feelings, decides abruptly to leave the supper table—and his native place. After this, Gianetto—by artful manipulation of the talk and aided by his best friend, Tornaquinci's good Tuscan wine—draws on Neri to accept a wild wager, which is to take him into an assembled company of Florentine gentry, clad in a suit of plate armour, and bearing a pruning-hook on his shoulder. Gianetto then goes off to spread the report that he is raving mad, and the scene closes.

In the interval, Neri has been duly strait-waistcoated, and Gianetto, covered with his green cloak, has passed into his room and spent the night with the unconscious Ginevra. At the beginning of Act II., he is explaining to her, in the morning, her little mistake ; at the announcement of which, her chief display of emotion is of fear lest Neri should get loose. This in fact he does, but is speedily recovered by the ushers of the Medici; and his behaviour under the ordeal is certainly not such as arouse a confidence in his sanity. Gianetto, now confident in his success, embraces Ginevra before his face. And the curtain falls.

Act III. is devoted to baiting the madman. First by the traditional fool of a doctor—having a certain resemblance, by the way, to the doctor in ' La Commedia della Peste '—and then by three girls, whom the now helpless victim has courted and ruined aforetime. But one of them has a soft heart ; and she, having calmed him, persuaded him to escape the imputation of violent madness by confessing to lunacy of a harmless kind. This scene is a very good one. Gianetto returning, sees through the trick, and very nearly succeeds in betraying Neri into violence again. But, finally, the doctor authorises his being handed over into the custody of his friends, and Lisbetta offers to assume the character. Gianetto, who has attained, apparently, a general order to deal with the situation, allows his release, and Neri goes off, not able for the moment to give vent to his feelings. Gianetto, however, out of an apparent miscarriage of plans, has evolved a revenge a thousand times more subtle and more deadly.

> I hold between my fingers
> The finest thread of all, and out of it
> I'll tie the knot of death.

The hastily mentioned name of Gabriello gives a hint—no more—to those of keen wit, of what this may be. And . . . and . . . Neri or no Neri, he will go and visit Ginevra to-night.

In the last act, Ginevra and her maid are discussing the situation together. Neri breaks in on them, orders

Ginevra to await her old new lover as if nothing has happened ; threatening her with death if she disobeys him in any single particular. Then he follows her into the room. What comes next is stupendous in its simplicity. There is silence. The stage is empty. Then a rollicking love-song strikes up in the street outside, swells out and dies away again, as the singer passes along. Can anyone, I wonder, imagine the irony of this drunkenly cheerful ditty in the ears of those who sit breathlessly, helplessly, awaiting the ghastliest of murders ! Silence ! Then a moment's speech between the waiting-maid and Fazio ; she begging him to warn his master. Silence again ! Then a figure, taller and more robust than Gianetto, clad in a flame-coloured cloak, passes hurriedly across the stage, casting nervous glances here and there. He opens Ginevra's door and passes in. A terrible cry, and Neri comes out, wiping his knife ; and at the very moment, from another door, Gianetto confronts him. For an instant they stand face to face ; the great fellow trembling now before the coward stripling whom he has persecuted. ' You ? Whom have I killed, then ? ' ' Go and see, and then keep your reason—if you can ! ' Fazio rushes to his master. ' Fly, fly ! ' But Gianetto only gazes at the door. ' I am chained here ' : then as Neri comes out, with a quiet detached voice, in which no member of the audience could imitate him, ' Will he kill me ? No ! He cannot.' And Neri passes across the stage, gibbering and caressing the flame-coloured cloak which he bears across his shoulder.

The translations we propose to offer are from Act I. (the hatching of the plot), and Act IV. (its final consummation) :—

(*The dinner is served. The guests eat and drink with relish.*)
　　Torn. Some dozen friends I had invited here
To meet at table. Naitheless, we are few.

Gianetto (to Neri). If you had asked the famous Bandinello,
Who has so many goodly tales to tell
Of love . . . .
    Neri.   Yes, truly softening the brain.
Think on your own tale tangled fine already !
True, is it not, Gianetto ?
    Gian.   Folly, folly !
To think that man can measure for a woman
Her fancy and her curiosity !
    Neri. I do not measure it. I chain it up.
    Gian. Can you, then, chain the cloudlets of the sky ?
For woman's mind is as a rosy cloud
Of spring, that spreads itself upon the air,
Cradles itself, delights itself, being seen
Thus still upon the fleecy, infinite,
Sufficient sea of naught. The other clouds
Meet all about it, kiss, and intermingle,
Change tone and colour 'neath the shining sky,
That looks upon them with appeasèd love.
Which sky is even the husband or the lord,
Who, being by chance offended or enraged,
The little cloud shall loose its dainty rose
Of spring blossom ; swell, and grow black ; belch forth
Thunder and hissing hurricanes of rain.
    Ginevra. Good, good, I' faith !
    Gian.   Because a woman loves,
Seeing that others love, she eats the fruit
Freely in her own garden, when she sees
A robber in the garden at her side.
    Gin. Yea ! What a goodly thing is robbery !
    Gian. And therefore, lady, is it, you have chosen
A robber ?
    Neri. Say'st thou ?
    Gin.   Eh ! A robber !—Who ?
    Gian. Your Neri is a robber—undisguised.
Because, the instant he was 'ware how much
I loved, he robbed me of you.
    Neri.   If I robbed,
I am robbed in turn by her.
    Gin.   How do I rob you ?
    Neri. By all the pretty gauds you cost me, Bitch !

Gin. Well, leave me, then.

Neri.   A fair retort. I cannot.

Gin. (to Gian.). But tell me, you, how was I ever yours?

Neri (same play). How was she yours, I say?

(To the servant.)   Give me to drink, boy

Torn. (to the servants). Attention!

Neri.   Let us hear the way of it
                                            [*Drinks.*

You are more foolish than a lame-legged bench.

Torn. Come, come! Let's hear i' faith.

Gin.   I am curious.

Gian. (with insinuating grace). Wherefore?

Gin.   I cannot tell you.

Gian. (to Neri).   See how fair

A woman is, waiting a madrigal!—
Yes, for my story is a madrigal,
Lady, for you.

Gin.   Therefore, I am all ears.

Neri. See! you are hovering about this flower,
Like hairy hornets who continually
Flutter upon the ground, and buzz and murmur
Under the leaves, just to be noticed; but
Dare not set foot upon the flower itself,
Nor ever shall, seeing, within, the bee
Who sucks the honey that delighteth him.
                              [*Pointing to himself.*
And now get on, and to your heart's content
Spin out the story.

Gin.   Hush! you frighten him.

Neri. Fright, but not fight. I'll have him understand me.
That is enough.

Gian.   Of course, I would not quarrel.

Gin. On quick and tell me, then, how was I yours?

Gian. I never quarrel, never. But see, now,
I can say nothing more.

Neri.   He is all at sea

A second time.

Gian. (to Torn.). With your kind licence, sir,
I, too, will take my leave.[1]

                ¹ Gabriello has already departed.

Neri.   By Heaven! Will you
Put an affront on me? I tell you, stay!
There is no help for you. Or play the game,
Or take the beating. Choose!
    Torn. (energetically).   Gently, good sir.
    Neri. 'Twas not to you, I spoke.
    Gian.   To me, because
He knows I shall not answer.
    Neri.   Sayest thou?
    Gian. I say that if I were not what I am,
A very coward, you'd not dare to put
Such tricks upon me. Even the other night
You had not treated, as you treated me,
Another.
    Neri.   Hear, and lay this well to heart.
That in all Florence, not a single man
Frights me, one moment. The Magnificent
Himself—hear it who may—I fear him not.
    Torn. No one speaks evil of the Medici (*coming forward*)
In my house.
    Gian. (*holding him back by the arm*). Ah, me! See!
       they'll come to blows!
Help! Stop them! Help, I say!
    Neri.   In your house, sir,
I will respect yourself, but no one else.
    Gian. Me, too, I pray you ; make it cover me.
    Neri. (*composing himself*). Give me to drink, boy! (*He
      is served.*) And some day or other
At some or other feast or supper, where
Are met together all the moribund
Striplings of Florence, I'll approve myself!
I'll make them, like the very aspen leaves,
Tremble before me.
    Gian. (*comically to spur him on*). Heavens! It is falling in!
    Torn. What is't?
    Gin.   What's happening?
    Gian.   The roof is falling
Even at the sound of such a splendid tale.
    Neri. Tale! Were they very weaklings like you,
Even though I were not in person present,

Yet at my name alone, they trembled all.

Gian. At my name, too, they tremble. Best that this
You, too, should understand ; that cunning walks
Close after down the channel that your sword
Has hewn, and mocks you ; and that force trips up
Sometimes, although the fighting ground be cleared.

Neri. Upon two planted feet of bronze I stand
While you are fluttering like a flimsy rag.
Cunning ! I fain would see it at its work.

Gian. I you, in turn.

Neri. I'd like to see you go
To the house that has the pilgrim girl for sign,
Where at this moment all these foot i' the grave
Fellows are met together. You should go
Clad as you are, but your face painted black.
Two golden florins I would wager, sir.

Gian. Thanks ! I have taken beatings and to spare,
I hardly think I will adventure it.
But on my side, ten florins I will wager
That even you dare not adventure. . . .

Neri. Pah !
That is an enterprise for fools and dolts,
Therefore, I set it you. 'Tis not for me.

Gian. Then I will wager that you will not go,
Just at this very moment, to the shop
Of Coccherino in the Vacchereccia,
Where all the notable young Florentines
Are met together, whom you boast that you
Can make a mock of at your own sweet will.
You need not even lay a finger on them.
Enough that in their midst you show yourself
Clad in plate armour, bearing on your shoulder
A pruning-hook.

Neri. Why, everyone would die
Of fear, were they Medici themselves !

Torn. (*whom Gian. has nudged*). Could I but see you
there. Ha, ha !

Gian. I, too.
I cannot think the man lives who would do
Such thing as that.

Neri. (*firing up*).   How, then ! you will not give
The stake in hand to Tornaquinci.
　　Gian.   At once !
Here is the gold.
　　Neri.   I have done feasting then.
Is there plate armour here ?
　　Torn.   I warrant you
Enough to set a whole brigade i' the field.
Neri. (*to Gin.*). Why, then, away with you ! Get you to
　　house
At once, and wait me there.   I shall be late.
Lapo goes with you.
　　Gin.   Ah ! What way is this
To interrupt sweet conversation ?   (*Rising.*)
　　Neri. 'Tis time I showed these dandies what I am.
Quick, quick—away !
　　Torn.   You are too sudden, methinks,
Dismissing her.
　　Neri (*violently*). Women, to house !
　　Gin.   I go.
Oh ! How I go.   I would not tarry here.
　　Neri. You came to see your charmer, I believe !
Well, you have seen him.   You can go away.
Be off with you.
　　Gin.   I go, I go !
　　Neri.   Quick, quick !
　　Gin. I know not for my life what ails you men.
We bear you in our arms all the sweet gifts
That life is rich withal.   And still distracted,
You will have none of them, except at times
To us not fitting.   But a moment since,
All was so sweet.   To finish out the meal,
Then to tell pleasant, and then livelier tales.
And then, who knows, perhaps to take our pleasure
Wandering forth : the moon shines fair to-night.
　　Neri. To house, women, to house, I say !
　　Gin.   And men
Out to their mischief.   Lapo, let us go !
Wine is a deadly enemy to women.   [*Exit.*
　　Neri. (*shouting after her*). To house, to house, to house !

(When Gin. has gone) And now ourselves.

Gian. *(aside to F.).* Be ready, Fazio!

Neri.   Here, quick, the suit!

Torn. *(to the servants).* Bring that rich suit which the
Magnificent
Himself has worn in former days.

Neri.   Why, then,
The fun is doubled since I enter in
The cast skins of the Medici.

Gian. *(to Torn., who is advancing to help).* Have a care.

*(The servants bring forward a beautiful suit of wrought steel
armour.)*

Neri. Here, then, here! Nay, 'tis beautiful indeed.

Gian. 'Twill be too tight. Better take off your coat,
'Twill fit you better.

Neri.   True, true, I am stronger
Than is lord of Florence.

Torn.   I think not so!
Rather it seems to me Lorenzo is
Taller of stature and a goodlier man.

Neri. I say I am stronger than the Magnificent.

Torn. Pity you should not be as wise as he.

Neri. Oh! Fury has its joys as well as wisdom.
Who likes me not may let me if he can.

  (To Gianetto) Each of your florins is an hundred now,
So goodly grows the enterprise to me.

Gian. *(exciting him).* Nay, I am certain you will never
Reach the shop door.

Neri.   You shall see, old bag of bones.

  (To the servants who are helping him to dress.)
Draw in the leathers, look you, there! Lace tight!

Gian. Oh, then, you think that you may come to blows!

Neri. Such will my laughter be, I fear 'twill burst
Even this case of steel.

Gian.   The helmet, Fazio.

Fazio. Quickly! 'tis here, my lord.

Gian.   A noble figure.

Neri. Give me to drink here. First, I'll drink.

Torn.   To all!
Serve wine.

Neri.   My only sorrow is, Gabriello
Cannot partake our joy, being far away.
But such a tumult I will raise to-night
In Florence by my valiant enterprise,
That, where he is, rumour shall bear it him.
(*Drunkenly*) To the beard of him who has no debts, I drink.
     Gian. Certain that no one present is aggrieved.
     Neri. Next to the beard of him who plays the lord
O'er this effeminate and servile land.
Merchants and saints and thieves bow down to him
Ere sunset !
     Gian.   May the just God give it you.
     Neri. To you next.   Coupling your honoured name
With the asses and the goats Lorenzo feeds ;
Aided by all that valiant company
Of guzzlers, swizzlers, and tavern touts.
Who will not drink with me, the plague be on him !
     Gian. (*ready*). I drink.
     Neri.   And now the pruning-hook.
     Faz.   'Tis here.
     Neri. My lords, your armour is most beautiful,
Worthy a banquet of a hundred heads.
To wit—the people's ; and the Medici
Pruning-hook, I will make it speak I warrant
To all the sleepy goats assembled there.
     Torn. Well, get you gone ! We, too, shall have our laugh.
     Gian. Let us go see the fun.
     Neri.   Open there ! Open !
                              [*He goes out shouting.*
Open for death to pass, open for ruin,
Open for truth, open for massacre !
     Gian. (*pressing the door with the others when Neri's voice
          is no more heard, to Torn.*).   Quick, send the servants
          from the room !   Quick, quick !
     Torn. (*to the servants*).   Forth.   Get you quickly gone.
          Leave us alone.
     Gian. (*seizing Neri's clothes*).   Into the spider's web !
          Here, Fazio ! take
These clothes, and bear them, mark you, with winged speed,
Unto my house, and lay them on the bed.

Then run ; use your legs nimbly, so you reach
The Vacchereccia ere he doth ; go in
Into the school of one Grechetto called,
Master-of-arms, who lives beside the tower.
There will be many people.   Cry to all,
Asseverate with many oaths, that Neri,
Gone raving mad, has well nigh massacred
All of his people who were in the house.
Next, down the well has thrown the furniture,
And roaring, threatening, has sought the house
Of Tornaquinci ; and has clad himself
All in plate armour, with a lopping-hook
Of size stupendous, and is coming towards
The Vacchereccia, and swears he will
Be death to that ineffable Coccherino,
Guzzler, babbler, licker up of scraps,
And with him all who keep him company
There in the shop.   Run quick ! Cry aloud !—Away !
And I will to the shop and there will warn
Who may be there.   Away, my Fazio—fly !
    [*Exit Fazio.   Gian. turns to Torn., taking up his red cloak.*
You, cavaliere, to the Magnificent,
And tell him that such pranks are set on foot
As promise forth a fair and subtle end.
I, too, shall shortly visit him.   Adieu !
I hold this scoundrel in my hollow hand.
Away ! (*he rushes out*).

The second is the concluding scene of the play.   Neri
has just come out of the room where he thinks he
has killed Gianetto ; and the two are standing face to
face :—

    Neri. You, you !
    Gian.   Yes, I ! Whom think you to have slain ?
You were too hasty to avenge yourself,
And lovers more than one Ginevra has.
To-day, another who would execute
My death and your revenge, was living, but,
More than my death, was honey-sweet to him

M

Another night swooned in Ginevra's arms.
Years had he yearned it, so he longed for her :
And I, to save this paltry life of mine,
Said to him : 'Well, an you'll be schooled by me,
You'll find the road to her as I have done.'
And lent him thereunto that cloak of mine—
Just as I borrowed yours. And thus together,
Both you and I supplanted were by him.
You were my vengeance, and have made him ice
Between her arms.
    Neri.   Tell me, who was he ?
    Gian.   No ;
Have you not guessed the riddle ?
    Neri.   Hell ! No, speak !
    Gian. Him whom you killed, who lies a breathless heap—
He was your brother Gabriello.
    Neri.   No,
No !
    Gian. If you are not yet a madman, go
And look on him.
    Neri.   No, no ! [*He moves towards the room.*
    Gian.   Go, only go !
And after, keep your reason if you can !
                    [*Exit Neri. Enter Fazio.*
    Faz. Fly ! 'Tis high time ! Oh, good, my master, fly !
Dost hear !
    Gian.   I cannot, I am chained to evil.
        (*Neri is heard in the room gibbering.*)
Oh ! Mother Nature, if I cannot weep
The harm I do, can I not weep with pain
Not even to feel it ?
               See, he comes ! How now ?
Will he kill me ? He will kill me not—he cannot.
    Neri. (*passes across the stage with Gabriello's mantle over
    his arm*). Lisbeth, my pretty one ! My dear revenge !
Where are you ? I am seeking you—where are you ?

If I had any hope of having conveyed to the reader
the terse intensity of the original, I would spare him any

comments of my own. But as things are, we cannot do without a few reflections on what the play has done for dramatic art. To begin with : it is the one play I know, outside the English theatre, that has made blank verse a medium for conversation. In the original of the first scene I translate, one has no feeling that the sense is being hindered by the measure—nay, we are hardly definitely aware of the latter. And yet for all that, no such violence is done to the metre as by some of our Elizabethan writers. And when the author delays for a moment to expand into little pieces of pure poetry—which, by him, are never injudiciously thrown in—his verse is like the flow of water, which, from its broken pattering past rock and beach, from the hurry of sounding wave and breaking ripple, delays for a moment in a broad expanse of tranquil pool in which the clouds of heaven mirror themselves. To have achieved this is itself no small thing. But, further, the play discloses a power in the author's lyre to vibrate in harmony with the themes which he has imagined. Situations are evolved which are startling in their intensity : where the observations of ordinary life would—though, perhaps, natural in fact—sound upon the stage utterly inadequate, yet where, on the other hand, any elaborate poetical construction would show like elegant lace on a man condemned to death. It is in finding the right thing to say, at such moments as this, that one strong manifestation of Shakespeare's genius lay : such words, for instance, as fall from the lips of Cleopatra as she hastens to put the asp to her bosom, speaking of the maid who has just killed herself :—

> If she first meet the curled Antony
> He'll make demand of her, and spend that kiss
> Which 'tis my heaven to have.

The little speech of Gianetto, as he is waiting for Neri to come out of the chamber of death, is of this kind.

Equal to Shakespeare? Perhaps not. But hear it spoken in its place, and then tell me of any writer, save Shakespeare, who could have bettered it!

Again, a play may be even a great one without its story being original or novel. But if it has these qualities, assuredly the fact is no discredit to its author. If the germ of Sigr. Benelli's idea does not exist elsewhere, I do not know where to find it. And in any case it speaks like the spontaneous creation of him who gave it shape. In the working out, too, it is sufficiently true to the surroundings in which it is placed, and yet there is no parade of a local colour which would be inartistic, because superfluous. The character of Gianetto is a distinctly original creation. Ginevra is a person without feeling— a sort of Helen of Troy—desired by all, understood by none. She is in her place, but does not advance our knowledge of womankind. Neri might be a Homeric hero as well as a medieval Florentine. Tornaquinci may be found in our own day, irreproachably adorned with white waistcoat and tie, with an army of liveried flunkies at his beck and call. In short, it is a drama of action and character, universal in its appeal; original in plot, intense in power. It contains good dialogue and a few fine speeches; and, for all practical purposes, it maintains the three unities of time, place, and action.

'L'Amore dei Tre Re' is also in blank verse, but otherwise different in every essential particular. 'La Cena' is a play of outstanding originality, vigorous action, running dialogue with few long speeches, characters whose nature expresses itself rather by their deeds than by their words. All these points are reversed in 'L'Amore.' Instead of being of salient originality it is full of association; the action moves much slower, the speeches are longer and more deliberate. The characters are less interesting, and are continually talking about themselves. It lacks the dramatist's imagination, but has that of the poet in compensation. There are, no doubt, certain turns of expression, certain peculiarities of style common to the two plays; but such are the differences that a writer of 500 years hence would have but small difficulty in persuading that most credulous of audiences, a critical one, that the similarity of the authors' names was but one further instance of the length of the arm of coincidence. The same facts to us—better understood if in a mode less exciting to the intellect—merely argue an author of exceptional variety, of whose next work nothing can be predicted, save that it will probably be unlike the last.

The story of ' L'Amore dei Tre Re ' is a simple one. We are in the early days of Italian history. Fiora, a native princess, is married to Manfredo, a barbarian prince, whose father, Archibaldo, vigorous though old and blind, is quick in every sense but the one which he misses utterly. But Fiora loves Avito, an Italian prince, and the two have clandestine meetings; suspected, but not caught, by the blind father. Archibaldo's interest in Fiora is intense, and there is just a hint in a speech of hers, coupled with his answer, that it surpasses that with which an old man should regard his daughter-in-law. In the second act, Manfredo, about to set out for the wars, begs his wife, whose very footprints he worships, to wave him a last farewell from the tower. There, on the battlements we see her; while Avito, hid by the parapet, creeps up and kisses the hem of her robe, pours forth his passionate love, and all the while the waved scarf signals to the parting husband a message—alas! a false one—of faith and love. But as the husband passes, more passionate grow the lover's words; weaker, the wavings of the scarf, until, vanquished and regardless of all else in heaven or on earth, she falls from her perch into her

lover's arms. At that moment Archibaldo appears on
the scene. He fails to trap Avito, but catches Fiora,
and, as she will not confess nor yield her ·lover's name,
strangles her with his two great hands. Then Manfredo
returns, and, aghast at the scene, cannot pardon Archibaldo his share. The latter, saying ' Keep your dream !
I will avenge you. You must not look upon the death-
necklace your father's hands have made,' bears out the
body of the fallen and punished wife. In Act III. the
body is laid out in the vault ; but Archibaldo has spread
poison on her lips to catch the lover, who he knows will
come to gather the sweetness which romance bids
him—and us with him—believe is still flowering there.
Avito comes ; is caught in his death-agony by Manfredo ;
and the latter, after enjoying his rival's punishment,
commits suicide—even with the executioner's weapon.
The scene is closed by the appearance of Archibaldo,
who, finding his son in agony, guesses the event, and falls
prone, with a gesture of despair, over his body.

The associations which the story and situations of
the play call up are certainly many. The whole is
strongly reminiscent (though, oddly enough, this obvious
fact does not seem to have been noticed by native
reviewers) of Paolo and Francesca. Gianciotto has been
divided into two : the softer part of the affectionate
husband being played by Manfredo ; the hard warrior and
ruthless avenger, by Archibaldo. It is certainly noteworthy, but perhaps not strange, that the story of Paolo
and Francesca seems to be much in the author's mind
—as we shall have occasion to notice with reference to
another play. The love scenes, especially that in Act I.,
strongly reminds an Englishman of those in ' Romeo and
Juliet.' The reader will be able to judge for himself by
the extracts given as to how far this assertion is justified.
The scene in the vault, and the presence of the two rival
lovers ; one triumphing over the other, both eventually

dying over the body of her whom both have loved, is strongly suggestive of the same play. The strangling of Fiora vividly brings back the murder of Desdemona. To complete, or to thicken, the chain of coincidences, there is a speech of Archibaldo giving the surnames of some of his following ; in which there is just an echo, but without the crispness of the original, of the—

> Perce-Bedaine et Casse-Trogne
> Sont leur sobriquets les plus doux,

of Cyrano de Bergerac.

But if this play has neither the originality nor the dramatic force of its predecessor, it has an idyllic beauty which, had it been the author's first attempt, would have amply sufficed to make it and him remarkable. I compared its love-scenes to those in ' Romeo and Juliet.' Here are two short extracts, from the beginning of the love-scene in Act I. :—

Avito. Geronte with his flute has given the sign,
And yet too soon. Still it is perfect night.
Fiora. Let us go back, then !
Av.   No ! For, going back,
We should forget ourselves, and then the flute
Would sound no more.
Fio.   The shepherd, it may be,
Thy faithful one, this morning may have woke
More early than his time. Alike for that,
Wilt thou then fly ?
Av.   How sayest thou, alike ?
One moment that I rest against thy side
To naught is like.
Fio.   If it be so, come back.
            [*Again, after a little interval.*]
Av. Art sure the door is shut ?
Fio.   'Tis shut, 'tis shut !
I shut it at the first, you recollect ?
And the old man cannot see.

Av.   No, but he hears.

Fio. Trembling Avito! And an infinite peace
Is in my heart.

Av.   Yes, Fiora, yes, I know.
It is of that same peace I am afraid.

Fio. Give me thy lips and I will pay thee fair
Out of this peace; then ask my giving back;
Yea! Even desperately imploring it:
Because without thy lips I have no peace.

Av. If thou canst furnish me such sweetness forth
As I do long to cherish thee withal,
Consume me altogether with thy fire,
For I shall rise again.

Fio.   Yes, my delight,
My burning heart; and on thy mouth a flower
Each moment blows, and as I gather them
Fast on the instant, lo! they bloom again.

The second:—

Fiora. My love came down upon thee from the skies,
With violence unknown it lit on thee . . .
I'd cast myself upon thee from above
Imperiously rushing as the stream,
White vested like the seething of the stream,
Whispering, murmuring, sighing like the stream—
The stream of some flush river from the hills;
On thine embraces in their rugged might
Descend, and wear them, as the river wears
The rocks, into a thousand grains of sand.
And every grain should hold a beating heart.

Av. The mystic madness of the white-robed spouse
Here I await, as do the mountains wait
The silvery glances that the moon sends down.
And in the freshening stream thy kisses make
I'd hold me sound so long as possible,
To give thy milk-white passion longer time
For the sweet cruelty of consuming me.

Fio. Avito! Many dreams . . . eternal fever . . .
Avito! Life. O life . . . dreams, very dreams,
Enchantments linger . . . have no end . . . enchantments.

Av. Ah! They are dreams no more. The day dawns.
See!
Fio. Yes, yes! I see it. Leave me, then. Farewell!
The little stars have looked upon the sun
And tremblingly they let their eyelids down.
Av. Thus, then I go away bereft of thee,
Quite altered. None could recognise me more.
Even as a pilgrim or a shepherd goes. . . .
As I climb up Altura's heights, whose slopes
The dawn already whitens, and whose earth
A limpid green enamels, yea, her meads,
Her forests wild, shudder with precious hues,
I am confounded and I think on thee.
Among the emerald flashes I behold
Thee, thee! A rosy pearl enchanting me,
Stilling my fever ; and I bow myself
And call. Thy name among the babbling
Of birds, the perfumes, the encircling mists,
The sighs and aspirations of the hour, . . .
All binds me in a strange and living net.
Thy name I feed upon, thy name, thy name!
And I repeat it, Fiora, Fiora, Fiora!
And even so murmuring I fall asleep.

And if ever since Romeo first waited in the garden
and heard that unpurposed confession of love, speech has
more feelingly conveyed the rich bloom of the south,
the pregnant silence of the early morn—that love, whose
simpleness and deep passion breeds forth blossoms as
rich, as deep, as definite, as her sun does flowers—truly,
I am mightily mistaken.

Next a brief passage at the death of Fiora, which let
the reader compare with ' Othello,' v. 2, 91, not expecting
to find a resemblance thereto in a passage from our Italian
author but only a like adequateness to the situation. It
is to the last half of the passage that the observation
applies :—

Archibaldo (who has his hands on Fiora's throat).
Throat of audacity, deceitful throat !
Too strait thou art to close so huge a sack
Of lies, lies, lies ! O horrible betrayal,
Which thou my son will pardon ! Ah ! but then
'Twill be too late . . . then 'twill be weeping-time.
                                        [*He strangles her.*
Silence . . . deep night . . . a void, save that the air
Is filled with flittings of my soul on fire.
I never looked on her and I have killed her,
And in my utter depths of night henceforth
'Twill be the only thing that I shall see.

I wish I could end on this note ; but the play has its weakness, which in fairness should be disclosed to the reader. I do not mean of construction—those I have already dealt with ; but of expression in words, and of the relation of the author towards his characters. This is Archibaldo to his son :—

            It is true enough, I am blind ;
But he who seeks for good, as you do, he
Is blinder yet, and nothing will he find.
I who am lit within by my revenge,—
I grope within the shade where evil nests,
And I shall see him, I shall feel him pass,
And fiercely I shall cope with him for joy.
I am a pagan, a barbarian,
And I hold that fierceness is a finer thing
Than love, when I have treachery by the ears.

Unless my instinct deceive me, the images are involved and overcharged ; while in the last three lines there is that tendency to self-analysis which is wholly inconsistent with the pagan and barbarian which he, in the same breath, boasts himself to be.

Nevertheless, though still out of character, the same vein is used with better effect in the closing :—

O Lord, who hast bereft me of mine eyes,
Let me see nothing—make me blind indeed.
It is too hard a torture thou dost use
To try me, making me to meet the truth,
Yet granting not see't. No, leave me ever
Shut up within my wall of night. Blind, blind!

Lastly, I cannot help quoting this—Fiora to Avito :—

Oh, if it be but once, take me with thee !
Take me away from this strange shadow here,
Tedious and terrible. Avito, Avito !
I, too—cannot I follow where thou fliest ?
Shut in the mantle which enfolds thee there.
The watcher knows thee, he will do whate'er
Thou askest him. . . . To-day, only to-day !

Down to the last two lines, it is possible, though
mistaken. But, then . . . was ever more lamentable
lapse ? Surely, here Homer slept, indeed !

Lastly, a prose play, ' La Tignola ' (The Bookworm),
which I have seen acted, but have not been able to read.
I take the account of the play from my note-book as usual.

Act I. opens in a book-shop in Rome. Characters :
uncle, daughter, and nephew ; the latter is apparently
studious and really romantic. The uncle is trying to
get him to marry his daughter while he is in love with a
person of (as it afterwards proves) very light character.
Scene between the lovers wherein they sit posing over
a book, and he kisses her. Next enter a socialist duke,
who persuades nephew to desert the business at a moment's
notice and become his secretary—the latter hoping
thereby to win his lady. Act ends with a violent scene,
the old uncle being furious.

Act II. finds the nephew installed as secretary ; ill
at ease, envied by the other people of the house, and not
quite giving satisfaction to his principal, who finds him

wanting energy. He gets leave of absence, expecting
to meet his lady with whom he has an appointment, but
who, instead, comes to see the duke. There is a scene
between them wherein he pulls off her shoe, which is
left on the floor. Finally they go into his room together.
Nephew comes in, disappointed, finds the shoe and . . .
Curtain.

Act III. is five years afterwards. Nephew is married
to cousin, who flirts, of course. He is aged much, and
has become thoroughly 'the bookworm' in appearance.
After various visitors, his lady of former days comes back
to see him, unexpected. There is a little scene between
them, at the end of which he is allowed to kiss her hand.
She goes out. The uncle comes in and finds him in tears.
'What's the matter? Ar'n't you happy?' 'Oh, yes,
quite happy!' 'If you are happy what are you crying
for?' Curtain.

The play is full of good characters taken from life.
The nephew, the bookseller, an old professor who has been
teaching his pupils the same thing for the last twenty
years, the socialist duke—are all good types. The second
act moves well and is exceedingly natural. The scene
between the duke and the lady is in the worst possible
taste; but dramatically, I don't think it is much at fault.
The end of it is just one of those points—the man standing
alone with the shoe in his hand—where the simple passion
of the Italian actor seems to triumph, in spite of—nay,
perhaps, because of—the difficulties of the situation. But
the fault of the drama, as such, is that its main thread is
not disclosed until the second act. The first is interesting
enough as a series of incidents, but leave no definite
expectation in the mind.

Now our examination of these three plays leaves us
with this result : that each presents a new theme,
and treats it in a new way. Each time the author tries

ELEONORA DUSE

In 'La Città Morta'

his hand afresh he seems to put aside all his former researches and experiments, instead of developing his already approved powers, to turn almost restlessly to new problems: and yet to overcome them, often with some approach to completeness, always with satisfaction to the onlooker. Such work means both strength and variety. In modern life, men specialise too much. No doubt Napier Hemy paints the curl of a wave better than Turner did. But no man will have the soul of a Turner by perpetually watching waves, more than he would by perpetually gazing at a barn door. He who confines himself to what he can do best, will do hardly anything worth doing, and, with all his masterly reality, will still be unconvincing : lacking always that wide range and comprehensive motherhood of Nature, who has room in her lap for the dwarfs as well as the giants, and by the side of whose shining glaciers lie heaps of dirty stones. But in the work of our author there is not only the largeness of a comprehensive view : there is success in the individual attempt. The rugged dramatic force of ' La Cena,' the idyllic poetry of ' L'Amore,' full of mist and colour, the prosaic life and terse characterisation of ' La Tignola,' like a series of pen-sketches, crisp, vivid, practical ;—these, surely, are assets as well as promises ; money in our purse as well as indications of gold to be minted in the future. The one defect we have charged him with—a narrowness in his treatment of woman—is a grave one to us. But it is difficult for a foreigner to understand how much more national, and therefore more proper, it is to an Italian. For him, a woman is to be reverenced, but not examined: to call forth the masterful powers or subtleties of man, not to exhibit any on her own account : to be a shield whereon the light shines, a marble whereon the pattern is carved, a page whereon the story is written ; but not, by ill-judged action or speech, to disturb minds or influence action in the world. Which of the great women of Italian literature have any character, properly so called, or have let us into the secrets of their habits or desires ? Who knows how Beatrice wore her hair ; what shops Laura frequented ; whether pink or blue was Fiammetta's favourite colour ? And if in our own days a daring Italian has given his women characters and a mission, he has only succeeded in rendering himself the most unnatural, if the most thoughtful, of the important dramatists of his day.[1] Perhaps Sigr. Benelli's failing is, after all, one of the principal signs of his power, denoting that nationality, without which no writer can hope to become, for all places and for all times.

[1] Bracco.

CHAPTER III

COMING now to the second head of my subject, I am met by a dilemma: for either I must break a rule which should be on every boyish lip, or else give the first place to the least interesting branch of the subject. For not only is it my impression that the greatest Italian actor is the greatest of all Italian players, but it is clear that those who come after him form a splendid brigade; whereas, first-rate Italian actresses—especially in the realm of comedy—are rather to seek. Still, as I have done the ladies the unheard-of discourtesy of describing them as inferior, I ought, at least, perhaps to give them pride of place. At any rate, it will be making a decision.

I begin, then, with the actress best known to the English public: I wish I could be sure of speaking of her in a way that the same public would appreciate and applaud. But a writer of dramatic criticism would be worth very little if he gave popular, rather than personal, impressions. Sigra. Duse, herself, would be the last to deprecate any criticism offered in a serious spirit. It is not that I admire her acting less than, but that I esteem it differently from, her English followers; and I am fortified in my confidence by the knowledge that if English popular opinion is against me, at least a measure of Italian critical opinion is on my side.

I have not the passage by me, but I remember very well reading in the ' Secolo ' of Milan [1] an account of some performance of La Duse's, with general remarks on her style. The latter amounted to this : There was a time when La Duse was a splendid actress, with a fine all-round style. But she is no longer young and her physical powers, never very robust, are failing. Consequently, she has been driven to become a stylist in order to make her effects at the cost of as little effort as possible.

So far the ' Secolo.' I can only report these remarks in substance, but as to their purport I am quite clear. I can be more precise, however, in my reference to a well-known critic, who writes under the name of ' Jarro,' and whose observations, made many years before these criticisms in the Milanese paper, seem to contain a note of the same idea. He is speaking of her tendency, in the part of Cleopatra, to excessive and persistent breaking up of her sentences with pauses or breathing-points. And he gives an instance of speeches delivered with continual pauses in between the phrases. ' These pauses,' he says, ' are commonly used by her so as to hash up all her periods. It is a very defective method of phrasing, which comes either from an exaggerated attention to the art of speaking or *from some defect in breathing which she has contracted.*' Continued pauses for breath, of necessity show faulty or failing powers in an actress as in anyone else. And I quote this to show that even in quite early days it was suspected at any rate, that the actress had to husband her strength.

My own observations do not extend over more than five or six years. But I confess the impression made is what would be suspected from the remarks last quoted. I do not mean that she can at any special point be noticed as ' saving herself,' as the phrase goes, but rather that

[1] The date would be at least four years ago.

the whole of her tragic acting is now cast in an ideal, almost monumental, style, which is in itself less exhausting than one which depends in its nature upon the detailed and the momentary; more on a large, almost sculpturesque, presentment of emotions and events, such as we could imagine as consonant with the spirit of Greek tragedy, than on one harmonizing with that of modern times. This view is borne out by my own observation in the only two tragedies in which I was able to see her—namely, ' La Dame aux Caméllias' and 'Monna Vanna'; a comparison of which two plays will give, perhaps, the best clue to what I mean.

Neither is a native Italian play. Both are, in fact, written in French. But while ' La Dame aux Caméllias ' is written by a Frenchman of a characteristic piece of real French life, ' Monna Vanna ' is the work of a Belgian, a poet, and a dreamer. It has that air throughout, not exactly of unreality, but of ideality. It is made up of situations, words, thoughts, actions, that are consistent ; and would be true, always granting the premises. To witness it, is like walking through some beautiful arcaded hall whose spandrels are filled with gracefully inclined marble beings, so perfectly content with their positions and their attitudes, that, in spite of their life-like aspect, they can be trusted not to come down. To see Dumas' play is to jostle on the Boulevards—by moonlight, if you will, but an affair of toes and elbows, none the less.

To begin with, then, there is a difficulty. This Parisian atmosphere cannot be got in Italy. The greater seriousness, the greater directness, the greater intensity, of the Italian temperament, forbid it—whether on the stage or in real life. Moreover, most of those who play foreign character-parts, in such a play as this, only know their character-type by hearsay. The result is, that, in the opening scenes, we get an unnatural atmosphere where absolute reality is needed. This is a bad background on

N

which to paint any figure, however well executed. But further, the Duse herself has failed to realise the Frenchness of the lady she is playing. There is another part of the character that she has, I believe, deliberately failed to realise. Marguerite Gautier is dying of consumption. Here is a disease whose effects are perfectly well known, and in which Nature—if the word can be used of any such mortal onslaught on her throne of grace —must needs be allowed to have the last word. Now let anyone, who has any doubt as to the *naturalness* of La Duse's acting, take the judgment of a doctor on her representation of this disease. I am not admitting my medico as a critic of the artistic rightness of her performance. That is another thing. But would a consumptive die exactly in the way that she does? I doubt it; and I am fortified in my doubt by the performance of another actress who, at least, is entitled to be heard. Comparisons, like other odious things, may be sometimes necessary. Again, I am not saying that at this point I preferred Madame Bernhardt's acting in its place. I only insist that it held more Nature and less art. And the 'Nature! Nature! Nature!' of Eleonora Duse is what has been driven into our heads, like the jangling of Swiss diligence bells, by people who have as little title to instruct us as the horses to direct the expedition.

Turn now to La Duse's performance of 'Monna Vanna.' If I have in any way succeeded in making my reader feel the atmosphere of this play, he or she will have guessed somewhat the qualities required of the leading actress. The character of the woman who, one degree more self-sacrificing than Godiva, was willing to give up even her virtue that thousands of human beings should suffer no more, was a delicate thing to have wrought, is a delicate thing to handle. It must not be given to budding actresses fresh from the lycée. It needs

experience of life, experience of stage-craft, an absolute
confidence in the effect of any gesture, look, intonation ;
for the least mistake would be fatal. It needs, further,
extreme grace of movement, extreme elegance of pose.
It needs, in fact, that supreme art, weaving together the
tissues of gesture, speech, and glance, to form a being who
appears absolutely real and yet obviously and utterly
removed from everyday life. In the presentation of
this ideal figure, the actress was inspiring and wellnigh
faultless. In that of the modern and national personage, she was often not more than moderately brilliant.
In the first, I have compared her with another actress
(Irma Gramatica) with critical interest. In the latter, she
must remain incomparable. I think this may suggest, to
some extent, the style and scope of her tragic powers.

There remain the realms of comedy. ' La Locandiera '
reveals a side of her which is certainly less well known
in England, but as certainly more near perfection. Indeed,
her *acting* is perfect. Nevertheless, her Mirandolina has
one blemish. It is ungracious, I am told, to notice that
an actress has wrinkles. An actress, perhaps ; but the
character is there for our comment. Mirandolina is a
buxom and vigorous woman, and La Duse plays her as
such ; but she does not look buxom and vigorous : and
this goes the further to destroy the illusion because of its
otherwise absolute perfection. This defect once stated,
however, criticism may lean back in its arm-chair. It is
as impossible in Italy to sit down and write a description
of the play as it would be in England to do the same for
' Much Ado about Nothing.' And Mirandolina is La
Duse and La Duse, Mirandolina ; just as, for the English
theatre-goer whose memories go back ten years, Beatrice is
Ellen Terry and Ellen Terry, Beatrice. To explain either
would be like lecturing on the making of bread. For
the English reader, the atmosphere of Goldoni could only

N 2

with time and difficulty be revived or translated ; and here we have only a few short and crude phrases to spare. We had compared the total effect of actress and play together in the two different countries. As a whole, the same elements are found in each, only in different places. Ellen Terry's acting had that quality known as 'charm'— something delightful, but peculiar to the actress and not to the part; while it is in the dramatist's work that the real character is to be found. In Italy, the situations are reversed. The charm of Goldoni's women, and Miran-dolina among them, lies in an atmosphere which is to be found in nearly all his plays. It is the actress this time who rises above her particular self, and, through the conventional manners and behaviour of the time, endows the part with a personality of its own. And so her Mirandolina is, in the result, just one whit the greater, because you are charmed by a charm that you are sure will not be repeated. Once separated—ah, me, with what sighing ruefulness !—from Mirandolina, you are assured that the actress will not again serve you up the same pretty curtsy and toss of the head, the same humorous tear-drops at the beginning, and skittish triumph at the end.

And what is 'La Locandiera'? The play, gentle reader, is the story of a siege. But not that siege of earth-works, lines of circumvallation, water and marsh, dyke and dam ; pursued and resisted by bristling spears and belching fires. It is the siege of a poor man's heart ; and the assailants, in nowise less terrible in their kind than the ruder weapons of war, are smiles, glances, and bows ; with underminings of humility and mock service ; frontal attacks of open reproaches ; heavy artillery of sighs and tears. Never was citadel so valiantly defended as the heart of the woman-hating cavaliere : none ever so ruthlessly put to the sack on its fall. I do not know with what feeling the ladies leave the theatre, but if one may speak for his kind, the men go away with the sense that life in an inn must be a perilous thing— nay, with a suspicion that the hidden dangers round about their feet, even in the pleasantest of places, are many ; and a wonder whether it were their greatest happiness to know them and avoid them, or go on easy and careless, even at the cost of falling into an ambush and being soundly trounced every now and then.

The fascinations of La Duse's Mirandolina were made all the more striking to the present writer by reason of a performance of the same play, seen by him a few weeks beforehand, by the company of a certain Dora Baldinello. The company, in general, far surpassed the Compagnia Duse in Goldoni comedy. Their playing was more brisk and lively, and the characters of the three men were better sustained. Dora, herself, was a sturdy, healthy person, and her Locandiera was good enough until you had seen La Duse's. But, then, it was as the thrush's song beside the nightingale's : one was sweet and pleasant, the other was enchanting.

Well known as she is, perhaps a word of description may be welcomed. Her face is dark, mobile, and expressive ; but of an expression which, while not refusing to harbour joy, leans naturally towards melancholy. She is not particularly tall, but looks so on account of her extreme leanness of form. Her arms and hands, beautifully wrought, are so thin as almost to justify the forms of some of the primitive Italian painters. Her speech is rapid, even for an Italian. Her gestures, graceful indeed, are just a thought too quick—almost, one might say, too fretful—for a northern eye ; and she has the habit of gesticulating with her hands near her face, which composes in an awkward outline. But it is in her attitudes of repose that the acting power of the body is best seen and some of her statuesque movements in 'Monna Vanna'—as that in which she stands with her hands at her brooch, ready, at a word, to tear away the mantle which is the only cloak to her nakedness—are truly never to be forgotten.

After this, without question, the first of Italian actresses, I think I am entitled to put the name of Virginia Reiter. The surname suggests Teutonic origin, but there is no suggestion of the Teuton, either about her person or her art. She is short ; but stately, graceful, of ample form. Her one defect is that she is too frankly and obviously a lady; not a bad one, perhaps, in these days ! La Duse has been called by a well-known Italian critic ' La Donna Nervosa.' There is no hint of nerves about Virginia Reiter. Her art has that rare gift of strength and elegance combined ; and her beauty, that character which comes from inward sanity and intelligence. Were any author to be so rash as to present Pallas Athene on the stage, she, and she only, of all the actresses I know—even in spite of her shortness—would not disgrace the part.

I saw her in ' Adrienne Lecouvreur ' and ' Madame Sans-Gêne.' For the reason above stated, she was clearly more at home in the former. Well as she played Catarina —and she played her very well—there was never that air of the clumsy woman ill at ease in her fine clothes. You felt that she had all the grand lady in her if she chose. She could not be really clumsy or ungraceful. She sailed by, through, or over (as the Thames Conservancy tickets say) the would-be great ladies by her side, as our old 'Sunbeam'[1] here, through a tale of puffing 'vaporetti.' But as Adrienne—well, she was an actress playing an actress, and she played to the life. Adrienne is not called upon to be clumsy : *is* called upon to be vehement, to be

---

[1] Lord Brassey's famous yacht was lying off the *molo* of Venice at the time of writing.

Photograph by

Nunes Vais,
Florence

GINA FAVRE

In ' I Buffoni '

passionate, to inspire awe and love. Her recitation of
the passage from 'Phèdre,' at the head of the great lady
who had provoked her, could hardly have been improved
upon. While having all the intensity possible, it yet
stopped short of that obviousness which, in such situations,
so often and so tiresomely makes it ridiculous that the
other characters present should ignore the applied
meaning of the passage. And her death scene was as
ghastly and painful as could be wished. Virginia Reiter
is a fine actress. I am sorry to have seen so little of her.
After her (always reminding my reader that I make no
claim to be exclusive), I mention Gina Favre. A medium-
sized, elegant person with a clear-cut face, an unduly long
nose, and rather pointed chin. On my showing the
photograph to a lady friend, it was greeted by the remark
that it might be a man's face. The reader, therefore, will
not be surprised to hear that she played the part of Jacasse
in ' Les Bouffons,' and played it in such a way as to suggest
an excellence in the lighter parts of Portia. I think her
strongest point is an intelligent variety. She would
study any part you gave her, and get something out of
it. Were I to start on a world's tour to play every
imaginable kind of play, with only one leading lady, it
should certainly be she. I have seen her play Micheline
in ' L'Âne de Buridon,' Elisabetta in ' Fiamme nell'
Ombra,' and Anna in ' Romanticismo '; the heroine
in ' La Dame chez Maxime,' Isolda and Ophelia, and
she always gives a capable, and often a brilliant,
rendering of her part.

The play she chose, and rightly, for her 'Serata d'Onore,'
the last time I saw her act, was in ' Les Bouffons ' (before
alluded to). I should not hesitate to say that she is the
only actress living that I could see in a man's part with
undivided pleasure. Her clothes sat naturally upon her.
Her shape seemed to have nothing to suggest the dressed-up

woman ; and only once, throughout the whole evening, was she betrayed into a gesture not proper to a man. The performance gave just the mettle of the dashing young spark, which the woman's pace tempered to an idealism, proper to the old time and artificial speech; while her varied and expressive tone, and the subtle and intelligent face, found their constant opportunity in the vicissitudes and stratagems, through and by which the young cavalier won his way to fortune and a bride.

Her delivery in more important passages is referred to later on. But she has a nimble tongue too, in ordinary dialogue, and her ' di mi un po ' (just tell me now), or ' mi raccommando ' (untranslateable Italian formula with a peculiar sarcastic significance), have from her lips a piquancy quite her own.

Then there are two actresses of the name of Grammatica, sisters. The first I saw very long ago, and I have no impression left of her acting. Of her sister Irma, I own to having felt a doubt. Her acting seemed always admirably planned ; attitudes always well chosen, and she always seemed to be doing the right thing, or expressing the right ideas ; added to this, she had a splendid style of delivery, though not a beautiful voice. Yet for all this you were not carried away. You could not tell why. In talking her over with an artist who has had great experience of the stage, I heard that some years before she was thought a person of wonderful gifts—even promising to equal La Duse herself. Then she had to undergo an operation on the throat ; and since then, it seemed—as he put it—that she was merely a mask of her former self.

Such losses of artistic power seem infinitely sad. Sadder, perhaps, when the victim still keeps, as in this case, enough to raise her above the crowd ; enough to interest, enough to disappoint.

Photograph by

TINA DI LORENZO

F. Benvenuti,
Florence

If, in my approach to other actresses, I have had the advantage of the mysterious and the unexpected, for one, at least, I had been carefully prepared. Her appearance has been made known by the camera, the caricaturist, the poster-designer, successively. Her great deeds, and the havoc she has wrought, are they not written in the chronicles of the queens of the Italian stage ? Surely, for this paragon, I must allow myself a front seat ! As surely, any near approach to her person would be dangerous. How to protect myself so that, like Odysseus, I may hear the voice of the siren without leaving my bones on a distant shore, or my heart before a distant shrine ?

I don't know what better expedient may be suggested. Mine seemed to me a flash of genius. I sought out the most charming of my lady friends in Venice and persuaded her to accompany me to the theatre. *Divide et impera !* Fine old motto. And it is owing to my following its sage advice that I find myself the day after, cosily writing descriptions, looking out towards the sunset and the tower of the Friari, instead of sighing like a wasted fire and seeking a rhyme to ' beauty ' that no sonnet-writer has used before.

Tina di Lorenzo ! The name suggested to me a little, elusive, dark-eyed thing. The sort of creature on whom you might chance in some peaceful green hollows, feeding a goat ; who, in response to your eager request, would give you to drink out of the cool, clear stream ; look bewitchingly in your face and then vanish, leaving your heart uplifted with fruitless desire. Such impressions are made to be shattered : consequently, I was neither surprised nor annoyed when the curtain drew up and disclosed (besides a mere man) an ample feminine form—let me not for a moment suggest that Tina di Lorenzo will become fat !— crowned by a fine head, strikingly adorned with two sapphire eyes. The outline of the face has a slightly Jewish turn. Her arms and legs (for she did not deprive us of the privilege of speaking with authority on both points), while being shapely, looked really muscular. I tried my own forearm before the looking-glass, and was not altogether pleased with the comparison.

One cannot imagine her without her ripe beauty and her strength : but it is not in these that the personality lies. The moment the curtain rises she is in action, and she remains in action till it falls or she goes out. An electric vigour and brilliance communicates itself to everything she says, does, or looks. She dominates the scene. When she is not speaking you instinctively change your point of view, and regard what is passing from the listener's side. Her sadness, her meditation, even her repose, have in them an active quality which force you to regard them as the prelude to further action ; and for that action, half-oblivious of the immediate stage present, you instinctively attend.

It is but a few days ago that I was writing that it is hard to find on the Italian stage an actress who could hover between sunshine and storm, lightly touching both in turn, plunging deep into neither. I wrote too soon, for I had not then seen Tina di Lorenzo. I have read it of her, that she has confessed to having an inclination towards sadness. I have not found this evident. Her balance seems to me as perfect as her brilliance. Her art is sound and polished ; the brilliant flashing eye, the graceful gestures, the pose—never statuesque, but queenly, were it not for the slightest touch of the termagant—these are used truly and rightly in the service of the Muse of Comedy ; could the actress be brought to confess to being the servant of anything but her own paramount self.

And here lies the very, the only, defect of the whole matter. I suppose I may trust the account given by one of the leading Italian critics to the effect that she was a stage favourite at seventeen. That is twenty years ago; and for the best part of those twenty years admiration has been showered upon her. Her acting suffers from this : not acutely—that stage has passed. It must be years since that, under such influences, her style crystallised—with warmth, not cold this time, but still the metaphor holds—into an over-uniform brilliancy of surface. The actress who could not let the smiles go, the admiration, the enthusiasm, relax for one moment ; and who, in the over-insistency to keep, almost betrayed the fear to lose : all this is written on her ; albeit, in cold characters on a person and a face that no longer betray concern.

I put next another beauty of the Italian stage, who, without forming a great contrast, is nicely distinguishable. It is as if two profiles approached each other within a narrow space on the same sheet, and yet the lines were always moving apart. Tina di Lorenzo is on the stage with her beauty ; Lyda Borelli, for her beauty : therein unique among Italians ; though in England, I think the case seems common enough. Apart from her looks, she has no p sonality ; none at least which will survive when they hav faded. The former actress, again, may seem slightly vulgar in some of her actions, but they could be left out. In the latter, the very beauty seems to be vulgar, and to need a tawdry background against which to shine clear. The very lines of the profiles distinguish themselves in character ; for, whereas Tina di Lorenzo's chin seems slightly receding, that of La Borelli is somewhat over long and prominent ; so that, in the one case, old age might end in fleshiness, and in the other, in nutcrackers.[1] If I have characterised La Borelli's beauty

---

[1] Not suggested as a probable or immediate catastrophe !

as vulgar, I by no means wish to suggest that it is not striking and real. It would perhaps be even perilous, but for its obviousness. No one could overlook the fine profile, the easy powerful pose, the clear flash of the eyes, the masterful sweep of the limbs. A dozen painters could give us an effective portrait of her. Her beauty could be inventoried and handed down to posterity with the greatest ease. But that mysterious indefinable charm, which should have illumined all these clear-cut splendours, is not felt by the looker-on of to-day.

I, perhaps, was both fortunate and unfortunate in the parts in which I saw her. The first, because I had a strong light on her personality from two sides. The second, because the extremes made a somewhat violent contrast. Between Pierina in ' La Modella ' and ' Salome ' there is a great gulf fixed. And perhaps if I had seen her in some ordinary society part, both her effects and defects would have been a little less striking. I make this reservation and apology because I feel that it is the lady herself who has lost, rather than I or my readers. Indeed, from seeing her performance of Pierina, I seem to know something that I knew not before—of how and why ordinary young men go down like nine-pins before a certain class of stage beauty. You see the music-hall and studio siren in action, and the sight is both diverting and instructive.

You saw enough of the workings of the charmer in ' La Modella.' In ' Salome,' you saw too much. The part, perhaps, is an exacting one. The play is full of suggestions of something weird and mysterious about its personality. Of men whose eyes she charms, of women whose minds she frets and puzzles. A creature who should frighten and entice at once, inevitably, imperceptibly : whose image should leave no effect on the mind except the over-mastering desire to see it again.

The very arts—or, perhaps, the very obviousness of the arts—which make the character of Pierina ruin that of Salome. Her acting and her dancing are all one intelligent but obvious effort. She moves and turns, she writhes and twists, she trembles and rages ; and yet, to one watching her closely, there seem no spontaneous actions springing forth charged with inevitable meaning, but rather things telegraphed to their place by the central intelligence, and, like trapped messages, letting out their secrets by the way. Perhaps I saw too much, for I was quite near to the stage. Near enough to see the square inches of her widely exposed bosom heaving with what should have been tragic emotion : near enough to see in play every muscle of her splendid face ; or when, erect, it darted scornful glances here and there, or when, like some serpent's head scarcely raised from the ground and almost touching that other head—carrion now, warm life a moment since—it was the only part of her visible.

What ought I to have felt ? A sense of the mysterious and the spiritual in the great drama of life and death ? Of the ever mystic feminine, which for a man, and just because he is a man, translates breezes into longing sighs, moonlight into radiant madness, simple scents into incense burned on rosy altars before invisible gods ? But of all this, not a trace. I gazed on the splendid form in play with the same cold admiration with which I have looked down into an engine-room ; the joy in a magnificent machine.

'These mysterious specialities are easy to ask for ; not so easy to find. You criticise a representation : Will you tell us who could have done it better ? ' Such a question, only half-formulated, perhaps, passes through the reader's mind. The question might have been an awkward one, but, as it happens—like a chess-player to whom a powerful attack gives the opportunity for a brilliant combination—I am grateful for its apparent difficulty. More grateful still, because it gives me the chance now to do something like justice to the actress of whom—but through no fault of my own—I have had to write what seemed cold and unappreciative words. A mysterious personality which shall impress itself, powerfully, but without details; a magical but unrecordable charm; a fascination without beauty; a royal manner without formality; a grace unapproachable; and that elusive spiritual power, which defies description and yet is more powerful than any describable thing; a physical form so light and fragile that it would seem that it might be crushed, like an empty egg-shell by the hand; and a spirit so potent that it should survive the catastrophe of universal destruction;—these are the qualities of Salome, and these are the qualities of but one actress, but one woman, whom I know—Eleonora Duse.

Therefore, she will go down to posterity unrecorded, but unforgotten; no writer will succeed in portraying her, but none will be able to pass her by. Our children will demand what manner of woman she was. We shall answer. Our direct replies will seem empty as a death-mask: and only by a hundred little recorded things will they come to have a knowledge of her; as we on earth know our satellite rather among the pointed shadows of long arcades, than by the explorations of Galileo's glass. If what I have written seems vague and insufficient, again, in a higher sense, it is no fault of mine. I lower my eyes from beholding the lights of the firmament and go back to the description of things within the compass of a writer's pen.

Next, please—Evelina Paoli! One of those distracting personages, chiefly feminine, who by their mere appearance scatter into a heap the nicely built edifice of the theorist. According to all our reasoned conceptions of acting, she ought not to be on the stage, and yet we cannot think of her as anywhere else. She does not represent character or life ; her voice is not beautiful or suggestive. She has no great play of feature, nor more than a moderate share of good looks. But for the wonderful play of her hands, she has no strong out-standing gifts. She is always recognisable, and yet has not that personality which makes up in an actor for want of mobility ; which makes us careless of what part he play, so it be that he will play himself. In the course of some half-dozen performances not only have I failed to understand a single character that she was playing, but I have not even arrived at understanding the character of Evelina Paoli herself. And yet her vocation is unmistakable. Put her among twenty women in a room, you would pick her out as an actress at once.

Certainly she has a considerable reputation in Italy ; and when his last verse-play was produced, D'Annunzio —who, I suppose, could have had practically anyone he wanted—chose her to represent the leading figure of the tragedy. I did not see the play ; but from reading it, I cannot say that he could have chosen much better. D'Annunzio's rapture at my approval may, however, be tempered by the confession that I totally failed to un-derstand the character of Basiliola herself. And all this suggests a reflection : to wit—that as the stage is nearly as large as life itself, so there may be room in it for the mysterious, as for other things ; and that it may be good for us sometimes to have the indefinite before our eyes. Our readers will recall what Massimo, in ' Come le Foglie,' said about the pictures. May not we take his advice and enjoy those stage-players whose performance we can take (figuratively) and hold out at arm's length, each reading therein his own thoughts and desires, his own actions and failures?

I ought not to leave out the name of Maria Melato, who played in the company of Virgilio Talli. Indeed, her position fully entitles her to a mention. As this seems a rather ungracious introduction, let me hasten to say that it is not for want of satisfaction in watching her performances that I hesitate—if I hesitate at all—but because I do not find her an easy person to portray. She has been with her present company upwards of two years. That would prepare us for finding that fidelity and persistency were among her chief characteristics; and this is fully brought out by her acting. She is young yet—I believe well within the twenties; yet without being in any way thereby limited in her art, she gives you the impression of a tranquil and steady nature; simple and thoroughly moral. It may be a guide to her estimate of her own powers that she chose for her ' Serata d'Onore ' ' La Piccola Fonte ' of Robert Bracco ; the patient, suffering, middle class, ordinary wife of the society poet. She is also admirable as the girl, somewhat prematurely wise and certainly abnormally patient, in ' Come le Foglie.' For all that, I think her light comedy is her strongest point. And the early scenes in ' La Commedia della Peste ' were played really comically, and yet with a fascinating delicacy and absolutely without exaggeration.

In person, she distantly reminded me of Gina Favre, but is darker and gentler in appearance. She is broad-faced and broad-shouldered, yet elegant and graceful, and reminded me a little of the domestic cat. Her one trick is, in sitting full face to the audience, to bend her neck and extend her elbows, joining her finger-tips at the same time across her breast, so as to accentuate the impression of breadth. She can wear fine clothes handsomely, but yet seems more at home, and perhaps even

more graceful, in a plain gown. Most characteristic of
all, she seems to play as if acting was not the exciting,
soul-racking thing that some of its critics would have it,
but a sober duty and a simple pleasure. And when
she comes on—as she often is called to do—to bow her
acknowledgments, her smiles seemed a part of her,
and are not, like those of many actresses that I have
watched, guillotined by the fall of the curtain.

In that company which, when I saw them together,
was led by Gina Favre and Paladini, there were several
members of interesting personality, if not great actors.
Lotti, who did the elderly men's parts, was more than
usually good, and Baghetti, the ' amoroso,' certainly more
than usually popular. But we are among ladies now,
and the one who, for me, most helped to make the
company illustrious was a certain L. Rossi. L. Rossi !
It sounded uninteresting as it stood thus on the programmes ; but the discovery that her name was Luciana,
gave it quite another turn. Luciana Rossi !—Try it
yourself, if you have any knowledge of Italian speech.
It is like Homer's ' Poluphloisboio Thalasses ' : or, better
still, like the hush of the grey-blue Adriatic as you walk
along it between S. Elizabetta and Malamocco. And verily,
her own voice had a low sweet sound. So low, sometimes, that I used to allow myself the extravagance of
a front place that I might catch every word that fell
from those gentle lips. Her face was sweet and pale,
though not strictly beautiful ; but it was in her form
and movement that the real charm lay. Of rather over
middle height, she was as slender as a woman can be
without being pronounced thin. Such a slenderness as
will reveal every ugliness ; develop every grace. How
I remember the first night when she and Gina Favre,
who did not always act with her, vied with each other
in brilliance of dresses—I think they sported five between

o

them in the course of the piece,—mutually surpassing each other in elegance and acting power! How I remember her as Solange, in 'Les Bouffons,' as she played with her bird, turning her head now this way, now that, and gently touching the bars of the cage with the slenderest of fingers! But most of all in 'Il Marito in Campagna' (The Husband in the Country). She was the wife, Baghetti the husband; Gina Favre did not play that night. 'The Country' gave no obvious justification for Baghetti's fickleness. However, the wife is a prude—principally by force of necessity and a mother—and it is not until the middle of the third act that she wakes to the fact that she must part with her prudishness or her love. With some reluctance she chooses the former, and appears before her spouse in unutterably graceful *décolletée*, but—last remnant of the prude—a handkerchief held lightly on her bosom. I see her now: that bend of the fingers which was Italian before Botticelli, the whole body posed—they were of a height—so as to get slightly below him and look up in his face. And, as she looks, slowly the pressure relaxes; lightly the little prude's curtain flutters to the ground. There is music; the others are dancing. A moment's pause as they gaze at each other! and then, before you are even aware of any approaching motion, they are in each other's arms, floating round the room. Baghetti was a good dancer, and she . . . well, I have since seen Ruth St. Dennis, Maud Allan, Sahary Djeli, and a host of minor stars, in their symbolic elaborations, but never did I see the 'poetry of motion' expressed as by a simple valse danced by this Italian girl.

And now, in this gallery of principals, I must find a place (surely, justly!) for one who is quite supreme in one branch of the art only—namely, old women: nay, her limitation is stricter still, for she chiefly plays old women of high position and vigorous personality; but within these limits she is supreme. I have never seen anyone, for voice, gesture, facial expression, and pose, to equal her. Her name is C. P. Andò. She is not tall, nor thin ; nor, one would say, really old. Her voice is powerful and clear ; her enunciation, whether for short brisk repartee or longer speeches, perfectly splendid ; her delivery, while full of variety, never too fast or too slow. Her power of the pathetic is nothing short of magnificent, and her rich strong voice, with tears in it, brings tears into the hearer's heart, too. I think I am right in saying that I never saw her play without being recalled, at some point, in the middle of the act to bow her acknowledgments. I know that I am right in saying that I never saw her play without feeling, at some point, more moved than I cared to own. She played all parts, from the peasant woman to the duchess ; and in each of them, while perfectly suiting her gestures and speech to the character, she seemed to brush all externals aside and go right to the heart of the real woman.

There are various actresses who on their reputation might be mentioned. Italia Vitaliani, whom I saw as Paula Tanqueray : to which part her style was well suited, but she did not strike me as powerful or penetrating. There is Olga Gianini (Novelli's leading lady), of whom I cherish the same impression ; but I was unfortunate enough to see her as Portia—of the meaning of which part she had not the slightest conception. There is . . .

But what is that rustling at the door that has been disturbing me for the last five minutes ? I can see a light figure pirouetting round the ante-room between each knock. I can see the little move of disgust at the continued unresponsiveness within. Very well, Signorina, we will keep you waiting no longer. It is but a touch of the handle and in she skips ; as lithe, as bright, as girlish, as when I last saw her—I should be sorry to say how long ago. Permit me to introduce you, ladies and gentlemen, —Dina Galli. She is tall, but not too tall ; she is short, but not too short. Full of youth and mirth, with a touch, but only just a touch, of the real seriousness of life. She is slim and light to a marvel. A waist she has, but it hardly matters ; no man would ever find it with his fingers if he were looking into her eyes. Had she— instead of clumsy old Mother Eve—had to resist the attacks of the Serpent, our troubles would have been spared us : for she would have slipped through some hole, defying him to follow her, leaving a laugh behind. She is one of those beings, one feels, who has not yet felt the necessity of sadness, because she has not yet felt the burden of wrong. A creature who would be naughty and perverse to the point of being utterly bewitching and provoking ; but only because, childlike, she has never known ill-usage or distrust. You could conceive yourself taking any liberties with her, so long as they were taken in honesty and good-will ; but pass that ivory fence and no tigress would scratch you so deeply on the other side. She is not really beautiful : her movements are not always perfectly graceful, and she has dispro- portionately large hands ; but any minor imperfections are forgotten in that irresistible charm. Such is Dina Galli. As to parts she plays, I will mention one, the most characteristic of her, ' Mademoiselle Josette.'

Were I under sentence of execution, and had I the choice of how I should spend my last evening, it should be given up to a performance of this play, with Dina Galli in the title part. Josette—for the benefit of those (few, I hope, in number) to whom the play is unknown— is a young lady of eighteen, who has a godfather of forty, whom she dearly loves, but also an English lover, one Joey Jackson, whom she believes she loves more. Now,

DINA GALLI

Joey is off on a tour round the world, and it appears that, for certain reasons connected with a will, Josette must be married before she is nineteen. She therefore comes to her godfather, who luckily is a bachelor, at some unheard-of hour of the night, and actually entreats, cajoles, compels that unfortunate to accept this astounding plan! —That he shall marry her just, and only just, to have a marriage; that after a time she shall be allowed to divorce him; and then when Joey returns from his twelve-months' tour, she, now her own mistress, shall marry him, with all her colours flying, and the godfather shall go back to bachelor life as he was practising it before Josette entered actively on the scene. The marriage 'pour rire' takes place. The strangely assorted couple go away on their honeymoon. They are pursued by the parents interested in watching the developments of this unforeseen match. The husband is followed also by his old friend, who has been left in charge of a certain lady in Paris, and who finds the task a difficult one. Finally, a lover presents himself to Josette and the godfather-husband fights him; and little by little the two are driven to play husband and wife in stricter earnest than they intended. The climax of it all is that Joey writes to say that he has 'boxée'd' the Grand Vizier of a certain aboriginal African state, and has been condemned to four years' detention. In the end, Josette finds that she does not regret Joey. André is in a similar case with regard to Marianne; and the play aptly concludes with the return of Joey, announcing that, to liberate himself, he has married the daughter of the Grand Vizier, who had taken a fancy to him, and offering André ample compensation in cash. Of course, Josette is the life of the play, and for me—for anyone, who has seen her— Dina Galli is Josette. Some of the situations are delicate, and are only saved by an extreme lightness of touch. Yet

Dina Galli never failed to carry conviction—you know that you could no more have resisted her preposterous demands than André did. Her flirtation with Valorbier is carried just to the right point ; so also her teasing of André with descriptions of an old colonel, who, taking her for an ordinary married woman, will tell her risky stories of a monsieur, a madame, and a Zouave ; and the contrast is perfect between her girlish love for Joey, and her scene where, after the reception of the news of Joey's four years of detention, she takes leave of André, sitting moodily between two thoughts, and then steals back, slipping between his hands into his lap, and with lips and eyes as well as voice, whispers that she loves him.

It is such a moment as that in which Faust enters into Margaret's chamber. We feel that the curtain does not come down a moment too soon to hide from us something into which we have no business to pry.

I went to see her again, after an interval of two years, and I confess that I went with a certain amount of trepidation. Would the old charm remain, or would she, or I, or both, have changed in the interval ? Could she have possibly begun to put on flesh ? I might have kept my fears at home. It was just the same ; and it was delightful to confirm my first impression—that she was better as a good girl with a spice of mischief, than a naughty person with a touch of good nature. Her performance of an American oil-princess, married to a French marchese, was fascinating. Her American accent was quite superb ; and I can see her now, standing, fanning her cheek after having successfully conducted a flirtation by way of revenge, and saying mischievously ' Adessow non si sentey pew il puzzow del oliow ' (Now, perhaps, you don't smell the oil any more). All this was very good, but even better, perhaps, it was—in another part—to have seen her dance. It seemed, as compared to other stage-

dancing I have seen, like looking at daisies in a meadow
after coming away from a hothouse full of cactuses. It
was perfectly arranged, and yet seemed absolutely spontaneous. She was all herself, and yet blended perfectly
with her partner, who was the grotesque of the play;
seeming to sacrifice neither to him, on the one hand,
nor to beauty on the other, and yet to bring herself into
harmony with both. Physically, it was an affair of
wrists and ankles rather than any large swing or bend
of the limbs; the ripple of running water, rather than
the leap of the cascade. Psychologically—if such a
preposterous word can be used of Dina Galli's pirouetting
—it was the dance of wit and self-possession, as opposed
to passion and abandonment. I have spoken earlier of
Luciana Rossi and her dancing. The latter's was in
a valse—a social dance—and yet you had no thought
but to remain a spectator. Dina Galli's dance was a
fancy performance in the rehearsal, and yet all your
stars called on you to oust the fortunate Guasti and
join in.

And now, between the two scenes of the act—one filled
with fluttering skirts, the other set off with broad shoulders
and manly brows—we will have an intermezzo, if you
please! While the ladies are chatting and laughing in the
green-room over their—let us hope—successful appearance
before you; while you are turning, each one to his or her
neighbour, and passing opinions on the performances,
on the politics of the day, or even on your own selves;
while the fans are still fluttering in the boxes, over the
'platea' there is a general movement of shoulders,
telling that the point of interest has changed once more.
Once again the lights go out, the curtain rises, and all
eyes are turned towards the proscenium.

The lifting of the curtain discloses some commonplace room—a library, in ordinary life; but in the middle,

just opposite to the prompter's box, a plain table with two official-looking green-shaded lamps and a pile of papers. What is in store for us now? There is a slight pause; then enter the figure of an old man, in evening dress. He is clearly very old, but very full of life. 'Vigorous' hardly describes him, because though the vigour is here, it seems to spend itself in maintaining a splendidly erect carriage and an almost sovereign dignity. So straight a back I never saw before in so old a man, in spite of the burden which ill-natured Time has laid: not on the same back, as is popularly supposed to be his way, but elsewhere. His head is bald, and his face deeply lined: the mouth, only partly covered by a moustache, drawn downwards at one side. Time has drawn—is drawing—tighter and tighter the cords, but he cannot dominate the strength of the old man's bearing, nor quench the fire in his eyes, nor muffle the ring in his voice. A paramount self-control there is, which will only go you feel,—and *will* go suddenly and without warning,—when the house becomes finally uninhabitable and the noble spirit seeks refuge elsewhere. Signori, your loudest hand-claps! Signore, your rarest smiles! It is the father of the Italian stage — Tommaso Salvini!

I should have said, had I been asked, that Tommaso Salvini had passed from the world ages ago. His Hamlet delighted our fathers when we were running about the football field. We, in England, have heard no more of him for those centuries of adolescence which separate boyhood from manhood. But here he is, ladies and gentlemen—in the living flesh! And as living, in the case of an actor, means above all things speaking, let us hear what he has to say.

The occasion is a celebration of the memory of Gustavo Modena, whose statue has recently been set up in the

Photograph by

Nunes Vais,
Florence

TOMMASO SALVINI

Giardini of Venice.   It appears that this Gustavo Modena was a very distinguished actor ; a power ; a man with ideals for remodelling the stage ; and, lastly, and to conclude, was the maestro of Tommaso Salvini.   And Gustavo Modena was as much greater than Tommaso Salvini (according to Salvini, who was born, Signore and Signori, on such a day, and the range of whose experience is a little beyond the common) as Tommaso Salvini is (according to certain critics of the day) than . . .; but no one dare put a name beside him, so we go on deteriorating ; and the marvel only is that in this our day anyone is so presumptuous as to act, or any so fatuous as to go to the theatre.   All this, besides being current and indubitable fact, is the theme of the discourse ; adorned with much sound advice and many wise opinions.   As, how foolish it is for the second-rate actor to fancy that he can make himself great by making himself conspicuous.   How a man could only become a great actor by learning to forget himself.   How actors of the lecturer's day came back, preening themselves, fresh from the salvos of applause ; and were riddled with contemptuous pity by the wiser ones, who knew that to please the crowd is to be of the crowd.   And how the sorry attempt of the modern actor to wear Nature as a cloak for his idleness and incapacity, is bound to end in exposure and shame.   And then his voice ringing out, and his eyes flashing—in spite of his two-and-eighty years—he leads us up to the altar of the stage and bids us bow down before the images of her high mission, her moral influence, her lofty and educating power.

And if there are some of us who believe that the actors of to-day are as great as ever they were ; if there are those who see to-day a movement which may raise them, both as men and artists, by education and by ideals, to a point beyond anything they ever touched ; if there are those who believe that to look to the stage for education, for moral culture, is simply the worshipping of graven images;—none the less, they shall bow down: not before the memories of past greatness or the future of impossible ideals, but before the living form of the present: not before the theorist, who has imagined, but before the actor who has achieved.

There is much that this noble figure, of a man who has done his good work and yet remains to grace the world, would give us to reflect upon; but I am sure that Sigr. Salvini, Italian, and therefore chivalrous to his finger-tips, would not prevent any longer the entrance of those who are waiting, less worthy and even, at times, neglectful though they be. Out of compliment to him, we will take first his son, Sigr. Gustavo Salvini, whose reputation in Italy fully entitles him to a high, though not a foremost, place. Report has it that, as to methods of acting, he and his father are not of one mind. That may well be; this much is certain—that they are very different men, and that the fire of the father of eighty is lacking in the son of forty, whose style instead a rather scholarly correctness and studied elegance informs. He is not the handsome man his father was—nay, still is; his voice, even now, has not the same ringing tones; and his face and bearing strike one as those of a man who might have been a distinguished man of letters, or a diplomatist, as well as—or, even better than—an actor. I saw him play King Lear and Orestes. He was better in the latter part. He passed among his classic surroundings with an aptness and success that suggested a man a trifle out of place, perhaps, in the present day. His only apparent fault was a desire to build pose on pose which should be plastically effective, needing an extreme agility; so that his movement, in changing from one position to the other, gave sometimes the idea

Photograph by

Nunes Vais,
Florence

DE SANCTIS

of an india-rubber ball. But he was wonderfully successful in timing his emotions to the slow measure of
the tragic verse ; and, by so doing—though throughout
there is not one detail of absolute nature,—by keeping the
convention all in harmony, he produced a piece of striking
reality. His King Lear could only be criticised by
saying that it did not impress. Everything he did
seemed to be right—the force always proportionate ;
nothing was apparently weak, nothing was exaggerated
or excessive ; and yet when it was done, you did not come
away awed or terrified. You witnessed the performance
with pleasure, but you forgot it with ease.

I will take next—I do not profess to be following any
order of merit—one of whom it is the fashion among
some Italians to speak slightingly, because 'he studies,
poor fellow ! ' but who, nevertheless, has a splendid, a broad
style, and would, I believe, stand, with one exception,
the best chance of satisfying the more critical section
of the English public : Alfredo de Santis. He is a
sturdily built man of rather less than middle height with
a face of no very striking features, and, unless the
action of sitting down suddenly and resting his head on
his clenched fists can so be called, absolutely free from
tricks. And yet without these, without any ultra-violent
methods or personal peculiarities, he absolutely commands
attention. I saw him in 'Monsieur Codomat,' 'Diana
of Ephesus' (already referred to), and as Jean Rouchon in
' La Maison d'Argile' of Emile Fabre. He was excellent
in all three. Monsieur Codomat is simply a character
study of a French bourgeois architect. I should be very
much interested to hear what a Frenchman thought of
his performance, but, to me, it carried conviction as a
reality which certainly was not Italian, and with which
I was not familiar. Jean Rouchon, again, is a character
part, though of a very different kind. He is a young

fellow who has been brought up below his station by those who are interested in keeping him down. He is a good engineer, but nothing more. And the spectacle of this lad, full of character, but quite aware of his educational handicap, suddenly called to assert himself on his sister's behalf and his own, among people who rank themselves as his social superiors; his mixture of awkwardness, affection, ability, dourness, and pride, are a gamut of notes on which De Santis played with admirable effect.

If these are parts of characters to be played with the head, the maestro in ' Diana of Ephesus ' is a part of passion mainly. The story has already been told. The contrast between his carriage and look here, as the easy man of the world, and his bearing in ' La Maison d'Argile,' was more than admirable. His love-making is just what is needed, and suggests that he would play with splendid effect the scenes between Richard and Lady Anne. And when his plot fails; when, after the poor boy's suicide, the woman turns from him ; when he unwittingly kills her and sends her to join his rival ; when he is left alone, defeated and impotent, beneath the vault which, even in its incompleteness, is the sign of his enemy's triumph over him : the way he looks from the dead woman to the living art ; takes his wrath and despair in both hands and raves at the forms that he is powerless to complete or to rival, over the body that he is powerless to revive ; makes it difficult for you to recognise the actor who, three night before, as M. Codomat, was disputing over investments, making love for lucre, sniffing, signing documents, haggling over one per cent.

We will take next, Ferruccio Garavaglia. He is hardly the all-round actor that De Santis is. One is not to the same extent sure of him. He is a brilliant pianist, who is yet guilty of wrong notes, and to whom, therefore, it is not the same perfect rest to listen. But he is far

more typically Italian, both in face and manner, and his
acting has an intellectual subtlety which is at times
superb. His face is absolutely unforgettable, one that
you could never fail to recognise. I met him in the
Piazza the day after I saw him act the first time. The
profile would look in place on a Roman coin, though the
nose is slightly beak-like ; approaching a type that I had
always supposed Cyrano's would have reached, until
Coquelin showed me what Cyrano's nose ought to be.
Figure of middle height, back very slightly curved, step
light, and gait swinging, he seemed hardly to burden
the stones of the Piazza ; though looking bulky enough,
with his great black cloak flung loosely over his shoulders,
from which the striking face with difficulty issued.

In his art, he distinctly reminded me of our own
H. B. Irving. I do not know to which of the two this is a
compliment. His acting had, however, rather more of
the intellectual, and less of the sensuous. The variety of
means was rather greater. His elocution was beautiful,
almost faultless—a splendid example of the actor's art.
So much so, that when he began to speak, it was like
passing suddenly from a stormy sea into calm water. I
think he was at his best in Sudermann's 'The End of
Sodom.' There the variety of emotion, the slight turn
he has towards the disagreeable, his power of representing
cleverness, callousness, coarseness, in one and the same
individual, found a splendid opportunity. I am sure he
would do well as Neville, in Pinero's 'Letty.' It is a
pity he does not try.

I also saw him as Hamlet. I had also seen H. B. Irving
in the part. The latter, although his easy actor's art
carried him through with credit, was too hopelessly modern
to succeed. The sight of Hamlet sitting on a table swinging
his legs is an intolerable one. Garavaglia had not this
same drawback : and his Hamlet, though not at all

points equally good, is certainly not a negligible quantity.
An initial difficulty which one has in judging of Shakespearean performances in Italy is the badness of the acting
versions.   It is said that this is so to allow for the taste
of the Italian pit; but the treatment is not consistent.
Some parts are well, even elegantly, versified ; some are
badly paraphrased ; some are minced and hacked about ;
some are omitted altogether.   This version of ' Hamlet '
leaves out the opening scene with the Ghost ; has no
inner scene to which Hamlet and the Ghost withdraw;
and the scene with the king praying is done in the hall
where the theatrical performance has just taken place.
The effect of these savings in time and scenery is
disastrous.   The ' Methinks I see my father ! ' ' Where ?
Where ? ' loses its thrilling effect when the spectators have
not the spectre in *their* mind's eye.   In the ghost scene,
the sense of distance and remoteness, the mystery and
importance in the confidence, is lost ; and again, without
that vague impression of sanctity that an altar, the
burning lights, and all the trapping and suits of religion
give, the hesitation of Hamlet in drawing his sword
becomes mere weakness, cloaked by a contemptible
pretence.   I think, perhaps, the ghost scene, from its
importance, lost most from these changes.   The Ghost
was not on the scene when he spoke his long speech,
and one had the impression that his voice came up from
the ground.   Whether this was intended or not, the
result was to destroy the awe which follows on his
' Giurate ! '   Whether it was from this cause or not, one
cannot say; but I don't think Garavaglia's acting here
was as good as it afterwards became.   In the scenes
with Rosencrantz and Guildenstern, reduced as they were,
he was very good and natural, effective without an
over-reaching after points.   His scene with Ophelia was
excellent too ; his speaking of the soliloquy very telling

—especially his way of dwelling on the word 'dormire,' a word which suggests the act in a way our English 'sleep' hardly does. Several times his inflection gave phrases a —to me—new suggestion; as when he said 'He that plays the king shall be welcome.' One's thoughts immediately flew to another who was playing the king with less title to our sympathy. One excellent piece of business he did. Hamlet's advice to the players had always seemed to me a rather formal lecture for a young man—albeit, a prince —to give to time-worn professionals. In reading the passage, one remembers that it is Shakespeare speaking; but not when it is given on the stage: and in its delivery you generally get the lecture-like quality to the full. Garavaglia had a scene in which he was noting up and distributing the parts to the players, and he delivered his remarks, punctuated by little pauses and the gestures of writing and reaching out to each in turn, so that not only was the lecture broken up, but what remains seems to arise reasonably out of a practical matter with which both parties have to deal.

Certain points—to my taste, at any rate—wanted modifying. He was always a thought too much inclined, in the great scene (otherwise splendidly played), to maul his mother about, and his manner at the end, after he has wounded Laertes, of going for him with his hands, and wringing the confession from him, is certainly not to be commended. Shakespeare intended Laertes for a gentleman, and although tempted by his real grievances, the latter strayed a moment from the paths of honour, the author meant to show in the speech, 'Exchange forgiveness with me, noble Hamlet,' how much his real self had returned.

Finally, there is something peculiar and even weird, but none the less very effective, about his way of dying. He is still on foot, though tottering. The trumpets have been heard. Hamlet has given his dying voice in favour of Fortinbras. Then he picks up the foil and looks for a moment with a strange look—half-pleasure, half-regret—on the instrument of so many deaths; slowly and deliberately he wipes it on his left hand, making that all bloody; and, seating himself in the chair of state, with both hands outspread like some strange Eastern image, he awaits calmly the coming of the last messenger.

I have spent some time over this performance of ' Hamlet,' because the subject is eternally interesting to an English reader. See now before your mind's eye a small, square-built, tense-looking man, with an eye like a hawk and a back like a board. His face is rather pale, his lips graced with an accurately waxed moustache. His clothes might have been—as Caran D'Ache so humorously imagined of President Carnot—cast in two pieces and automatically clamped upon him. He does not look young, and you cannot imagine him growing old. In his voice there is none of that attacking and yielding rapier-play that so many fine actors have, because every speech seems so final a thrust that there is need neither of defence nor recoil. Have I set him before you with any degree of reality? It is Flavio Andò.

He is an actor of considerable reputation, having played lead to La Duse. His power and character would give distinction to almost any part. He might even play Romeo, and though no part could be more utterly unsuited to him, no one would laugh. He does play romantic characters which are not too young—as, for instance, Count Lambertini in ' Romanticismo,' and Cattaneo in ' L'Ultimo Doge.' But he is at his best in modern comedy, and in such parts as the middle-class husband who triumphs easily over the aristocratic lover, or the adventurer who, penniless as he is, by his astuteness, makes himself and his dress-coat necessary to the grandees all round him. Whatever Andò does as an actor is easy, decisive, complete. You may not like him. You can find no fault with him.

An actor of whom I have seen little, but of whom that little fully bears out his reputation among cultivated men, is Ruggero Ruggeri (*anglice*, Roger Rogerson). Of his personal appearance I can say little, save that he seems slender and rather tall. The two parts in which I saw him, while being widely different, were alike in this: that they represented characters far removed from modern life. Aligi, in 'La Figlia di Jorio,' is a pale, wasted, dreaming young shepherd, who is made the victim of a sorceress. The scene is laid among the mountains and superstitions of the Abruzzi. The story moves slowly, tragically, through a series of pictures—as the progress of the sun casts on a spacious chapel-floor and wall the mysterious hues of its windows, in which, though soft greens predominate, some sanguine is always to be found. 'Tutta di verde mi voglio vestire [1];' but from this soft green background of remote and primitive life the awe of the tragedy detaches itself. Herod the Tetrarch, on the other hand —whether in the Bible story or in Oscar Wilde's play— is very different from the pale young shepherd; but he has this in common with him: that he is a personage around whose still form the tragedy is draped; or who sits at the entrance that leads to it, like some huge, supporting statue in a cathedral porch. The figure is large, monumental. It can hardly be said to act. But what importance to the story it has! And Ruggeri created this figure with a make-up almost Assyrian; he suggested a right kingly presence even in the undignified state of satiety and maudlin passion: a passion, evil and unrestrained, but rather as the marsh that oozes than as the river that breaks forth. His

[1] 'All in a green green robe I'll grace me.'

P

continual ' Dance for me, Salome ! ' came almost as the repetitions of a set phrase by an oracle, whose voice, though the priest's and a human one, was yet solemn, mysterious, and sad. The passion was contemptible in its humanity, but the form it occupied was royal still; as if a band of rebellers and libertines were soughing out their exhausted antics in halls of a deserted palace. And in the last moment, when over the prostrate form of the writhing Salome, his tall figure on the stairs towered high, and his terrible voice rang out ' Guards, kill that woman ! ' the tragedy was fitly closed : and the shields of the soldiers descending upon her, crushed out, in one death-blow, the petty sensual sounds of the story—like a herd of wretched prisoners shut in for ever by the clang of an iron-bound door.

The reputation of Giovanni Grasso in England is such that, although not strictly speaking an Italian, he cannot be passed without a mention here. I was unfortunate in seeing him under more than one disadvantage. For, firstly, he was acting in a music-hall, and therefore had a peculiar audience to satisfy ; and secondly, not being in his native land, he, on the one side, lacked that sympathy which comes from a perfect understanding of every point ; and the foreign auditor, on the other, that ease of appreciation which comes from being soaked in the language in which the performance takes place. Nevertheless, after making all possible allowances, I cannot but believe that his Italian, rather than his English, reputation is a just estimate of his worth.

I saw the Sicilians in two pieces : the first, a highly abbreviated version of ' Cavalleria Rusticana ' ; the second, the third act of ' Othello.' We may note in passing that the dialect of the Sicilians is a very limited one—perfectly easy, in the main, to follow without any previous acquaintance ; and it is difficult to believe, after what we have heard about the extraordinary mixture of languages in Sicily, that it is what they speak in real life. Moreover, the prima donna, Signa Bragaglia, speaks pure Italian all through, and speaks it, we may add, in a way that makes it a pure pleasure to listen to. In 'Othello' all spoke Italian.

In 'Cavalleria Rusticana,' the part of Alfio, which Grasso chose, hardly seemed to give the actor his opportunity; but he certainly managed to suggest a burly, reserved, terrible man—one very ill to offend; and made one think it probable that he might well be a very great actor, if only he had his chance. But it was the old story of the 'nisi imperasset' of the Roman emperor. In 'Othello' he had his chance, and he failed.

This seems a bold assertion in face of the praise that has been showered upon him, not only by the general public, but by the critics as well. Luckily, in this case, the ideas relating to the part have been so well inventoried that it is easy to refer to specific points as to which the critic is the least likely of all to raise any question.

First, then, we will take the delivery of the farewell speech. The way—not the only way, but the best way—in which this speech can be given, has been told us by Hazlitt in describing the acting of Edmund Kean, and to his essay on this subject the reader is consequently referred. Instead of delivering it as the solemn leave-taking to all his greater hopes there described, Grasso ranted it, but ranted it ineffectively. Take again, his entry on the words 'Avaunt, begone! Thou hast set me on the rack!' It should be the bursting in of a powerful man at the white heat of agonising passion. Grasso came in as one filled with a modern nervous agitation; looked restlessly about him; drew aside the curtain as if to see if anyone was lurking behind.

Again, having flung Iago to the ground—but without

having put that fear either into us or Iago which comes
from moral power and is far greater than that excited
by the display of mere physical force,[1] he lifts his foot
as if to stamp on him and then thinks better of it—an
infamous gesture, and one wholly unworthy of Othello.
Again, on the line :—

> If she be false, oh, then, heaven mocks itself !

there was no sense of the gloom of suspicion melting
before the sunshine of Desdemona's presence. Again,
when he said ' Blood! Blood! Blood ! ' there was no
sense of the animal side of the man's nature surging
to the top ; the powerful creature bestially athirst for
a material revenge. Any hard-worked gondolier, bent
on refreshing himself, would have cried his ' Bírra di San
Marco, hey ! ' a dozen times more terribly. In fact, while
he was not successful, on the one side, in interpreting the
character of Othello ; while he missed the strength and
simplicity of the soldier which make for his undoing—and
at the same time make that undoing so pathetic—he did
not, on the other side, light his performance with any of
those electric flashes which we expect from the Italian
temperament, and which dispel doubt and annihilate
criticism by a display of natural brilliance or force. One
felt—whether justly or not, it is difficult to say—that he
had a nervous fear of being set down among the blood-
and-thunder school of actors, but had not at command
the finer interpretative powers wherewith to replace their
more rough-and-ready means. I could name a dozen
English actors who could give a juster interpretation of
the character, though their physical powers might not
be equal to carrying it out. Equally, I could name a
dozen Italians who, if the slightest hint were given them
of the possibilities that lay in the lines, would strike us far

[1] See the description of Novelli's acting, p. 232.

more strongly with their physical powers. I do not believe
—and, after all, this is the true test—that one in a hundred
among the audience knew when he was crying for the
blood of the betrayer, or when his anger was melted to
naught before the sunshine of Desdemona's smile. But
this is not so before the kings and queens of the theatre.
We know, without being told in words, when Sarah
Bernhardt is in love, or when Novelli is threatening
revenge. Nor do we forget the sight or the sound for
several days and nights to come.

We have not yet in our gallery the form of any purely
comedy or character actor. Half a dozen competitors
spring forward, eager to sit for the portrait—all of them
most acceptable to the Italian 'platea'; but, as we are
sole judges here, come forward, Alberto Giovannini, and
make your bow!

An actor, every inch of him, and there are not a
few. When first we saw him, he was playing what is
known as 'juvenile lead,' but he has gradually leaned
more and more towards character or clown parts. It is
difficult to say in which he is best. He is a tall, slender
fellow, still obviously young, and easy and graceful in
his movements when he chooses. His face, except for
a rather long and prominent nose, is inconspicuous, and
would make up to anything. There is no reason why he
should not play any part in the piece. Male, of course
understood—you correct me. But I am by no means
sure that I would agree to the reservation. If no suitable
actress were forthcoming, at a pinch I would certainly
let Giovannini try his hand—not to speak of the rest of
him—at some stalwart matron or damsel in distress,
confident that he would neither guy the part nor fail to
make it effective.

If it had been his fortune to have been born an Englishman he should certainly have belonged to the Elizabethan

stage, and the two parts that I most fancy him in are Falstaff and Touchstone. He has given proof of just that wit, diffused, genial, and babbling; that mixture of clumsiness and adroitness, of good nature and selfishness; which would have been perfect in the one : as well as that dry, concise, yet withal, humorous manner, which would have perfectly expressed the spirit of the other. And, while absolutely at home in a modern part, he has, when he plays old comedy, that air of making himself something far off, without thereby becoming unreal.

But since it will probably give the reader a juster idea of him, to describe him in what he does than in what he might do, we will take two parts of his which, by their perfect contrast, show him the really admirable actor that he is. And since the old world properly comes before the new, let us begin with his performance of Sennuccio, in ' La Commedia della Peste.'

He makes the character to the play what Mascarille is to 'Les Précieuses Ridicules.' He dances, capers, flashes hither and thither; and, with ready and easy movement, holds its not always skilfully constructed scenes together. His ever-recurring figure decorates the progress of the play, like the continually repeated 'putti' in some old Italian frieze.

Those who have read the description of the play will understand how easily his part might degenerate into farce. Giovannini seemed to know this : to be, out of very bravado, continually treading on the very verge of the precipice and never falling over. What other actor, I wonder, could have done his business of crawling on the ground and pinching the girl's legs without the comedy degenerating ? But, somehow, he has an air which deceives you while you are watching him—and, after all, this is all you need—into thinking that commonplace, and even coarse behaviour, is coarse and commonplace no more. He avoids the elegant—that he must leave for his betters; but he steers past the rough—for that would be out of the spirit of the time. And he leaves you with the impression of a quaint, whimsical, resourceful individual; inoffensively bumptious, on the one hand,. and bluntly submissive on the other: a personage whom you know you could never meet and yet whom you fully believe in. No one better than he knows the effect of attitudes; and in this play he takes full advantage of his knowledge. And these attitudes have often an inner, as well as obvious, meaning. The one in which he is illustrated opposite p. 138 is a good instance. The audaciousness of it and the suggestion of the Serpent and Mother Eve are very happy. But from the moment he comes in and sits down in mock meditation, with his hand only half-covering his smile, to the time when, with a last Parthian witticism, he trots out after his master, he fills the play with pictures, among which an artist might well choose with difficulty.

But if he is convincingly unreal, he can be convincingly real as well. In ' La Tignola,' he has a part of quite a different character : the young bookseller, with aspirations, making love to one who is above him in life and beneath him in love ; pursuing his aspirations towards something greater in life as in love ; who takes the place of secretary to a politician, and there finds politics unsatisfying, while politics find him incapable. Then comes the moment when his mistress betrays him, and the evidence of her unfaithfulness is a dropped shoe. Never, never, shall I forget the look of utter and submissive misery with which he took it up and looked at it : a look more intensely pathetic for the youth of the man. It was—in humbler surroundings—Othello's soliloquy of farewell; but pronounced by one who, instead of meeting death on the swift sabre, must live and work on, patiently, drudgingly, God knows how many weary years. In the last act there is practically no action—it is just the elaboration of that look. You see the drudge at his life's work. It is not a happy picture as Giovannini draws it, and you are glad when the curtain comes down.

We are taking actors in no particular order now, but just as their images present themselves. Ettore Paladini, formerly head of a company of his own, with Gina Favre for his leading lady, and now director of the Compagnia Argentina, deserves more than a passing mention. His style suited hers, to my thinking, better than Garavaglia's does; and several of the plays in which I saw them together went exceedingly well. He was an actor with a robust and sincere style. One peculiarity of his was a very marked lameness. It says much for the really artistic point of view of an Italian audience that they can look past such an incidental blemish provided that the characters are well conceived and in other respects well rendered. He played Lamberti, in the immortal ' Romanticismo,' better, I thought, than did Andò. The note of patriotic aspiration in his voice rang more simply true. His playing of the old major-domo, and his scenes with La Rossi, in ' I Buffoni,' were delightful in their quaint comedy. But I think, on the whole, he touched a higher level as the stern old priest, in ' Fiamme nell' Ombra,' than in any other part. It is not at first sight a pleasing character. The spectacle of any man— but especially of a priest—refusing, or hesitating, to receive back to his house a sister, is a thing that needs a good deal of accounting for: and I doubt whether any explanations after the event, whether anything short of witnessing her actual sin, could justify it at the bar of our sympathies. But he made a very human thing out of this stern old man, and gave us an insight, too, into the time when saintliness did not always keep apart from hardness: the time when, while his eyes gazed at the stars, the steadfast pilgrim sometimes crushed out the warm life that was creeping at his feet.

Virgilio Talli is a man of equally serious aims, but would hardly, I think, be mentioned in the front rank of actors were it not for his powers as a manager. In the latter capacity he is referred to later on. In person, he is short, rather broad than otherwise, and clean shaven. His face is well adapted for the expression of character and thought. It holds much, and holds it well; but gives rather the impression of a good, handy drinking-vessel, rather than of an elegant goblet. In his style he is correct: something like an inferior Andò, only with less acidity and rather more pliability. He is a good character actor at times; plays, among other things, Valentino, in 'La Piccola Fonte,' with great effect; but in general, he gives the impression of being a pattern which he himself has devised—a part of his own dream.

Sichel, when I first saw him, was playing in Dina Galli's company, but has since set up for himself. I should think that both had suffered from the change. Dina is left alone with other spirits—chiefly male—as frivolous as herself, and misses the background of his dry, humorous personality; as a rose, the gnarled post about which it was wont to climb. And it is unlikely that he, on the other side, has found anyone who, by her flighty manners and her good heart, could so delightfully contrast his whimsical patience and harmonise his patriarchal indulgence.

Let us take next, Armando Falconi, who is interesting as forming a comparison in a character which they both played, Panhard, in 'Signa Josette.' It shows very well the character of the two men's acting, and the way they severally get their effects. Incidentally, it furnishes a comment on acting generally. For there are practically two styles: one of which proceeds from without, the other from within. One relies on rendering things seen, the other aims at giving effect to things felt. One is an affair of clothes and physical sensations, the other presents character and emotion. Sichel's Panhard is in no way remarkable for anything he does. One could not, two days after seeing him play, have said where he was or what attitude he assumed, at any given point of the play. But my impression of a good-natured, perplexed, and put-upon old man, is distinct and lively, as I write now, some four years after the performance. Falconi's presentation, on the other hand, one recollected mainly as the study of an utterly drowsy man. Panhard arrives, at one point of the play, so tired that he cannot sleep. He is drugged, and then dragged out of bed and made, among other things, to play second in a duel. Now seeing Falconi play, brought me no nearer to the character of the whimsical old man. I should not have been able to recognise him in his acts, nor know how to beguile him into leaving me legacy. But it did show me how a sleepy man—and one drugged, to boot—would probably behave. He made one act, at least, of the play exceedingly diverting, and the audience was enthusiastically pleased. But I doubt whether the author would have felt himself as much indebted to him as to an actor who did not so cover up the character, which was a special one, in a set of clothes which we most of us wear for seven hours out of every twenty-four.

Falconi's acting was always pointed and always diverting, but never without this particular defect: he saw external effect to be got out of a character, and, worked up, until, like some sky, in a picture gallery, of an exaggerated blue, it killed all the delicate lights and shades that lay near. In ' Infedele,' he played with an extraordinary appreciation of the fussing ways of the professional lady-killing bachelor ; but his exaggerated preparations for the entanglement of his victim rendered him absurd before she came on the scene. There was nothing left for her to do ; and her victory over so self-sufficient and so paltry a thing certainly did not stand out as that feminine triumph which the critic's description had led us to expect. Not the least of Falconi's titles to fame is that he is the husband of Tina di Lorenzo ; which evidently difficult rôle he has filled, both domestically (if report says true) and artistically (as to which the public can judge), with discretion and success.

Another actor of this class is Gandusio. In Italy his reputation is a high one : standing in relation to Falconi something in the relation that Hare stood to Kendal; though the comparison must not be pushed too far. Gandusio is what is known as ' brillante,' [1] and certainly is a player of unusual versatility. I heard him play in three different pieces for his ' Serata d'Onore,' all totally different in character, and all with success : the chief one being Arlecchino, in a Goldoni comedy. To say that he was an outsider, playing before a Venetian audience, and that the performance was received with much laughter and applause, is to make any other comment unnecessary. He has, beyond, perhaps, any other, that actor's confidence which will pull through somehow a performance of doubtful success, and sometimes even one of doubtful taste. Probably, a simple straightforward gentleman, such as Kendal excelled in representing, he would find most difficult of all to play. He has easy, rather than graceful, manners on the stage ; and is capable of speaking faster than any other actor I have ever heard.

[1] See p. 258.

No doubt there are many more of the same class on the Italian stage equally, or almost equally, deserving of mention and criticism. Opportunities of theatre-going have not been infinite, nor is space unlimited. It is in reparation of any such injustices that the dedication of the book is offered. We must get on now to a description of the two great actors, worthy rivals in the public estimation, whom we have left till now.

I have, myself, heard four names mentioned by Italians as those of the greatest actors on the Italian stage. Of these, two act in dialect, and are described in the chapter dealing with the dialect stage. The partisans of Benini are few in number and of a special temperament : those of Ferravilla, rather men of the old school—*Laudatores temporis acti*—whose judgment, though founded, no doubt, on honest conviction, is delivered with additional satisfaction and confidence, in view of the fact that the object of its appreciation is not very likely to be seen by his hearers again. Both these two actors appeared to me as men of very brilliant but special gifts—the cavalry or artillery officers of the great army of players, and not possessing the wide knowledge of the operation of all arms on which it is necessary that a commander-in-chief should be grounded. We are left with two, oddly enough, having the same, not very common, first name—Ermete Zacconi and Ermete Novelli.

I remember in my youth—I hope none of my readers have had to undergo the same process of slow poisoning—having to study the subject of Jurisprudence. The foundation of it all was a system laid down by one Austin—not Alfred—which all teachers began with, and nearly all abused. The reason of this was obvious. It was so definite and complete that to disregard it was impossible ; to acquiesce in it was to reduce yourself to a cipher. But one began after a little to marvel at the universal way an apparently reprehensible system was sown broadcast by the teachers of youth.

Something of this kind, in my humble opinion, takes place with regard to Ermete Novelli. It would be, of course, a gross exaggeration to describe him as abused by nearly all. He has at least as many partisans as all the rest put together. But the reason why he is not held as universal king, is, we believe, that—if a pun may be excused—to be a novelist has no novelty; and that the ordinary conversationalist, who would dissolve insignificantly in praise, can make himself cheaply illustrious by scattering sneers or setting up rivals.

Therefore, we have vaunted the characters of Ferravilla, which few have seen. The delicate art of Benini is contrasted with the more rude and commonplace effects which anyone can understand : an appeal to an opponent's false shame which is hardly ever without response. Therefore we have erected the stalwart figure of Zacconi, whom I readily admit, if there were no Novelli, it would be very easy to accept as the leader of the stage. We will take him the first of the two, keeping Novelli till the end. If these descriptions have given to the reader, in the perusal, anything approaching the pleasure they have to the author in the writing, he will understand with what eager anticipation we keep to the last the task of writing on so splendid a theme.

When a man hesitates in his steps, he calls on all external circumstances to explain his hesitancy. The lateness of the hour, the badness of the light, the slipperiness of the road, will be feverishly invoked to excuse a faltering footstep or an uncertain line. He, on the other hand, who has assurance within him, will march confidently forward, heedless of difficulties which ought to perplex him, and obstacles which should be enough to turn him aside. It may be thought that we have not seen enough of Zacconi to pronounce so definitely on his merits. I answer, that some matters and at some times, our perceptions show us a form whose reality we cannot doubt, though reason cannot assign its foundations. It is like a mountain, whose clear peak soars above the mists which encircle its base.

I have such a conviction, as regards the acting of Zacconi, though I have only seen him twice. I may plead, however,—if I must plead,—that I saw him in two very characteristic parts : one in comedy, one in tragedy—parts in which his most ardent admirers agree that he is at his best.

'Cardinal Lambertini'—not a great play in itself—is by Testoni, a Bolognese ; and the central figure and title-part is a real character who flourished in Bologna, in the seventeenth century. It is in his progress through four acts, of very light intrigue and somewhat scattered incident, that the action of the play consists. It is a part which, with its strong local character and flashes of local speech, is very dear to the Bolognese pit. And it seemed to me that Zacconi, himself a native of Bologna, conceded something of his actor's art to make it go down with the crowd. It was not that he exaggerated or burlesqued it in any way, but that he resorted to easy means of getting effect which took away from the genuineness of the representation. I remember, especially, a fretful and frivolous gesture of the hands near the face, and a head more bowed than was consistent with his make-up or the liveliness of his discourse. It did not seem to have the reality of an old man played by Ferra-villa. It was very brilliant, but, on the whole, an affair of external marks, which were not always inserted in the right place.

The other play, ' Tristi Amori ' (Sad Loves), was of

ZACCONI
In 'Il Cardinale Lambertini

a totally different kind. Anything more remote than the society levity of the Testoni's cardinal, from the work-a-day simplicity of Giacosa's advocate, cannot be well conceived. Certainly, if I had only seen Zacconi in the latter part, I should have had no fault to find. He was as free from tricks as De Santis, and there was just that slight feeling of greater breadth that longer experience and, perhaps, more power can give.

It was a piece in which you could see no marks of the brush or the chisel. The real simple figure, simply existed ; and you no more had sense of the art of the maker than you can perceive the strings of the sunrise. By an apparent disregard of all points, he made the poignancy of the drama more intense. He let the spilled blood of injured love run purple on the marble flooring of his simple soul, instead of making futile efforts to scoop it up and hold it out to view. Never shall I forget how he leaned over and patted his wife on the shoulder, talking of older and harder times that they had suffered together, when the poor wretch was almost screaming with a sense of misery and guilt. The absolute confidence in her as the utter satisfaction of all his wishes, expressed in little things such as the daughter's name ! He had wanted to call her after the mother, but it had been represented that this might lead to confusion, ' Allora abbiamo agginto un ge ' (so we added a ' g '). Whatever was appertaining to the wife—name ' Emma ' included—was, of course, perfection. If not that, then the nearest possible. The man's simple manner and open confidence makes the situation absolutely heartrending. And when the discovery, by means of collateral facts, the bearing of which is beyond dispute, is forced on him, the same simplicity of bearing makes the man utterly terrible.

Such was Zacconi to one who saw him but twice.

He might easily have doubled the satisfaction for
every meeting, by which the acquaintance was pro-
longed.

And now after all these lesser people of the skies
have twinkled and faded; stand forth, Ermete Novelli,
moon of all the heavens ! But, indeed, we need not talk
in metaphors ; and there is no need to tell him to stand
forth: for, as in spirit, so in stature, he towers head
and shoulders above all his compeers on the stage. It is
hard to conceive an Englishman of his build who would
not be clumsy ; but his extraordinary lightness of gait
makes him seem less massive than he is. His face is
large and extraordinarily mobile. His thoughts appeared
in it like clouds reflected in still water. It is the ever
changing shadow spread below the heaven of his mind.
The only actor I know who had anything of this power was
Henry Irving, and he was far behind. Have I described
him at all ? His face !—I hardly think that I should
recognise him by that in the street. The face of Papà
Lebonnard was broad, genial, simple, patient, yet with
a reserve of strength: Sigr. Travetti's was long, pale,
and careworn : Louis XI's seemed rather broad in the
forehead, and had a line of extraordinary determination
about the mouth : Hamlet's seemed to have a low forehead and an extraordinarily long, straight nose: Shylock's nose was, of course, that of the obvious Jew, but
the face had breadth and power—a face that would have
cowed poor Travetti into three years' silence. But the
face of Novelli ?—I know it not, though I have seen
photographs in the shop windows of a person bearing his
name. Sometimes I wonder whether there is any actual
Novelli, just as we discuss whether there was any actual
Homer ; and whether the linking together of these various
characters is not merely a trick of the stage manager.
These things we meditate in the repose of our chamber,

but an electric spark always tells us when we are in the presence of the actual man.

If I tried to follow Novelli through all the parts in which I have seen him, I should lose myself and weary my readers. The best part for an English audience to see him in would undoubtedly be Louis XI, because there he would challenge comparisons with, I suppose, the greatest English actor within living memory. And great as Irving was in the part, Novelli has just that natural ease in sustaining himself in it which distinguishes the eagle from the flying-machine. It all *is*. You have forgotten the foot-lights and the proscenium, the carpet-grass and the painted flowers. The king in all his greatness is before you ; death in all its awful simplicity is at your feet.

I will not say that his acting is free from blemishes, but they are such as come from the colossal power of the man. In ' The Merchant of Venice,' for instance, when the sentence is given, ' You must prepare your body for the knife ! ' the mad fury of Shylock, thirsting for blood, is so bestially huge that although the whole of the audience in court close in to screen his victim from him, they seem hardly guard enough : and Portia's tiny ' Tarry a little ! ' is no more than one ear of corn blown into the sea. Again, in the play scene in ' Hamlet,' when he approaches the king on all fours, pinning him with his eye, with a motion as constantly accelerating as that of a falling stone, the danger appears so imminent that there is, to the memory, afterwards, no reasonable explanation of how the king got out of the room alive. If he ought first to play Louis XI, in England he certainly ought last to play Hamlet. His death scene would never be endured. He dies, no doubt, as a man pricked with deadly poison would die. A series of vast hiccups convulse his body. I have a recollection of his legs being

Q

jerked up so that the soles of his feet were visible. Finally, on the last convulsion that looses soul from body, the latter, relaxed suddenly, rolls from the throne down a flight of steps, hitting the ground with the thud of an absolutely inert mass of eighteen stone.[1] It is a marvellous piece of real life, but not Hamlet as it ought to be played. Nevertheless, there were wonderful passages in his Hamlet —as there must be, to my mind, in anything that Novelli does. His play scene was grand, and, above all, in the scene with the ghost, he made you feel the reality of the presence of a being from the other world. They say that in the presence of spirits, animals cower and tremble, though the cause of their fear is invisible to us. Something of this seemed to come into the actor's bearing. He did not cower or tremble, but his whole being seemed touched into a sensibility not explicable by anything we saw or heard.

I think, of his tragic efforts, his playing of Louis XI gave me the most pleasure, as being the most simply and unaffectedly great. Shylock—in some ways, perhaps, even finer—was marred by the background. The supporting figures matter more, and their mishandling did more to distract the eye. In comedy, far his most popular part is ' Papa Lebonnard ': the play being a translation of a French original. The part was played by two of the greatest of the French actors, Antoine and Silvain ; and in the French edition there are pages of descriptions of these actors with whom, as not the least of the triumvirate, is coupled the name of the Italian. The French do not readily admit foreign actors to rank with their own in typically French parts. That they, who are—here, at all events, not without excuse—prejudiced

[1] A recent work of theatrical reminiscences by Mr. William Archer attributes similar excesses in his death scenes to Tommaso Salvini; so that the fault would seem one inherent in Italian acting.

critics, should have allowed his right, seems so interesting that I have printed these criticisms in an Appendix.   One sentence may be quoted here: ' Thanks to Novelli, the name of Lebonnard will not be effaced from the anecdotal history of the theatre throughout the world.'   There is also a letter from the director of the Français, M. Jules Claretie; two photographs of Novelli, and a sonnet addressed to him by his living rival.   I doubt whether French popular and critical opinion ever paid such tribute to a foreign actor before.

Therefore, whatever satisfaction we feel, it is not well to comment on a performance already so widely known. For my part, I always think his most brilliant feat, in the range of comedy, a monologue in the character of a young priest, which is, I believe, a favourite piece of his. Everything combined to make it striking.   Great changes of character are said to be among the lesser of the actors' difficulties : but we could not but be impressed when the curtain—which had cut off from our view the body, writhing in the throes of quick poison, of a brutal and passionate man—rose and displayed to us the figure of a dapper young priest, sitting in his chair with his coffee on the table beside him.   From that chair, for the twenty minutes during which he recounted his experiences to us, he never rose.   And while his most excited gestures were to sip his coffee, or—when his parochial dilemmas and social entanglements became more than usually agitating to an innocent devotee—to place both hands on the arms of his chair as if in the act to rise.   But the experiences tripped out, treading on each other's heels : and doubt, perplexity, confusion, consolation hunted each other over the broad furrows of his face; humour chuckled in his voice at his own blunders; wit sparkled in his eye—even while his tongue recounted its own mistakes.

I make here—or do I renew?—a solemn protest against a certain kind of judgment that I often hear expressed. On no subject are our views so likely to be perverted by occasion or circumstances on the actor's art. Weariness, a bad dinner, a hot theatre, will often be enough to degrade to our eyes and ears the most splendid efforts. These things are perhaps inevitable : and in the individual must not be harshly criticised. Less tenderness, however, is to be shown with those who, in spite of ignorance of a people's language or unfamiliarity with their nature, arrogate to themselves the right to pronounce a judgment upon them. We have heard from a young critic, who guides our steps from the lighthouse of one of the daily papers, an opinion unfavourable to Italian acting : founded (as appeared upon examination) on *one* performance of a typically French verse play which he witnessed—ignorant of any word, tired, ill, and after thirty hours of travelling. Nor does it ever occur to observers, expert or otherwise, that a little knowledge of the customs—not to speak of the language of a people —is necessary to appreciate their dramatic art or to determine the relative greatness of their players. Further, I find it difficult to extract any principle on which theatre-goers bestow their praise or censure. One likes personality ; another requires that the actor should be merged in the part : so that one actor is blamed for a limping walk and another banned for lack of a large nose. One critic is charmed by an appealing voice, another by a flashing eye. One expects correctness, another is taken by impulse. One prefers his art obvious, another likes it concealed.

Are there any canons by which we should award to one actor above the other the Laureate's crown ? What questions do we put to these who come to claim our suffrage ?

I think the first is sincerity : namely, that they are not trying by a series of well-worn tricks to produce an effect on unpractised spectators ; but, on the contrary, are trying to convey to their hearers the idea of a character—never mind how slight or artificial — which they themselves have conceived. Granted. And if our competitors fulfil this condition, what shall we ask next ? I think that their style is easy, elegant, free from tricks. Some more fall behind here. What is the next test ? Perhaps a largeness of conception and execution, which shall be applicable to a greater number of characters, personages, times, and emotions.—Fewer pass the test this time. What next ? We are getting curious, now. Let us ask who of them have some notable excellence — eye, voice, carriage—that captures the sense and remains in the memory ? To those who can satisfy us, what further test shall we propound ?

I think that they furnish us with some sensation that is altogether new, strange, and admirable. That they lift us out of ourselves, and, for our pleasure and advantage, carry us now and then into a realm where we cease to fret, strive, or suffer : a realm wherein our sensations are glorious, but incomprehensible, and which we could not visit but by their power. Among those that satisfy this last demand we need not make comparisons. They are all first class : we need not dispute about a Senior Wrangler !

No one who had seen Novelli act would question the sincerity of his art ; but a short conversation, as far as the memory will serve, may be quoted for the benefit of those who have not yet had that advantage. The author asked a photographer, of whom he was seeking Novelli's photograph, whether he had ever seen the original. ' Oh, many times ! ' ' Off the stage ? ' ' Yes.' ' What was he like ? ' Really the witness could not tell. One day he would see a being striding along, erect, head in the air, with the bearing of a king. Soon after, he met a decrepit, woe-begone individual, whom he could barely recognise as the same man. His very clothes seeming to partake the misery of their wearer as completely as (this is not his illustration) the feathers of the Jackdaw of Rheims after the curse. When Novelli enters on a part, he clearly lives in it. His plays must be of importance to his family. Obviously better to sit down to dinner with a tender-hearted old Lebonnard than with the subtle tyrant of France.—Passed. What next ?— Ease, elegance, freedom from tricks ? I challenge anyone who has seen him play, to find any trick of gesture, intonation of voice, peculiarity of gait, which is common to his various parts. He enters into the character; and his realisation of it comes out clothed with all the externals required to convey its personality to those who see him. What next ?—Largeness of range ! It would seem like the act of the put-up heckler at a public meeting to ask of the man who plays Shylock and Travetti, Hamlet and Papa Lebonnard, Louis XI and Corrado, if his art is a wide and comprehensive one. King and merchant, clockmaker and office drudge—they each appear in their own image, clothed with their own manners and habitual action. To see Lebonnard put the watchmaker's glass into his eye, you would swear he had done it every day of his life. The sceptre of King Louis is held by a hand born entwined about it, and again Travetti turns over papers with just that air of habitual action which gets into the fingers of a busy office drudge. Put the crown on Travetti and it would become merely one of thorns. Put rags on Louis and none would mistake him for aught but a king ; and the evidence would not merely be in a noble and lofty bearing, but in the very touch with which

he tore up a bit of paper or signed his name. The last
I heard of Novelli (for, alas! I did not see) was that he
was playing some part in a play by Maxim Gorki. The
latter was present at the first performance, and on its
conclusion he made a speech, saying that if he had not
seen it he would not have conceived it possible that a
foreigner could so enter into and illustrate the Russian
peasant character. Whereupon author and actor fell
into each other's arms!

To turn to our next question. Natural justness
of movement, wonderful expressiveness of face have
been already hinted at. But his voice! Who that has
heard it will never forget it? Now roaring in frenzy,
now crying in wrath, now pouring out in pity, now
expanding in serene contemplation; without rising or
sinking, increasing or diminishing, it seems to become
invested with a new moral quality which, in spite of
difference of language, conveys his meaning to the hearer.
It is like an infinite organ whose many stops, changing at
the will of a master intelligence, breathe out through the
same pipes, hate, love, triumph, sorrow, pity, contempt,
arrogance, irritation; patient despair, unquenchable
hope, infinite compassion: which at times, sinking to
a point where music seems scarcely maintained in
sound above the throes of silence, now swells, now roars,
now rises, into a magnificent harmony; whose variety
composes into a passage, uniform and tranquil, but yet
full of inspiration; towering and tremulous with emotion
and thought.

Lastly, if mighty movements are to be sought, which
as eagles' wings shall lift us into the infinite, it will be
a trivial play—and he does but too often put up trivial
plays—in the course of which, we do not pass into Paradise
for the price of our eighteen-penny stall. I can remember
well hearing him say (in ' Travetti ') ' This promotion

comes too late.' It is impossible to try and convey the effect of these simple words. We understand them at a glance. If all the grammarians of the two hemispheres met together and discoursed upon them for a week, we should know little more about them than we do now. But just hear Novelli say them with that organ point of his, and in a moment you will feel a sense of something that is far beyond all speech.

Perhaps no description can ever hint at the power of suggestion in such a simple phrase by a great actor. Let us turn to something else that more nearly approaches actual proof. When, in 'Louis XI,' he is on his knees trying to pray, he is approached by someone whom he does not hear and who startles him. Recovering himself in a moment, and furious at having let slip even the least suggestion of fear, he turns and looks at the man with a royal wrath in his eyes. I can see him now. He was in profile on the stage. From about the fourth row of the stalls on the right, I watched his long curved figure (he seemed quite thin), bent on one knee, the sword hanging diagonally, the legs and arms mail-clad, the body covered with some hanging garment. He did not move a hand or touch his sword, he only turned his head and looked. I was aware of a real physical fear, and with an effort got my gaze free of him. I looked at the foot-lights and the prompter's box. No, there was all that in between us; and surely he could not jump! I was comforted. But I had had exactly the same sensations of personal fear as when, a small boy, trespassing, I evaded just in time to see the angry face of the proprietor glowering on the other side of the hedge.

One other moment I will mention in Sigr. Travetti. He has come almost to the bounds of his patience. Harassed and ground down, he stands for a moment

wondering if life, as he is trying it, is really worth while.
Workmen labour, he muses, but they have no appearance
to keep up : their life is a reality, their money is spent
on real things. What is the good of living this life of
empty pretence, when all around is contrary—poverty
gaining, disorder growing in the home ? How much
happier to live as the workmen do, even as the beasts of
the field . . . ! And, as he thinks, the voice ceases to sound,
but his lips move still. Then this motion ceases, but the
face is irradiated with thoughts : thoughts of a time
when sham and make-believe shall be no more ; when
boys shall have outgrown perverseness, women vanity,
men irritation ; when a peace, now dimly imagined,
shall descend and comfort thread-bare souls ; when the
hard-worked ' impiegato' shall pass to where, by some
miraculous change, power is not an advantage or
poverty a reproach.

Illustrations do not always make clearer ; but I will
try one more here. As a boy, in my climbing days, I
remember coming out of the hotel door at Zermatt, after
a shortened night and the inconveniences of a cold shave,
scanty wash, and hasty breakfast. Day was just dawning
and the first light fell on the black mass of the Matterhorn,
tinting it with rose ; and, under the influence of a breeze
not felt below, tiny wisped clouds arose and moved around
it in graceful dance. And, as I looked up at the mountain
far above me, sleepiness and discomfort slipped from me
as a discarded dressing-gown, and I soared away in a
strong flight far from the littleness of the world. As
before the mountain, so before the actor. The thoughts
circling about his face seemed to carry the mind away into
a region of spiritual coolness and peace : into places
clear and open, far from restless people and racking
cares. It was a moment of complete self-abandonment :
time was not for a little while, and it was with a strange

mixture of gratitude and bewilderment that the feet touched earth again.

I will leave Novelli here. We all have our preferences and aversions. For myself, I would not lose the memory of his acting to see any actor, present or past, English or foreign, who could be named.

CHAPTER IV

THE ITALIAN STYLE

STYLE in various arts is affected by different considerations. The art of architecture—to take, perhaps, the best illustration—is moulded largely by the limits of building construction and the requirements of practical use. Balconies developed in Venice, because of the limitations of the ground ; buildings, such as the basilica and the baptistry, from the particular use to which they were put. In the art of acting, likewise, we find what we may term its architectonic conditions of great importance. If you take as three types the Grecian theatre, the medieval open platform, and the modern stage, it needs very little thought to show how different a manner of speaking each in its turn must have produced : the Greek, with a large but scientifically designed theatre, which to a certain extent carried his voice ; the medieval player on a platform with his public on three sides of him, obliged to come right forward to speak his lines, and then retire to make room for others ; and lastly, the modern theatre, a building carefully designed for giving room in a given space to the greatest number of spectators and for providing the actor with the readiest means of reaching them.

These things go some way towards determining a style : but within the proscenium itself, development has been busy in our own days, and nearly all the changes made

235

have been with a view to realise the actual scenes, where, before, the presenters had been content with suggestion. Improved apparatus, improved machinery, better stage conditions generally from the spectacular point of view, have made great differences ; but they have been chiefly noticed by critics as influencing the art of the writer and the arrangement of the play.   It does not seem to have been considered that they may have a very important effect on the art of the actor as well.   More probable-looking sunsets, trees and skies that are not quite so obviously paint and cardboard, swords that seem steel, and corpses from which the sawdust is not streaming : surely these things may affect the way in which a knight delivers his defiance or a lover sobs out his woe !   I have heard that Edmund Kean ruined himself by wearing real lace collars, which in his passion he tore to shreds.   Whether it is true or not, at any rate, it is, as the Italians say, ' Ben trovato.'

But there is another thing : one essential to the conditions under which the actor performs, and operating in various ways—a condition which separates his art from almost every other.   All other works of art may conceivably be produced at a distance from those who enjoy them.[1]   You in Boston, Massachusetts, may read a poem which I have written in county Fife ; Danes and Canadians, Scotsmen and Japanese, will find Giotto's tower rigid marble, though the bones of the architect have long ago crumbled to dust.   But for the creations of the stage, the joint presence of actor and audience is indispensable. It may have been prepared beforehand, but only as a child in its mother's womb : it needed the touch of the actor's hand to bring it into life.

Other artists, then, are influenced by their subjects, and it is with them that they must be mainly in

---

[1] With the partial exception of the work of executive musicians.

communication.   The painter must live largely in the midst of the scenes which he chooses to represent ; the sculptor have continual visions of the nude form : and, as the writer moves over the desert or amid the busy throng ; as the musician, among the hum of human voices, or the sighing of winds and the roaring of cataracts, so will the expression of his art vary.   But with the actor it is different.   The conditions of his theatrical life, the variety of characters which he may be called upon to represent, make it impossible that he should choose his ' ambiente ' and maintain it.   While, on the other hand, if he does not understand the audience to whom he is called upon to translate the author's thought, the character which he is striving to represent will wellnigh fail to come into being.

It is this that, while it makes the actor's art transient and elusive, makes it interesting as well.   The playing of the same piece, night after night, to the same audience would be a physical impossibility.   But every night the audience changes, and almost every night the actor's way of playing must change, just as certainly as a man must wear different clothes in different weathers.   What is true from night to night, is also true from nation to nation : and the same characters, to get the same result, cannot be played to a German, a Frenchman, an Englishman, alike.[1]

We have, then, two main elements which tend to affect a national style.   A third, in the present case, is undoubtedly the transitional state of development in which Italy is found at the present day.   This, as it has been already spoken of, may be briefly dismissed here as tending to produce the absence of style rather than the thing itself.

[1] A consideration that should affect our criticism of foreigners in Shakespearean parts, *when they have been worked out for an audience of their own people.*

I will pass on, then, to speak of such differences in the theatres themselves as seem likely to affect the actor.

The principal differences in the auditorium in Italy are the greater size for the same holding capacity, and the fashion, which is probably the cause of this, of dividing the tiers into boxes all round instead of giving up the middle to rows of seats. The result which would be expected from this would be a more oratorical style of delivery ; but, as a matter of fact, the tendency in this direction is rather more than counteracted by the greater quickness of the Italian ear afterwards alluded to. The disposition of seats in the theatre has also a slight significance. It has, I think, the effect of localising the point towards which the actors play. In old days, with us, the pit had an overwhelming importance which it no longer retains. In Italy, the state of things now is what it was with us a hundred years ago. The corresponding part of the Italian theatre, the ' platea,' is chiefly filled by men. The boxes are the resort of the ladies. Many of the seats on the floor of the house are occupied by individual solitaries who have little else to do than watch the spectacle. The box holds a party, and encourages conversation. The serious interest therefore comes from the former place ; for the gallery (*loggione*), even were it of equal importance, is too high up to influence the actors' mode of delivery. And I think I am not mistaken in an impression that the actors play chiefly to the pit, but distribute their bows chiefly among the boxes.

The scenic effects and methods of production are to a certain extent to be considered as the result of the social conditions before referred to, and as influencing the actor, if at all, in a similar way. Nevertheless, a good deal of what is simple, direct, unembroidered, in the Italian style of acting is due to simplicity in the production of the plays. And I believe that, if the latter were more elaborately produced, if the details of dress and scenery were considered as they are in Paris or London, the changes would produce a corresponding effect upon the Italian style. Whether for the better or the worse, however, I will not here express an opinion.

We come now to by far the most important point : the question of Italian manners and character. These affect the actor both directly in himself and indirectly in his audience.

It were too long here to discuss the Italian character in all its detail [1] ; but it may be briefly said that it presents certain strong contrasts with the English. It is simple, direct, exact, intense. It is passionate : it is not senti-mental. I noticed recently, in some essay on the characters of animals, that the latter have strong desires, which, when ministered to, pass from them quickly and completely. In this respect the Italian is the nearer to the animal. His desires are stronger than ours while they last. But, though affairs of passion, they have so much of reason in them that they are capable of satisfaction, and when satisfied they pass utterly, leaving no trace behind.

They are a people gay, but not merry. Their laughter has a different sound from ours. It is not less sincere, but it seems to come from a different place. It is— I cannot find a better illustration—like the voluntary, as distinguished from the involuntary, muscles of the body. A blow from a man's fist is no less real a thing than the process of digestion; but the one a human being can control, the other he cannot. So the laughter of the Italian seems to be a momentary and conscious matter, of which the effect will be quickly over. Almost as soon as the joke is passed, the smile will have vanished also.

[1] The best analysis of it I have ever seen appeared in the May number of the *Fortnightly Review*, 1910, by Miss Tuker.

Whereas the Englishman will go chuckling on till the jokes and the laughter run indistinguishably into one another.

But, perhaps, even more important as regards the actor, and certainly less observed, is the question of manner in conversation.   This affects the actor directly and strongly ; and the difference here between England and Italy is important and wide.

In ordinary life an Englishman has only one conscious way of expressing his thoughts—his voice.   The Italian his three : voice, gesture, and facial expression.   All three may be, and often are, used to convey a fact or to explain an idea.   It is true, no doubt, that an English-man's face changes, and changes a good deal, with the current of his talk ; but this is not quite the same thing. In one case, it is intentional and primary ; in the other, it is unconscious and derived : not an aid to, but a consequence of, speaking.   This proposition, if true, has an obvious pertinence to the matter in hand ; and that it is true, I think, a little reflection will easily convince the reader.   Has the ordinary man any idea of the changes taking place in his face or the movement of his hands while he is talking ?   As regards hands, he pro-bably uses gesture very little ; as regards his face, how-ever expressive it may be, he would be a very self-conscious Englishman who considered what it was doing.   As regards his voice, however, I believe that the case is quite different ; and that we can, if we think of it, be aware of a conscious effort to modulate, raise or lower, sharpen or soften, in order to express the feelings that are passing through our minds.

With regard to the Italian, I am satisfied, by close observation, that the case is otherwise.   To take the question of gesture first.   I used to think that the gestures of an Italian were just a wild medley : expressive, if of anything, of a generally impulsive and excitable nature.

This is no doubt the first impression of many other Englishmen. In reality, nothing could be farther from the truth. These gestures, apparently disordered, suggesting chaos at first sight, are, in reality,—like the underground wires at the General Post Office—to one who has learnt their ways, the type of all that is orderly and scientific. They express the Italian love for detail, accuracy, and spring from the prosaic faculty of exact description. And a noticeable thing is that the higher you go up in the scale of speaking, the less the gestures tend to express picturesque and minute detail ; the more, to indicate states of mind. An organ-grinder or a gondolier will portray backwards and forwards, numbers, the passage of food down the throat, &c., with an unmistakable sign-post accuracy ; the man of our own class, not to the same extent. In the actor, these indications have reached the vanishing-point ; while in the public orator they have disappeared altogether.

As regards the voice, it needs no argument to show that the Italian uses the same conscious modulation as we do. There remains the face. Again, a careful observance of Italian faces will satisfy anyone, I believe, that their faces are a conscious medium of expression to the same extent that our voices are. Their faces and hands are both wonderfully still when the mind is not working : when it is, they both, together with the voice, leap into expression at once : they are here, there, and everywhere in a moment ; and in a moment they are still again, with a tranquillity hardly known to us.

The stillness is, perhaps, if you watch it carefully, even more astonishing than the motion. There is none of that fidgeting of fingers, shuffling of feet, twitching of faces, that one sees so much of among one's own com-patriots. In England, fingers, whether of idle or business men, are continually on the move ; whereas in Italy, you

R

may watch, say, a dozen to twenty men about you in a library for minutes together and see hardly any movement save to turn over the pages of the book. This restfulness of the hands is the result of their use. A man keeps a walking-stick to play with, but his tools are used and laid aside.

But these three means of expression are not merely co-ordinate : they are reciprocal. Gesture will help speech, expression, gesture, as occasion demands. The little changes of face, to express some physical sensation, are positively ludicrous to us. I have seen a man twist up his mouth in a perfectly absurd correspondence with his action, when struggling with his coat-sleeve. An Englishman's resource, in the like situation, would have been swearing or using slang. Observe, that in neither case is there any question of its being done ' for effect.' I was the only person, for the moment, within sight of the person referred to, and I am sure that he was not even aware of my presence.

It will be seen, then, that, in this respect at any rate, the Italian comes into the field with a very considerable natural advantage. Past question, all these three modes of expression must be used on the stage ; and, if in the one case they are natural, in the other acquired, there is no doubt as to who will have the advantage—so far as acting is concerned.

It may seem to some readers as if by a long and devious path we had arrived at the proposition—familiar to most Englishmen—that every Italian is a born actor. Such, however, is not the case, by any means. The aphorism is not a sound one, to start with. No man was ever born into the humble callings of blacksmith or wheelwright : far less into the difficult arts of violinist or actor. What we have in reality arrived at, is that the Italian is differently and more richly equipped for *becoming* an actor—which is a vastly different thing. Those with more varied powers are often, if not always, more difficult to train; and it is exactly this lively ' bozzetto ' of the actor in the ordinary Italian that makes him so difficult to turn out into the finished masterpiece. These distinctions are made with a view of suggesting that the art in Italy must have a different result, which will in turn be the outcome of a different training. For while the English actor needs something which will arouse or enlarge his powers, those of the Italian are already in active existence, and will need, rather, ordering and restraining, to bring them into harmony with the others who occupy the stage : a toning down and not up, to make them part of the symphony.

With regard to Italian voices, their power of expression is both greater and less than those of the average Englishman. The organ is, I believe, an instrument on which the expression of the same pipe can be modified by the stop used, so that fresh sensations can be conveyed to the listener though the pitch of the note has not changed. Using this as a comparison, the Italian voice contains most pipes ; the English, most stops. I have heard an Italian complain of the poverty in modulation of an English voice—and from them the complaint is a just one. But, as justly, an Englishman might complain to an Italian that the latter's voice was wanting in those mysterious shades of meaning which his own ear is accustomed to enjoy. It is Touchstone, I believe, who engages to find an expression which will fit twenty different occasions ; and he finds it in ' O Lord, sir! ' which he pronounces in twenty different ways. The Italian would have no difficulty in finding a remark suitable to each occasion : much, in delivering them in more than one way apiece.

Now, turning from real life—to which we have hitherto

mainly confined ourselves—and looking at effects upon the stage, we shall see that the Italian actor's art bears a relation to life different from that which the English one's does : a result which our critical sagacity had not altogether failed to foresee. As regards gestures, we shall find it modified to this extent ; that, although they are by no means lacking in variety or reality, they tend—as, indeed, we have had occasion to notice—less than in real life, to accompany the obvious fact and more to suggest the hidden emotion. Art, here, has gained out of an apparent loss ; for it is obviously a far finer use of gesture to make it express something that words cannot say than merely to emphasise what they can. The self-expression is then complete. Here the reader, if he recalls what has been said as to the psychological nature of the Italian drama, will see how it all fits in. Which is cause and which effect, it would be difficult to say ; but it is, at least, a happy combination that the actor's art is most interested in representing, by gesture, that side of life which the writer's art is most concerned to portray. Here, also, incidentally, is a refutation of those who talk as if holding up the mirror to Nature and to real life were the same thing. We have seen that we can arrive at a better expression of Nature by doing something that real life does not do ; and this is one of the great strongholds of the actor's art.

Certainly, this particular branch of it has been carried to a much greater pitch of perfection in Italy than in England. La Duse is known among her own country-men as ' dalle belle mani.' I am afraid that when I saw her play, the language of the hand was as yet almost unknown to me. Of all the actresses whom I have seen recently, Evelina Paoli has by far the most expressive hands. I have thought her hard and artificial ; she has not the power, or does not care to use it, of reading character ; her attitudes are often strained and over-posed. But the hands !—It is like the wind blowing over a forest in full leaf : every atom of surface seems to vibrate to the influence of emotions else unseen.[1] It may seem to some of us that the hand is but a lame exponent of thought : that in its regard the word ' language ' is an exaggeration. Yet what are words ?—Combinations of twenty-six letters, whose variations can be mathematically proved to be finite and exhaustible. A can be nothing else than A, nor Z than Z. And what is that to the inexhaustible variety of a graceful hand, whose surface, even when still, might be drawn a thousand times, giving a thousand different profiles—and which in motion can multiply thousand by thousand ! Watch it, now raised or lowered a hair's breadth ! the fingers now slightly detaching themselves—quivering, clutching together convulsively ! What death-wind is passing ? Now the hands marry, are raised, and pressed together in prayer ; but oh ! not that tranquil prayer of the devout, with the fingers laid each alongside the other, and hand calmly pressed against hand : here the fingers only touch at the root, and the tips, and are pressed and bent like a yielding arch. What sinful woman's last chance is here ? What miserable wretch's last hold on life ? Then they part with a motion as if every part were throwing every other part a thousand miles. Then . . . but perhaps it is little use to make pictures. It is an art that cannot be learned by the book ; but, once learned, it will give such pleasure that the student will feel that he could almost go to the theatre with wax in his ears that no siren's song should divert his senses from the pure pleasure of the hand.[1]

[1] The only English player whose hands have such a power, so far as I know, is H. B. Irving. I have been able to read his thoughts by his hands when it was a strain to catch his words.

The expression of an Italian face changes less than an English actor's would in a like situation ; but it is not on that account inexpressive. In a certain aspect, it is the reverse of the voice. The latter has an apparent activity which is sometimes disappointing : the former, an apparent impassiveness whose power of expression is astonishing. We look at this marble mask, and suddenly become aware that we are being seethed with passion or flooded with grief. Agony seems to fill it as water a reservoir ; but it is only by the light shining on the surface that we know of the power beneath. I have seen an Italian actor's look glow with hate or passion, as I have watched a piece of metal heat through all the phases of red and orange up to pure white. Each moment you would think that emotion could go no farther ; but yet it grows ; as if the man was revelling in the luxury of soul-consuming ; would have passion swell to the uttermost possible, ere the rough hand of action should be allowed to break in and mould it to a use.

I can give no better instance of what I mean than the performance of Palmarini, as the husband, in 'La Crisi.' He is an actor of no particular note, but he did his part as a strong-natured man who was feeling it all the time. *You*, too, felt the shame, the utter misery, as if they were your own : and in the last scene, when he stands over his, now for the first time, feeling and repentant wife, his face, although you are aware of no change in it, has become a sombre background, against which the figure of hope gradually detaches itself ; perceptible, like a spirit from the other world, by some other sense than that of the eye.

With regard to elocution, most Italian players deliver well : the best, splendidly. Absolutely nothing could surpass the incisiveness of Andò or the elegance of Garavaglia. Among the ladies, Irma Grammatica and C. P.

Andò come as high as any. When they fail, they mostly
fail from some falseness or affectation in their art ; whereas
ours, in like case, fail from either absolute want of education or the power to assimilate it. But crass failures in
Italy are few, and many successes might be remembered.
If one is to be picked out, it shall be Gina Favre's delivery
of the little fable of the Zephyr in love, which adorns
the third act of ' Les Buffons.' [1] I have, perhaps, a
partiality for this actress, which comes from old associations. But when I speak of the beauty of this piece of
recitation, I am not afraid that the blear-eyed lamp of
prejudice has misdirected me. Her voice has a softness
and suggestiveness that is rare among Italians ; her way
of pronouncing the simple phrase ' Un giorno ' brought
to the mind, unconsciously, ideas of—

> Old, unhappy, far-off things,
> And battles long ago.

And yet she in nowise overweighted the pretty trifle,
but gave it just that artistic inconsequence which it
would have had from the lips of a French actor : and
the rippling melody of the refrain—I can hear it now—

> ' E chiedeva la fanciulla chi filava la lana.'

Oh, it was like some stream, gushing fresh and pure
from the mountain side, made to run and ripple between
the marble balusters and the cypresses, the ordered
walks and the bedded flowers !

Italian actors are apt at times to speak very fast,
and also at times very low. As regards pace, the Italians
certainly speak faster in real life than we do. Their
language demands it ; for the man who has to say
' medesimo,' while we are saying ' same,' must out with

---

[1] A translation of this will be found in the Appendix.

it, or be hopelessly left behind. But the curious thing is that the Italian actor speaks, on the whole, faster than the man in real life ; whereas the English actor speaks slower. It must not be supposed, however, that the Italian actor is always rattling. When he does, there is usually a reason. He uses this exceedingly rapid speech, as a rule, firstly, for explanations or narrations which the author has put in just to tell the audience of the facts, but not to form part of the drama proper ; facts which are to be got through as quickly as possible and without any particular expression : and secondly, to convey dash and spirit—a sort of devil-may-care atmosphere, or an easy sociability. But there is another thing which explains this mode of delivery. Speech is to their minds, after all, only one key to thought : those who try—as, haply, the Englishman does try—to follow by that alone, are apt to get left behind. The recitation of a practised actor in farce is, at times, like the running-out of a salmon-reel at full speed. But, helped by his gestures and his face, the mind will record the gist of the words, and, a second or two after each paroxysm has ended, be aware of what has been going on.

I think that in real life, the Italian talks louder and more emphatically than the Englishman ; but it is certainly not so on the stage. This loudness is sometimes mistaken for and described as harshness. An Italian's voice will rise to a scream or a roar, either with the vibration of passion or the conscious intention to make itself heard. When the obstruction to conversation or the cause of excitement has vanished, it will automatically cease to vibrate. And every Italian knows how to use his voice for effect, just as, till recently, every Italian knew how to use a dagger. When he gets on the stage, therefore, he has not so much to learn about enunciation : and I suspect that the art of the Italian conversation has something to do with the conversational nature of the Italian art. Certainly, it is true, that on the stage they expand to a degree that our stage would hardly allow. Observations are tossed in here and there like hastily arranged flowers. Sometimes this is done with very happy effect; and the conversations of the various groups, where many people are on the stage together, are made images of reality. This is right, where the personages or remarks are subsidiary; for, on the stage, the background may always be more naturalistic than the main figures or events. In important situations, on the other hand, it can well be over-done—and often is, by the less good companies.

But as regards the lowness of speech which often accompanies these remarks, another reason can be found in the excellence of the Italian ear. My own, I have been told, is a fairly sensitive one; but I have often had remarks made to me by Italians, in actual life, which it needed all the straining of which my ear was capable to catch. The Italian actors, naturally, take advantage of this power; and, though their theatres are large and not remarkable for acoustic properties, speak at times much lower than our performers do.

Let us pass on to another observation. This time, not to the advantage of the Italian, so far as acting is concerned. They are, generally speaking, men of thought and intellectual discussion, rather than of action. Most Englishmen, who have been to a public school, would be more ashamed, or would more easily admit to being ashamed, of not being able to swim or throw a cricket-ball than of not being able to discourse on political economy, or to quote Ben Jonson. With the Italians, the reverse is the case. They like to be thinking or expressing their thoughts, be these profound or trivial; but doing things is not a delight to them. Now this absence of action, this very repose that we have been praising so, lately, comes at certain points to be a drawback upon the stage. That each actor in turn should speak his speech with all the fluency of gesture, expression, and voice, and then fall into statuesque rigidity, is not conceivable ; nor is it tolerable that the often numerous personages on the scene should be entirely devoid of movement. In English real life, the supernumerary figures might be occupied in some easy and noiseless way : in Italy they would either be talking or in repose. Now, talking is not admissible, under the circumstances ; and the need of the Italian to find some means of filling up the background often leads—with second-rate men, at least—to an idle fidgeting, a restless swinging of the knees to and fro, in a seated person, quite foreign to Italian real life. So great, indeed, is the difficulty evidently felt to be, that I have known a side group of actors talk almost as loud as those actually delivering the text of the play.

With their personal movements on the stage, I own to being a trifle disappointed. Travelling about through Northern and Central Italy, one is impressed with the fact of being among a race, strong, supple and easy in their movements. I have seen Tuscan peasant-girls who were one's ideal of women, physically: stalwart and broad-shouldered, yet graceful and light. I have seen an Emilian grape-treader, whose size of calf and neatness of ankle made me blush for my clumsy little English tibia. Go, again, to a 'latteria' and watch, at work or in repose, the arm of the man who whips the cream all day : go— but, perhaps, no one wishes to dispute the Italian peasant with me ! Male, he is apt to be a little short-legged, but that is his only common defect. In general, he is easy, graceful, and strong ; while certain walks of life—for instance, gondoliering (if that may be described as a walk)—

produce men surely strong and graceful above the common.[1]

Men in the higher ranks of life maintain this advantage, to some extent ; but their wives and sisters hardly as much as could be wished. The average Italian gentle-woman is dressed without much display, and yet in bad taste. Clothed in strong colours, with ill-designed and badly disposed ornamentation ; combed and curled to excess ; and, lastly, stayed with remains or exaggerations of last season's Paris models ; she hardly makes the most of her natural beauties : as to hats—'let us draw a veil,' I was about to say ; but she generally does, producing the effect of irregular bunches of feathers stuck in a gramophone-funnel of stupendous size.

Will the ladies forgive the incursion of a mere man into that holiest of holies—a lady's tiring-room ? Men ought to suffer in silence, I know ; but there comes a time when outraged nature will cry out. It was bad enough before, when the stiff armour extended only to the waist : enough, none the less, to make that gradual curve over every inch of the body an impossibility. Imagine a fashionable lady, even of three years ago, in the attitude of Burne-Jones's Circe ! But still this armour, hallowed by tradition—armour against the fiery dart of Cupid, who knows ?—was claimed and conceded as a necessity. But now that it has extended downwards, from the waist, and has taken hold on the flanks as well, the apprehension, dear ladies, is imminent and real : the fear that the supple elegance that we knew aforetime may be strait-jacketed into a rigidity like that of a tortoise ; enlivened only by the trotting of feet at the bottom, the pattering of fingers

---

[1] A gondolier carried my box, weighing little short of 200 lb., to the top floor of one of the great Venetian palaces, without a rest. I asked him what was his limit, and his answer was 'Fino a cento cinquanta' (Chili ; i.e. about 320 lb.). An English porter suggested 80 or 90 lb. in a similar London house !

at the sides, and the nodding of a head at the top. And as for the stage : fancy, Tristan making love to an iron-clad Isolda, who lay like a patent chimney-pot in his arms ! Or what would become of the sweeping curtseys, or the hundred-and-one other unnecessary graces with which the queens of the theatre are wont to delight our eyes ? Pray you, sweet ladies, if indeed it be not possible to reform it altogether, reform it indifferent well !

The tendencies of modern life affect, among other things, perhaps more important, the Italian stage. The scene of many modern plays is laid in modern times : and it is a healthy sign that it should be so. But while dresses, both male and female, remain what they are, a graceful stage-picture is impossible. Some people may say that this is of no consequence : that it is the business of the stage-picture to be not elegant, but real. But if this is true, what is the use of improving every day our knowledge of scene-painting and scene-setting ; of studying delicate effects of light, compiling magnificent sunsets, evolving delicate boudoirs, elaborate parks, quaint villages ; of building up stupendous castles, or hanging in air mysterious gothic vaults, if the figures to which all these things are a background or a covering are carelessly or hideously attired ? I have often, in England, heard a round of well-merited applause at the rising of a stage curtain. Whoever felt inclined to clap his hands before the window of a dressmaker's shop ?

I am afraid that a momentary agitation has carried us back again into real life. Let us go back to where we were when *frou-frou* came rustling by. Remarks on the Italian audiences must be reserved till a later chapter ; but the public so definitely affects the players' style that it is difficult to avoid a word or two here. The quickness of the Italian ear has already been referred to as influencing the actor's mode of delivery. The nature of the people has also undoubtedly much to do with a matter that has already been referred to in the chapter on plays : namely, a tendency almost to do away with farce by treating it after the manner of comedy. Bear-fighting is not in the Italian character, and it is on bear-fighting that farce depends. The same man who, in England, would nudge his friend with his elbow, in Italy would stir him up with a pointed word. They are an intellectual people, and the intellect is the *corpus* upon which the attack is made. This fact, in some degree, limits the actor's appeal ; but in compensation makes it possible for him, within those limits, to use a lighter tool and to produce more delicate effects.

Arising out of the same cause—namely, that the audience is composed of men living more largely in the land of ideas—is the fact that in an Italian play it is possible to prolong a situation in which there are no words ; nor any action save the passage of thought. A typical one, from Marco Praga's ' La Crisi ' (the play has already been described), is thus set out in the stage directions :—

Piero, who has accompanied Raimondo, dragging himself with difficulty as far as the dining-room door, remains on the stage, fixing his eyes on Nicoletta, who is motionless the whole time, stretched on a couch. Then with slow steps, he comes towards her. He takes a low seat, and sets it at the side of the couch near her head. He sits there, bending over her—silent, waiting—like a mother watching over a sick child. Curtain.

And these directions were faithfully carried out. There was no attempt to abridge the lingering painfulness of the situation by one iota. Into its slow dragging moments a hundred vivid facts could be crowded. Yet here, there was practically no external action ; for the few deliberate movements of the man are not what is interesting the mind of the looker-on. No ; this one, illumined by the second-sight of the inspired play-goer, is watching that which would be invisible to the man suddenly brought in from outside : the train of doubts, shames, despairs, repent-ances, hopes, following each other through the throbbing corridors of the prostrate woman's brain, and the spectacle of agony and triumph wrestling for the mastery on the man's uplifted face. Situations such as these may not be a necessity to a well-ordered drama, but they certainly enrich the scope both of the playwright and the actor. The only instance I have seen of the same kind of thing in England, was at the Little Theatre, with its small house and its special public ; [1] and I have been told of a somewhat similar one which was tried as a conclusion to a recent and successful modern comedy,[2] but which did not survive the first night.[3]

After making all allowances which could possibly be claimed for them, it must be conceded that Italian actors do not drudge, as do their English or French compeers. One night, Garavaglia was not acting. ' But,' said the ticket-seller to me, ' " La Fine di Sodoma," and then two nights of "Hamlet"! You see, he wants a rest !' Fancy an English actor crying out for a rest after playing even Hamlet for three nights running ! The Italian's way of acting may be, in its nature, more exhausting ; but the difference seems disproportionate.

Another evidence of the lack of hard work is the fact that the Italian actor is hardly ever word-perfect in his part. You hear, with the average Italian company, the run-ning sound of the prompter's voice : and this, apparently, is no more thought a blemish by them than the supporting of architecture with visible iron stays. I do not mean that the voice of the actor waits on that of the prompter any more than the instrumentalist in the orchestra waits

---

[1] *Denton, Lab.*   [2] *Don.*
[3] These two situations are given at the end of the book.

on the conductor's baton. If the prompter stopped, the
actor would not stop immediately, but he would finally,
no doubt, get into difficulties. We feel that he ought
to be able to do without that help, and that he has no
real justification for needing it.

There is something of a tendency in Italian acting,
generally speaking, to lack a little of that easy variety
which is one of the actor's chief charms. Not, indeed,
that they are without the man of all-work. On the contrary, he breeds like the rabbit ! But they want the man
who can be all things at once, in the course of a single
part or a single evening. Italian acting is in this respect
like Italian weather : it has many sorts, and each excellent
in its kind. Its smile is the hey-day of beatitude, its
sorrow has the gloom of the funeral-pall, its thunders
roar terrifically. But it cannot, as a rule, pass from sunshine to storm through the delicate half-tones of an April
sky ; never letting us feel either that the shadow is very
deep or that the clouds are very far away.[1]

I should be sorry to have to pronounce definitely on
the question of which is the Italian actors' strongest
department. It is as character actors that their more
ordinary players undoubtedly shine most brightly. I
have seen, in odd moments and in out-of-the-way places,
performers whose acting, as an art, was exceedingly poor,
but who made the evening pass pleasantly by the way
they gave life to eccentric personalities. The higher up
we go in the scale, the less the actor seems to rely on
this power. As high-comedy actors they do not touch
the brilliant and artistic performances of the French,
but they have, in compensation, a kind of middle comedy,
which is more genial, on the one hand, than anything
that French acting can show ; and more artistic, on
the other, than is to be expected from any but the most

[1] See p. 186.

finished of ours. In representation of the great tragic passions they are supreme. They show a natural force that is almost overwhelming. But even this has its drawbacks ; for it tends—unless controlled and directed by an intellect such as is possessed by few of any race— rather towards the animal side of things ; and leads us into exhibiting a suffering or a love such as we share with the beasts of the field rather than with the angels in heaven.

I think we might resume the matter fairly enough by saying that if we can have an actor of the necessary intellect, we will prefer tragedy ; if, of a more ordinary type, the kind of middle comedy before alluded to ; if, of the most ordinary, then character acting, without question.

If we have found it hard to decide what the Italian actor does best, it will not be so hard to make up our minds as to where his weakest point lies : oddly enough, on the side where we should least expect to find it.   I was trying to settle in my own mind an ideal Italian company—one that is, which should, if brought over to England, fairly represent the talent of the national stage. I had no difficulty in filling the posts of leading and second actor and actresses ; ' brillante, padre, and madre nobile ' ; with performers of the very highest class : but could not satisfy myself with a lover who should be more than ordinarily good. No doubt the difficulty is an accidental one, owed to my lack of experience. No doubt the man could be found. But it is suggestive, nevertheless, that a play-goer of average experience should not yet have come across a lover of the quality of—shall we say Henry Ainley ; or, rather, of Henry Ainley as he was, when taken from the Bensonian hot-house and bedded out, to dare with his blossoms the vicissitudes of the theatrical weather, and perhaps suffer in his roots from the proximity of a great Tree ?

That the Englishman should excel the Italian as a

lover seems at first sight a paradox; but it is a paradox in whose explanation we shall find a truth. Is not the Italian as good a lover as the Englishman in real life? Of course he is; far better. And it is precisely the fact that love-making is such an easy thing in actual life that makes it, in its simple unadulterated form, a matter of so little interest on the stage. Putting on one's boots, or eating one's dinner, are topics of less scenic importance than the ravings of Indian fakirs, or the loves of Chinese princesses; and I am inclined to think that the more popular the spectacle, the more remote its personages are apt to become. Hence comes the fact, already noted, that Italian plays deal chiefly with mature men and women with whom the spontaneous passion of love has become complicated with other interests and other dispositions. Hence, also, the lover's part being of relatively minor importance, it becomes the property of an inferior performer, and will sometimes come into the hands of any nice young man who can bow and smile at the right time, and be trusted never to trip over the leading actress's draperies or draw off the leading actor's applause.

We have, hitherto, been speaking of the actor individually; and, in so doing, perhaps we may have left a somewhat ungracious impression. Perhaps it is inevitable in this kind of point-to-point examination. For, while it needs a certain amount of exaltation to appreciate what is excellent, we can recognise defects in our most ordinary and tranquil moods. I ask the reader, therefore, to allow for a slight correction from the critical to the true; assuring him—not, I believe, for the first time—that he will be better pleased with the Italian player himself than with anything that can be said on his behalf.

We can now go on to speak of the company as a whole. As regards their actual composition, I have a

s

list given me by an actor, which I reproduce here; without agreeing that all the units which he mentions are always distinct and recognisable.

They are, of the men :—

Primo attore : leading actor.
Primo attore giovane : juvenile lead.
Amoroso : lover.
Brillante : not translatable.
Caratterista and padre nobile : character actor and heavy father.
Secondo carattere : second character actor.
Generico primario : leading general actor.
Generici : other general actors.

The ladies :—

Prima attrice : leading actress.
Prima attrice giovane : juvenile lead.
Amorosa : lover.
Caratterista and madre nobile : character actress and mothers' parts.
Seconda donna : second lady.
Seconda madre : second mother.
Generiche : general actresses.

These can best be illustrated by reference to English companies. The leading actor or actress is obviously such a one as Wyndham or Lena Ashwell. The juvenile leads, such as Ainley or Marie Löhr. The distinction between juvenile lead and lover is one which it is rather more difficult to be precise about ; and I suspect that it is not always accurately maintained in Italy. The actor whom my informant cited as playing juvenile lead, certainly, often did the lover's part.

' Brillante ' is a type peculiar to Italian companies : either because the kind of part does not exist with us or because it is taken in a different way. Laroque, in ' Madame X,' would certainly fall to the lot of the

' brillante '—but, then, this is a French play,—or Dazzle, in
' London Assurance '—but this is a play of past days. The
type of actor in question would be at home in a Hawtrey
or Du Maurier part. He is, in my experience, the most
hard-worked member of the company, and will take any
character part if not too old. In fact, Giovannini, who
was cited by my friend, was about the best character
actor of his class that I have seen.

The rest of the men need no explanation. The ladies
follow on the same lines. There is no ' brillante.' One
distinction which I have seen observed is not noticed by
my informant. There is often, in French and Italian plays
founded on matrimonial relations, a slightly older, and
generally erring, married woman, who attracts the eyes of
the male characters, but does not appeal to our sympathies.
Such parts call for special treatment ; and the actress
who undertakes them has often great powers, but is
hardly ever the lead of the company. As an instance,
in Sudermann's 'The End of Sodom,' Gina Favre,
undoubtedly the leading actress, played the girl's part
—thus ousting the juvenile lead,—and Garavaglia's wife,
the part referred to.

Italian companies, according to the list furnished to
me—and I think it is borne out by the facts—do not
respect that distinction between the fathers and mothers
and the low comedy parts, which is to be found among
our companies. Probably, all through, the respective
lists of actors would be the best guide possible to the parts
that they are likely to be called upon to play.

Much might be said on the subject of by whom and
how these various departments were filled : but that would
be to praise the individual actor instead of criticising the
company. After what has been said in the Introduction,
the reader will not be surprised to hear that it is rather
the exception than the rule when the combinations are

really satisfactory. It cannot be said, to start with, that the leading players are generally fitted to one another. This arises from the deplorable habit of the actor marrying—or, in certain cases, not marrying—the wrong person. Indeed, I have wondered, sometimes, whether in some perfectly organised State—shall we say Sweden or Switzerland?—we should not find traces of a law regulating the marriages of actors; assuredly, in these democratic and pleasure-loving days, more important than those of diplomatists or princes royal. Whether from the last-mentioned cause or from the general conditions of the Italian stage, I cannot say, but the fact remains—that the companies often fail to present an artistic unity, because the leads, strong players in themselves, are incongruous beside each other. When I first saw Gina Favre, she was with Paladini, with whom her style combined well enough. But it struck me that she and Garavaglia were as ill-matched as possible: he with his keen and sombre elegance in its polished groove; she with her less intense, but more all-round, powers.

De Sanctis' wife played lead to him with very fair success; but, then, Ada Bordelli is an actress of no very clearly defined personality, though an actress of parts withal. Novelli's leading lady, Olga Giannini, has immensely improved by his side; but when I last saw them together, she wholly failed to respond to his Proteus-like personality. Evelina Paoli, again, tall, fashionable and serious, beside Andò's short and not sweet, by any means! Instances might be multiplied. In fact, on thinking the matter out, it seems as if there were but few cases in which the urn of Fate had made a happy choice. Some companies, again, rely chiefly on a few stock personalities, who are expected to appear every night, whatever the play may be. Each of them acts as a sort of theatrical Procrustes—adapting the part to himself, not himself to the part. Any well-marked personality will serve an actor of this sort ; and, if somewhat grotesque, so much the better. An almost dwarfish person, a pale monkey-like visage and a mouth awry, may be greater assets in this respect than the voice of a Kean, or the bearing of a Kemble ; and the fortunate possessor of the first-mentioned charms is immediately recognised and applauded by his public, whatever his part may be. That this sort of thing does not make for sound dramatic art, it needs no ghost to tell us. These character-bearers have thus much justification, however, in Italy, that they are the lineal descendants of the masks of older times. They serve the same purpose. They merit the same praise.

Companies formed in this way have, however, the advantage of a certain homogeneity. If three or four people are constantly playing the same parts together, it will be hard if those parts do not fit in together after a while ; and one will be spared the inequality and confusion that sometimes prevail.

Perhaps the most striking instance of such failure to combine, was the company in which I first saw Gina Favre play. Its members were, many of them, good actors : most of them strongly marked personalities ; and, perhaps, partly for these reasons they showed like a scratch as compared to a trained team. They were of all sizes and descriptions. Gina herself was young, active, and healthy-looking. Paladini, the leading actor, was middle-aged and lame. Lotti, who played the 'padre nobile,' certainly deserved the English description, for he was twice the fighting-weight of anyone else on the stage. La Rossi and Baghetti, who often played together, made the best pair, but it was rather like rose and pergola-post. The talent, which, if sorted and strained, would have been the making of two or three companies, almost seemed to be the marring of one.

These criticisms, however, are not to be made of all Italian companies; and we will pass on to a different picture. Chief—at any rate, until recently—among those which were remarkable for compactness and ' go,' is that of Virgilio Talli. The director himself is not really great as an actor, but he can have few superiors as a stage-manager; gifted, moreover, with the power of holding his company together in despite of outside attractions. Of the members composing it two years ago, five of the principals are with him still—and six actors playing together for two years can achieve a good deal. To Maria Melato—formerly his second, now his leading, lady—and Giovannini his ' brillante,' as well as to Talli himself, we have already given places in our ' tribuna.' But the strength of the company lies, not in any individual, but in the admirable way in which the scenes are arranged—positions, movements, &c., studied—every figure having its exact value in the picture. Again, one does not notice in this company, either that excessively fast speaking on the one hand, or the excessive prolongation of trying situations on the other. Extremes are avoided, voices articulate well, little suggestive bits of play are introduced : in fact, all those little grace-notes are cared for in a way that makes an artistic and consistent whole, and bespeaks a watchful personality behind.

Situations which illustrate the point, crowd into the mind. In ' La Buona Figliuola,' where Cesarina is paying her visit, ostensibly with the purpose of putting a veto on her sister's marriage, really with the intention of furthering it, the three old people are seated, the father (stage left), Cesarina near him, the mother and aunt to the right, and rather behind. She sows her seed and goes away, passing out by the exit at the back. Being a ' mantenuta,' she is treated with scant courtesy by the dwellers in this puritan household, and no one accompanies her to the door. As soon as she is out of sight, the father (Talli) moves slowly across the stage, the other two come forward diagonally towards the front—all three turning over in their minds the situation. Just as they reach the limit of their march, enter the son. The faces of all three are excellent, and the effect of the slow, thoughtful march is irresistibly comic. Another instance : several men are at supper; the host, a certain black-bearded, lady-killing prince, has been recording his experiences ; he is seated in the middle, at the table from which the others have risen. One of them, a young fellow, sitting to the right, takes up the tale and tries to cap his elder and worse. Just when the critical moment of his story is reached, the buffoon of the party, who is lying tipsily with his head in another one's lap, lifts up his face and kisses the other man who is bending over him, with a resounding smack ! The vulgar noise and drunken face contrast ludicrously with the rather pretentious love-adventure retailed by the young spark on the other side.

The delightful ' Commedia della Peste,' elsewhere described, affords endless opportunities for making pretty pictures ; and the opportunities were by no means lost. The scenes were charming, and suitable without over-elaboration—so were the costumes ; and the haphazard colouring, which makes an Italian podere [1] or piazza so fascinating, was used so that its wild-flower beauties were gardened scenically to the best effect. Here, in fact, and in the best Italian companies, I think we have a climax which cannot long be maintained : the point at which the pride of stage-craft has been aroused, and beauty has followed disorder, but has not yet been displaced in turn by her ill daughter, pomp: when the art of the accessory has been cultivated indeed, but not to such

---

[1] A farm : generally on a small scale.

an extent as to dominate the spectacle and to dictate to author and player.

The stage-management in the Andò-Paoli-Gandusio company was often excellent. Some of the scenes in the rather weak play, ' The Last Doge,' were very good ; and I have a lively recollection of certain pictures of the lonely old patriarch, surrounded by doubtful followers, confronted by bitter foes. Again, the very French ' Petite Chocolatière ' was played with a go and spirit which made it alive, and would, perhaps, have been something of a lesson to those who ' tantalised Tommy,' according to their own sleepy notions in London : and although the leading actress, La Paoli, was not well suited to the part, the excellence of the combination almost made this a matter of minor importance. Dina Galli's company, again, play with a great swing, and make their farces and *pochades* go with an ease and a certainty which is half the battle.

Most of the dialect companies, again, by virtue of their limited scope, play well together. I have been drawn on to speak of Benini's company in speaking of Benini. But, perhaps, I was most impressed with what homogeneous action could do in seeing, with only a short interval between the performances, ' La Locandiera,' played by the Compagnia Duse, and by that of a certain Dora Baldinello. I had never heard of this company before, and possibly—to quote Lewis Carroll's Bruno —' nor you won't hear of him again.' Dora, herself, was no more than adequate (what would poor dear Dora say at hearing herself so described !) ; but the whole effect was so good that, in spite of La Duse's presence in the other company, it was a doubtful thing at the time as to which performance was the best worth seeing.

I now come to that company which, say what you

will about it, is undoubtedly the most important event
in the Italian theatrical world of to-day. As such event,
it has already been discussed in the Introduction : as the
enterprise which produced Sigr. Sem Benelli's plays, in
the section relating to playwrights and their work. It
remains only to speak of it here as a force modifying
the style of the actor and the composition of the
company.

Of course, as an institution which promised so much,
it has been freely, and even harshly, criticised. If the
reader will turn back to the account given of the purposes
of its founders, he will see that the reforms proposed
by them attacked too high interests not to meet with
bitter opposition ; aimed at too high ideals not to miss
perfect success. The Compagnia Argentina has wasted
money and made mistakes ; these are the criticisms
against it. They sound very formidable. They are not
really so formidable as they sound. Waste of money is
a relative term. The cost of extracting radium may
seem disproportionate to the tiny particle produced, but
when that speck is found to act as no philosopher's stone
ever did, the money is held to have been well spent. If
the end is of sufficient importance, nothing necessarily
spent in arriving at it is thrown away. The question is,
then, whether, humanly speaking, the result attained
by this company could have been gained, and no tale
left of mistakes made and money spent without
apparent effect at the time. If it could not—and no
preceding attempt has disproved the proposition—then
the expenses of the Compagnia Argentina are not waste,
nor its mistakes wholly to be deplored.

The attempts at reform, speaking from the point of
view of the theatre itself, lie practically under two
heads, which are connected—perhaps, inseparable—and
yet distinguishable. These are : a change in the system

of management, and a change in the principle on which the actors are chosen.

With regard to the system of management, the two sides of the question are rather similar to the contentions of the opponents on the subject of military control : one side asking for a purely military aristocracy, the other calling for a lay element which shall check the purely technical view of the soldier from the larger point of view of common sense or public policy. Almost everything that has been said, in this connection, of the army might also be said of the stage—nay, in Italy, has long been said. No charge of tyranny against the council chamber has been spared to the actor-manager's office. The clean-shaven lips of the actor are charged with as domineering language as that which flows from those masked by the flowing moustache of the major-general. After all, on the field or in the theatre, man is best judged by his works. Let us see what the changes made by the Compagnia Argentina really are, and how they work in actual practice.

It was noticeable that, in running one's eye over the list of actors on their programmes, one noticed no very well-known names. I had seen a certain Ugo Farulli, a clever actor (I think a ' brillante ') and an amusing deliverer of monologues ; but his was not a name which would have commanded any particular following. Edvige Reinach, also, I seemed to know by name ; but I could not be certain that it was not in connection with the present company. Gabriellino D'Annunzio, son of the writer, is found among their members, and the fact has been held to justify a charge of favouritism. If this were allowed, the being a poet's son might prevent a man from getting any employment at all ; for in the minor parts entrusted to him, Gabriellino has shown himself quite equal to doing all that has been hitherto required of him.

I notice, in going over my notes made after the performances, that—except on the subject of a small play in verse—remarks about the actors and acting were the last things which came to the tip of the pen. The actors were neither criticised nor praised : they were simply passed over. They seemed merged in the personalities they represented. Such observations as I find are, on the whole, favourable. They refer, in particular, to a little piece called ' La Cena dei Cardinali,' which was given with both an elegance and a brilliance upon which it would have been hard to improve. It could not have been easy to give value to the somewhat artificial form of the play, and yet distinguish the characters of the three cardinals : one of whom had loved as a warrior, one as a diplomatist, and the last, an old, old man, who had loved very early and for love's sweet sake alone. Without these distinctions, the play would have been nothing more than three old men in red, seated round a supper-table repeating rhymed alexandrines. To give value to such a piece as this is the test of the finished actor and the polished company. It is very much easier to conceal want of training in moving tragedy or screaming farce.

Looking back, and having got away from the impressions created by the plays themselves, the acting stands out clear enough in the memory ; and it is easy enough to supply criticism. I though that Archibaldo, in ' L'Amore dei Tre Re,' dragged his speeches a little and failed to give the required idea of barbarian ruggedness ; though, from what has been said about the play, it will be understood that this fault is not to be attributed to the actor alone. Neri, in ' La Cena delle Beffe,' hardly suggested the immense brutal power which the part demands ; but perhaps his physical means were not entirely adequate. Ginevra, I did not like ;

but Gianetto was both free from faults and brilliant. Oddly enough, of these two, Ginevra was played by the actress who had created the part, and Gianetto by a new-comer. The others, as one thinks them over, were adequate—no more, no less. They made the picture: all helping, none disturbing it. The staging was good enough; but there were no scenes that made you draw in your breath on the rising of the curtain. The grouping and movement of the actors was good enough; but there were none of those clever little pieces of stage management which so took the fancy in Virgilio Talli's company.

All this is well enough, but does not suggest very wonderful achievements for some years of hard work, much earnest thought, and the expenditure of many thousands of pounds. Yet we must consider. There have been difficulties in the way, prejudices to be overcome, the opposition of interested rivals to be conciliated or defeated. So far as they have gone at present, the Compagnia Argentina has done a thing which has never been done in Italy before, which was very difficult to do in the present state of things; but which is, nevertheless, not very striking when done. It is the case of a girl who has flung her jewels away, and relies for the first time on her own personal grace in wearing her own simple clothes. Naturally, at first, she appears a dowdy by the side of her less abstemious sisters. It does not follow that she will not reap the benefit in the long run.

The word dowdiness, be it noted, however, is used metaphorically. The bows and trimmings intended are the attractions due to special reputations in the performers. As regards staging, the company compares favourably with its rivals and, indeed, exceeds most of them. Nevertheless, it does not give us any effects comparable to those that feast our eyes at His Majesty's or Bayreuth. Nor are the effects always perfectly judged : as, for instance, in the scene on the top of the tower, in ' L'Amore dei Tre Re,' in which the too-complete roofing went far to destroy that sense of space and openness which should have given its special value to the picture. Again, in the ' Midsummer Night's Dream,' the type of criticism passed has already been laid before the reader [1]—the remarks coming, be it noted, from a spectator who had seen the English performance of the play. It is only fair to say that, generally speaking, the performance seems to have satisfied those who have not had that advantage, and that pages of sumptuous praise might be extracted from the columns of the daily press.

To sum up : it is impossible, in estimating the work of a company like this, to bless or to curse, altogether ; but, on a dispassionate view, it seems evident that a great step forward has been made. The results are of a double nature. First, in the direction of establishing a permanent theatre with a settled home, a result which will inevitably have as its corollary the setting up of a body of critical opinion which will systematise the acting through the land : this, the first and most important. Secondly, in the direction of getting rid of abuses which have undoubtedly grown up from the too great powers of the actor-manager, and of setting up a better system to replace the powers destroyed. I do not say that the results are complete, but I do say that it is possible to hope for their completion : that the work done is, unlike that of so many reforming enterprises of this nature, not only destructive, but constructive. And I think that to those who have done so much, to the real pioneers after so many false starts and abortive attempts, we must confess ourselves very deeply indebted.

[1] Page 21, *ante.*

CHAPTER V

THE DIALECT THEATRE

I HAD hoped to discuss the questions connected with plays and players in dialect in the other parts of the book. But, for two reasons, the subject has grown to such an importance that it must have a chapter to itself. These are, firstly, the consideration that Italian critics of weight attach to the subject, and, secondly, certain false conceptions that have established themselves. I know that in writing as I must do, I should provoke a good deal of hostility, were it likely that the Italian critics would do me the honour to read my work. I can only say that the subject has been thought out, and that I will give chapter and verse for everything that is said.

In the first place, nearly every one of those who uphold the dialect theatre, with whom I have discussed the matter, has, in the course of conversation, given me to understand that these dialect companies were things of great antiquity. Investigation, however, tends to diminish the force of this generalisation. One—the Florentine company—was founded with great *éclat* about three years ago. The chief (if not the only) Milanese company—on the authority of one of the leading writers on the Italian stage—is due to the efforts of

Ferravilla, an actor still living ; and the revival of the
Neapolitan company, in like manner, to Scarpetta.
And in the very theatrical journal which was handed
me by a critic who was sustaining the theme of the
antiquity of the dialect theatre, I find the announcement
of a new company from the Abruzzi. It looks as if we
were in the presence of something more like a revival,
than a mere continuation of something in full force.
Side by side with this, I put the opinion or admission, very
generally expressed, that the dialects, in their actual use,
are diminishing. I have discussed the question with
various Venetians—the possessors, by common consent,
of the most important and literary dialect—and, besides
them, with natives of Piedmont, of Parma, of Marsala.
All agree that the dialects are losing their force : that
the upper classes are taking more and more to speak
pure Italian,[1] and that education is slowly affecting
the speech of the common people.

The first point, then, is that, instead of this theatre
having the sanction of antiquity, it is, in its present form,
rather the product of modern times. This would not be,
itself, a condemnation, were it a natural and spontaneous
growth; but I cannot help feeling that it is only one
instance of that tendency, already commented on, to rely
on a past which no longer has real life, rather than let
the true life of the time develop itself : that it is rather
the work of studious and intelligent personages here
and there, than a spontaneous growth among the
people. Ferravilla and Scarpetta are, undoubtedly,
strong and leading men. The Florentine Theatre is due
to an actor and a playwright jointly, both able men in
their way. It is quite a matter for speculation as to what
will happen after the active influence of the originators

[1] See Appendix at the end of the book—'Impiegati.'

has passed away. I suggest this consideration. I shall come back to it later on; because, besides the positive proof of the sources of its origin, I hope to add the negative proof in respect of the nature of its reception by the popular audience for whom it is intended.

To return to the main question; I think it is obvious that there is a disadvantage in splitting up the acting talent of a given population into a number of separate languages instead of retaining it in one. What compensating advantages can these theatres offer ? We may look for them under the following heads :—

1. They produce plays which have a permanent, artistic value.

2. They lead to a representation of characters which are in themselves interesting : in short, they ' hold up the mirror to Nature.'

3. The dialects are easier for the actors : we, therefore, get better acting over a larger class.

No. 1, I think, we may have little compunction in dismissing summarily. I have hardly heard it contended, by practical men, that the plays of the dialect theatre have any permanent value. Novelli plays one, it is true, but it is chiefly for the sake of the central character; and one doubts its surviving Novelli. In a book, which contains some very valuable descriptions of the Italian stage, the Contessa Martinengo gives a long account of a harrowing piece which set all Italy's heart beating. But where is ' I Mal Nutriti,' now ? I have seen no sign of it in recent years, and have never heard it mentioned in conversation.

As for what we do see, there is very little of the epoch-making about it.

We pass from Florentine to Neapolitan, and find just the same flimsy love-story, just the same young man who is hoping to marry a little below his position. Of the slightness of the stories and scenes, I will give two instances. In the last play which I saw of the Neapolitan Company, the whole of the last act consisted simply of the return of the company from a wedding, and the leave-taking of the young people. Take another instance —a whole play, this time. Theme, the attempt and failure of a young Florentine butcher to cut a figure in the world. In Act I. he is going off to Milan, and there are affectionate leave-takings. Act II. is occupied by speculations as to why his letters have ceased to come. In Act III. he returns, once more in a butcher's frock, and they all fall on his neck. The play is entitled 'Home, Sweet Home.' It would make a very pretty short story for 'Home Notes'![1]

I pass on to the second consideration—one that has frequently been suggested against me in argument. But since shortness of time and the presence of pre-conceived ideas had usually been the obstacles to developing an argument in reply, let us take our revenge now.

They 'hold up the mirror to Nature.' In what does this consist? The argument that can be put to an Englishman in a way that would not be possible to an Italian. Of all the great playwrights the world has ever known, who most held up the aforesaid mirror? There is no doubt as to the answer. But look in his works : will you find out from them where the fish-market was, what hour men dined, how many times a week the quality were shaved? Nay, he was sometimes inaccurate in such suppositions : as that there were convents in ancient Athens. Next, take a man who was working side by side with him—little inferior in reputation, in those days—Ben

---

[1] Since writing, I have the advantage of an illustration from the English stage. 'Bunty Pulls the Strings' is a dialect play—exact. Charming and (to us) original, no doubt. But, can the reader imagine a continued series of these plays—not to speak of a Devonshire dialect company, a Sussex dialect company, &c.?

Jonson. Run through his works, and you will be posted in the tricks of the time : the begging old soldier in Moorfields, the slang of the market, the evil practices of sham alchemy in unoccupied houses. And these things are not badly done, either, but are studied with real acuteness and fidelity. And yet, who reads them or acts them now ? The rust of age has crept over the mirror, and no one has been at the pains to wipe it clean.

Now the Italian dialect plays are leading Italian drama to exactly the point (only with infinitely less art) to which Ben Jonson would have led the English, if he had not had broader-minded writers beside him. The cases are in all respects parallel. But I go farther than this. Ben Jonson, so far as we know, was an accurate observer of men—of their hearts as well as their fingers. I do not believe, testing the question by those parts of the country in which I have passed some time, that these dialect-writers do more than superficially represent the life they propose to set forth. The barber stropping his razor, the cabman blowing on a five-franc note to see that there were not two of them—little characteristic ways and gestures like these there are, no doubt. Is the life and nature of the people really understood, or the characterization anything more than superficial? Let us examine. In the best scene in the most successful play of the Florentine Theatre, 'Acqua Cheta' (Still Waters), by the principal writer for this theatre (Augusto Novelli), a young lodger, of superior position, not a native, in the house of a Florentine cabby, is reading the scene of Paolo and Francesca, from the 'Inferno,' to the ladies of the family. And these latter are interrupting the reading with absurd comments : such as taking the word 'Dottore,' which Dante uses to represent Virgil, as meaning the 'Medico condotto'; saying, when Paolo and Francesca are embracing, 'And then enter the mother,' and things

of that sort. The scene is theatrically effective. Is it—
for this is the point we are on now—characteristic of
Florentine life ? The regional pride of Italians in their
great men is immense ; and, perhaps, no pride is greater—
and rightly so—than the Florentine pride in Dante. I
do not believe that any family in the city would have
exhibited themselves before a stranger in the way
described. Even in the lower classes, they have far
too much spirit and intelligence. From a Florentine
country-girl, who is married to a road-scraper, I have
letters occasionally, which are, though simple, among
the best expressed of any that I receive. I have been to
the Florentine popular kitchen, and discussed peculiarities
of local speech with a man whose clothes were rags, and
on whose skin the dirt stood in layers. I cannot persuade
myself that the women-folk of a respectable cab-driver
would have so degraded themselves when the ' Divina
Commedia ' was in question. If they had not understood,
they would have held their tongues.

I am well aware of what presumption it seems for an
Englishman to venture such remarks as this on a play that
has (for once) been played all over Italy. But I submit,
that the presumption is largely an affair of seeming. Very
often a foreigner can observe justly, what is hid from the
native ; and I have had certain advantages for observation. I have lived in a Florentine ' podere ' outside the
walls, and made friends with the ' contadini ': one of my
best friends in Florence is a lame beggar on Poggio
Imperiale. I have hung about the Piazza on Fridays,
listening to the men and watching their gestures, or have
herded myself with them, under the Loggia de' Lanzi,
when it rained. I have lunched daily with the workmen
—going often to the ' Cuscina populare,' where those who
feed at the cost of charity are sent. But I have never met
in these places any Florentine critic or man of position.

And I believe it is not impossible that these gentlemen are deceiving themselves in their belief in their power to realise what they do not seem to have inspected at first hand. To bring the matter home : What theatric critic in London would be qualified to say whether a stage scene correctly represented a certain department of Manchester east-end life ? And yet, this is exactly what takes place when the critic of a Roman paper praises the representations of Florentine street and market life.

The average foreigner, on the one hand, finds the superficial naturalness of the scenes pleasing. It is something new and interesting, and he has no means of checking its truth. It is pleasing, on the other hand, to the critic, who likes to see his own national life portrayed. The independent observer is in a midway position between the two. He has neither the interest of ignorance, nor the pride of possession. So he suffers ; but I believe it is his opinion that will in the end prevail.

For what is the real purpose of the theatre ? Let us ask this plain question, and insist on its being plainly answered. What is the purpose of any art ? Is it not to give us something that we would not otherwise have ? Apart from this, has it any right to exist ? That sounds obvious ; but, precisely because it is so obvious, it seems in danger of being forgotten. Why should we go into close theatres and sit up till twelve o'clock at night if the theatre has nothing to tell us but what we can see for ourselves by daylight and in fresh air ? If the theatre is to be the mirror of the externals of life ; well, we can all use our eyes and ears. Let us go out into the market and the Piazza and see what we can find there. I shall be told, perhaps, that the theatre is to be the means of letting us observe these things without the taint offence which curiosity brings. I wish I could think that this reason was a sound one ; but I am afraid that these considerations do not in practice prevent a certain amount of inquisitiveness on the part of our countrymen. But the Italian ? He considers life among his countrymen even more as a spectacle than we do. I was out walking on the Lido with a young friend, a native of the province. A storm drove us to take shelter among the ' capanne,' where we found also some fisher and long-shore folk. These he examined with a frankness of which I was half-envious and half-ashamed. Finally, he took the one nearest him—an old broken-down curiosity—by the sleeve, and swung him round towards me, ' Bel tipo, hey?' And this was as modest and tactful a young man in ordinary life as you could wish to meet. No ; I am afraid that if public modesty is to be its justification, the dialect theatre will seek it in vain.

It will be said next that it is the business of the dramatist to dispose and arrange : to make the seeing easier ; to choose out episodes remarkable in their effect ; weave them together in a united whole. By all means ; but let his whole be interesting as well as united, else he might as well put his episodes in a packing-case ; and let them be really something that we should not have remarked for ourselves. I hope I have not done these plays injustice in asserting that their themes are flimsy and insufficient.[1] ' Home, Sweet Home ' is typical : and there, I am sure, the description has been faithful. Let the reader decide. And as for their episodes, I don't think they match some of the scenes I have witnessed in real life. Let us take just one. Picture a broad room divided in two by a partition, across the end of which runs a counter ; behind which, again, through an arch, you catch a glimpse of the kitchen and its flickering fire. It is a spring evening, and the windows are open on to the canal, and the curtains lightly flapping to and fro. You are sitting dining, almost alone : the tables running across you, as you face

---

[1] ' Bunty ' has a more substantial intrigue than most of them.

the counter. At the table next the latter, sit the family :
the father, an old soft-voiced, bearded man, with his back
turned towards you. The mother, a keen-eyed, keen-
voiced, bird-faced woman, facing you on the other side ;
a brother, very like his mother, at a table on the left ;
and on the right of the father, but away from him, a
heavy-faced girl, the eldest daughter, the effect of whose
beak-like nose is diminished by the heavy cheeks, and a
sloping pre-Raphaelite line of hair ; while about the room
flits daughter number two—a little sylph of a thing,
slender and straight, in a dark-red frock and a deep-blue
apron with gold stars ; while the cook, with bare arms,
stands picturesquely leaning against the door-post of the
arch. They are discussing something seriously, evidently.
They turn towards the daughter to the right. She sits
with her cheeks on her hands, only throwing in a sullen
word now and then. Presently, the brother takes up the
tale, attacking her violently. What has she been doing ?
Whatever it is, she defends herself ; and he moves forward
so as to bring himself into the group. The cook dis-
creetly disappears. The guilty one gets up, and setting
her foot on the bench, throws out her right hand, bringing
her whole figure into profile in your sight. Her voice
begins to rise, they answer, all three at once ; above, or
through which, her voice soars distinctly audible into a
perfect shriek. The three accusing voices sink down.
One last-returning shout from the brother. Then she,
exhausted with her effort, throws herself on the bench ;
her face downwards on the table over her clenched hands,
and begins to sob like a lost soul. And the three talk
on in short jerky sentences, obviously about something
else, with a word flung at her here and there ; and the
sobs, little by little, die down, and the talk dies down
too, each finding it hard to perish, and reviving in little
intermittent outbreaks, till silence finally prevails. I

have seen nothing in the dialect theatre that moved like this.   I wanted to go up to the girl, put my hand like a father on her shoulder, and say ' Dinna greet, lassie ! 'Twill be forgotten by to-morrow ! '

Scenes like this have the advantage over the theatre in that they are real flesh and blood—life at first hand. The heart in which the thought grew is the one that palpitates : the face of the sufferer is the one wherein his pain or triumph is figured.   All the accessories are real, and the scenes take place in the very atmosphere under which they arise.   If the theatre is to do no more than reproduce them in a place where nothing is spontaneous, nothing is original or immediate, what counter-balancing advantages has it to offer ?

If real nature consisted in externals, the stage would be in a perpetual difficulty.   For, in certain respects, for practical reasons, nature must always be at odds with the theatre.   I will give an instance from another of these Florentine plays.   The hero is a barber, and, as the scene takes place in the street, he must be in the street too.   The itinerant vendors pass by, the people make their purchases, the cabbage-seller comes to the front of her stall ; and all this is absolutely like real life.   Then comes the barber, running out into the street, and remains there for three-fourths of the act.   This is not real life ; and you see it at once.   Florentine barbers do not pass their time—even their unoccupied time—in the streets.   If you tell me that the stage must have its conventions, I agree ; but with the proviso that they must hold good all round. Your play cannot be three-quarters the mimicking of external life, and the last quarter convention.   It is like a picture which is highly finished as to three-quarters, and the rest sketched in black and white.

But no terms in art have been more abused than naturalness and holding up the mirror to Nature ; and they are used, generally; by shallow people who have neither observed nature nor studied art. Nature in art does not consist in externals. A work of art may have every external mark to betray its origin and yet be convincing : it may be adorned with every outward mark of accuracy and yet remain a lifeless thing. Only this morning, I was in the Museo Nazionale here,[1] and looked upon a fragment carved in stone some two thousand years ago. A sleeping fury : ye gods ! what an awful thing ! It was in rough, grey marble, broken off short at the neck and stuck on a square plaster background. No possible stupidity could have taken it for a living thing. And yet this piece of fragmentary imitation was to me the quintessence of life itself. As I looked, I became aware—not by my eyes only, it seemed, but by every sense of the body—of a being near me in brief and fitful repose. The breeze was merciful, and did not raise her matted locks ; but its pity availed nothing, for the unrest within made the flesh palpitate, although nothing could be seen to move. The horrid curve of the mouth was there ; disdain glowed from the eyes, although they were closed. You could feel the bitter torment of perpetual cruelty ; the soul saturated with blood, the spirit agitated by passion : and all this covered by a mask of repose as slight and impotent as one night's film of ice over the deep sea. I grew, with the minutes, increasingly afraid of a creature that might awake and rend me : increasingly powerless to tear myself away. And all this before a cubic foot of worn marble that seemed to glory in its obvious unreality ! This is power ! This is satisfaction ! This is art !

And now I come to the third head under which a possible advantage is to be sought for : namely, the advantage of the actor. I had it argued against me, very temperately and wisely, by a young Sicilian, that the speaking of

[1] This was written in Rome.

Italian by the ordinary actor rather tied his tongue. I put it to him whether one must not distinguish between conversation, where words and feeling were simultaneous, and acting, where the former were already provided, and suggested that any educated Italian—and Italian actors come from an educated class—could pronounce the common speech without difficulty. He still maintained, with a pretty shrug, that something was lost. I also have to recognise that some of the greatest Italian actors, and several of the best companies, are dialect ones. It looks, at first sight, as if the dialect theatre might compensate its disadvantages both by producing fine individual actors and by furnishing that school of acting which we have said was so ardently to be sought for. Some of the best dialect actors—as, for instance, Scarpetta and Zago—I have never seen. Ferravilla, I never heard, except in Milanese. Niccòli, I understood, had a good reputation before he undertook the Florentine company; and, although I always heard him in dialect, I thought him a greater actor in his less characteristic Florentine parts. Benini I have heard in both dialect and Italian. I do not believe it makes an atom of difference to his acting, or to the fluency of his speech. One of his best, if not his very best, part is 'Il Bugiardo'; and, though there are masques in the play speaking Venetian, his part is in Italian all through. Zacconi, a Bolognese, I have heard once in pure Italian, once in a characteristic part with a continual interspersing of dialect. In the first he was made known as a great actor; in the second he hardly rose above the ordinary.

As for the companies, I have not heard any but the Venetian ones perform non-dialect plays. But when these did so, the pieces were given with the same verve and brilliancy as those in dialect. Now, the level of education is not higher in the Veneto than in other parts of Northern Italy ; it is markedly less, indeed, than in Piedmont and Liguria. On the other hand, the dialect of Venice is used higher up in the social scale and is more literary than any other in Italy. If a Venetian company does not lose by acting in pure Italian, therefore, it does not seem probable that any others need do so.

But suppose, for a moment, that acting in pure Italian does make speaking—temporarily, at any rate—difficult for the actor. Is the case proven ? Let us pause a moment and examine.

I have always resisted the notion that the theatre had a moral mission, but I should give up unwillingly the idea that it had a physical mission ; namely, to maintain and improve, first, the language ; but secondly, and to a far greater extent, the style of speaking, throughout the land. Now these dialect plays—whose bounden duty it is to hold up that highly polished mirror of which we have heard so much—not only do not elevate, but even necessarily degrade, the art of speaking. For these plays, to be characteristic, must deal chiefly with the lower classes, because the higher you go in the social scale the more people are externally alike, and the less scope therefore for characterisation by external means : and especially in Italy—not to speak of the difference of manners—there is a less marked dialect among the upper classes. Therefore, to begin with, the people who go to hear these plays are, on an average, listening to a speech less refined than their own. ' Facchini,' journeymen carpenters, cab-drivers, print-sellers, and the like, are the common personages of their stage. And their language does not tend to improve, though it may possibly amplify, the current speech of the day. But the mischief does not end here. On the dialect stage, being a ' facchino,' you must speak like a ' facchino '; being a washer-woman,

like a washer-woman. There is no such thing as idealis-
ing or adapting. The result is what might be guessed :
in ordinary stage speaking the pitch of the voice is
almost unaltered ; so that I have heard an audience
cry ' Forte ! ' (Speak up !). When there is passion to be
felt the voice becomes a shriek at once. And the listening to this uneven stream of sound is not made any the
easier by the fact that one-half of the audience is generally
engaged in explaining to the other half the state of affairs
on the stage.

But, furthermore, it is not enough that we are distracted by an inconsequent variety in delivery, but we
must have—within the limits of each company—a tedious
monotony as well. There is to almost every dialect
a peculiar lilt of the voice—by which Tuscan, Roman,
Neapolitan are known at a distance at which it is impossible to recognise the exact words : and this lilt it is the
business of the dialect actor, as a portrayer of externals,
to reproduce faithfully, even, perhaps, emphatically.
Consequently, unless transformed by any violent emotion,
there is a considerable monotony in the voices. Now, it
is one of the means used by a good actor to obtain
effects of character that he will use different modulations
of voice in different parts. As you take away the power
of the actors to do this, you also take away one of their
means to make variety in any scene ; and, instead of a
series of voices all variously ' stopped ' (to use the old
simile of an organ) to suit the various characters, you have
a series of rippling sounds, which have no individuality
save that which belongs to the actor himself; which is
precisely the one that ought not to appear.

And could the beautiful elocution of Irma Grammatica
and Garavaglia—nay, why not come home and say that of
Ellen Terry and Forbes Robertson—have been evolved
out of such a school as this ? And if not—it may be

an Englishman's prejudice, but I believe it is one that a
Frenchman, at any rate, would share with him—is not
the delivery of Hamlet's soliloquy, or Portia's apostrophe
to mercy, a nobler feat of arms than the imitations of
the manners of a coal-heaver or a cheapjack? Hold up
the mirror to Nature? Then go out into the woods and
fields, among the cities and factories, and find, if you can,
the pictures to which those marvels of art correspond!
And when you come home, wearied with your search,
think seriously on the question of which department
of ' art ' you can most readily forego!

With regard to the acting of the companies, as apart
from speaking, I have to make this admission—nay, I
do make it, readily, as a tribute to their work—that the
ensemble reaches a high level : higher, perhaps, than any
but picked companies like Virgilio Talli's or the Argentina.
It still looks as if—in certain departments, at least—we
ought to apply to them [for those schools of acting of
which we are so urgently in need.   But, oddly, and yet conclusively, enough, the very thing that gives them their force,
prevents them from using it.   Few dialects maintain more
than one company. Once educated in a company, therefore,
they must either leave it and cease to practise their art,
or stay there and prevent others from learning it.   In
neither case can the institution be described as a school,
where the aspirant cannot enter to learn, or, receiving
his diploma, cannot be admitted to practise.   In the few
cases where there is a plurality of companies, their
members might conceivably change places every now and
then ; but for purposes of development they would be
rather in the position of Dr. Johnson's islanders who made
a precarious living by taking in one another's washing !

And note, further, that it is not a case of enriching
something which, otherwise, is left as it was.   The dialect
stage takes away from the ordinary 'Scena di prosa.'

If it is strengthened, it will take away more. I am far from saying that all the occupants of the former would have come to swell the ranks of the latter. If by a universal decree to-morrow, all performances in dialect were forbidden, the stage would lose many members and acting gain a lesser number of recruits. But the number of those whom it employs is not the test for the usefulness of an institution—else that of house-breaking would hold a high place—but that of those whom it occupies well. And soon Italy will have to choose between two ways, whose parting will be made obvious. Her well-wishers want her to be aware of the necessity, and to be informed of the reasons, for this choice, beforehand ; and not enter unconsciously on one road, and then—too late—find it impossible to draw back.

Finally, it will be objected, to all these arguments : you cannot demolish an institution of this sort by theory. Your reasoning may be unanswerable, but all the reasoning in the world will not help you if the plays are really popular ; if the people throng to see them. Well, do they ? I took an ' abbonamento '[1] for the Florentine company in Venice. The theatre was half empty ; although the Andò-Paoli company which came before and Tina di Lorenzo who followed after, at prices one-third higher, drew full—even crowded—houses. I am told, I must not judge by the Venetians; and that Rome or Milan are the places to try. I come to Rome. I go to see a highly praised Neapolitan company. I find the ' platea ' three parts empty, and the boxes certainly not more than half filled : and even at a much advertised performance, to which the critic of the ' Tribuna ' devoted over two columns, the theatre on the second night was certainly no fuller than at the end of a successful London run ; though Dina Galli, at prices one-third higher, had

[1] Subscription. See p. 307.

her theatre full to overflowing. What is the meaning of it ? Perhaps that the dialect companies are so numerous as to split up their public? Look, then, in lists of the theatrical journals and you will find that the recorded dialect companies do not number one to ten of the others. Is it, in face of all these facts, the case of a really popular national spectacle, which has endured from ages back in the hearts of the people ? Or, is it not, rather, something which has been galvanised into life by the ability of a few active men, fed by a pabulum of intellectual and artificial praise ?

I know it would sound a dreadful thing to many Italians, even to suggest that the dialect play might disappear. This feeling comes partly from local pride—and so far, I have little sympathy ; but partly it comes, also, from an honest fear that one source of the strength and variety of their stage might be dried up—and with this thought my sympathy is sincere. They are afraid that the lightness of touch, the power of rendering characteristic life—all those various harmonies of local colour that go to make up a charming and varied background—might go too : they fear this, just as they fear that a more elaborate education might take away from the force and spontaneity of the actor. In neither case is the fear justified. We are not dispraising, but honouring, the acting talent of Italy when we maintain that its character is strong enough to live through discipline and correction ; and to gain in power, as well as in elegance, thereby. So also it is honour, and not despite, which makes us maintain that all these beautiful little bits of variety, all this characteristic and quaint whimsicality, is so deep ingrained that it will enrich as well a united, as a divided stage ; and will enrich a greater and more permanent thing. The real danger is just the contrary : that the background should become the picture ; that variety should become disorganisation ; and that its many parts, like a set of scholars lacking a master, should lose in irresponsible freedom that which might by obedience and unity have been cultivated to some good end.

I come now—and I come with hearty good-will, after all this necessary but ungracious talk—to pay my tribute to such of the dialect companies as I have seen. And first of these—would any other Italian be hardy enough to dispute their primacy?—we must put the Venetian ones; and first among these that of Ferruccio Benini. I remember remarking to a Florentine bookbinder, with whom I had been to the theatre, that it was curious that, though I had spent little or no time in Milan, I understood the Milanese company better than the Venetian! 'Not at all!' he said, and proceeded to favour me with the reason. (Some reason was always forthcoming from this bright-eyed, stout-armed little craftsman.) 'The Venetian companies give us the real natural thing ; for, every one is presumed to know something of Venetian. The Milanese dialect is edited for stage use. If they gave it us full flavoured, we should only understand half the play.' Full flavours, the Benini company certainly give us; and I had the further advantage of hearing them, with the speech they loved so well, ringing — if generally a somewhat disorderly peal—in my ears. On entering the theatre, my brain was full of the dancing lights on the water ; mystic glimpses down dark alleys : all the life which filled the comedies they love to represent, having passed, like lantern-slides, before me. Once inside the theatre, the atmosphere is perfect. Venice is ruined— hopelessly modernised! the wiseacres tell us. Well, here is a Venice without the steam and the strangers. Here is something which we can take part in and yet not spoil. Put aside actualities which are no longer real ; turn your back on shops dressed to deceive the eye, restored mosaics, machine-made leather-work, faked old masters, all the paint and powder with which Venus, too long risen from the sea, tries to revive the early brilliancy of her tired evening eyes. Step inside this humble unassuming doorway, ladies and gentlemen! The play's the thing, after all.

Is Venus, here, altogether lovely? Well, that, perhaps, is a question of individual taste. Personally, I think that an uglier set of personages I never saw collected in any one lot. The leading lady is—if a bull may be allowed—old and ugly enough to be her own mother. She never can look young; she rarely tries. But, how they play together! How they get the thing going, from the first moment to the last, until every garment, every property, every piece of furniture, seems, with every look, gesture, speech, attitude, to be part of such a real and concrete whole that it only lacks of perfection by the tantalising rapidity with which it passes away!

Benini himself is a fascinating person. Graceful, though bony and angular; adorably ugly in face—the kind of face which, though apparently expressionless, is a perfect index to what is going on inside. But if his face does not change its expression, his body does. I remember once some redundant phrase being dropped about a man ' smiling with his face,' and the objection made, ' You never saw a man who smiled with his back!' But I named Benini. I have seen him walk away, shrugging his shoulders; the hands, the long delicate hands, slightly spread out, while the elbows were close to the sides. If it was not a smile, I do not know one when I see one. At any rate, the house responded with a roar.

The two best parts in which I have seen Benini are ' Il Bugiardo' (The Liar), and in ' Una delle Ultime Sere di Carnivale ' (One of the Last Nights of Carnival). We have, of course, an excellent liar in Charles Hawtrey;

BENINI
In ' Il Bugiardo '

but I don't think his fibs come with the same spontaneous innocence as those of Benini's Bugiardo. You feel that, with such a graceful talent, he ought not, cannot, be fenced by the humdrum limitations which are for ordinary men. When he tricks the two girls, your sole anxiety is lest the pretty picture should be broken by the clumsy work-a-day hand that belongs to that hard-faced individual, Truth. When he misleads and distracts his poor old father— well, poor old fathers ought not to be misled and betrayed ; but—could you have resisted a son who slid so gracefully on to one knee with a ' Father, behold me at your feet ! ' ? And can you, being in front of, and not upon, the scene, with all your Æneas-like piety, refuse a laugh, when he peeps round his three-cornered hat to perceive the effect of his blandishments ?

But, perhaps, he is even more remarkable in ' Una delle Ultime Sere.' In ' Il Bugiardo ' he has a well-marked part. Read the play, and you will see that there is a good deal to be got out of it. Read the other, and you might almost pass by unnoticed the part that Benini plays. But, then, you might easily pass the whole play as entirely wanting in stage effect. In fact, its force consists solely in the extraordinary way, by the art of the dramatist, the different figures combine. It is just the touch of real genius that makes Goldini an exception to a sound rule. There is no plot. The only question is whether a certain young man, who is in love, will leave Venice or not. He is a designer of stuffs, and he has had a good post offered him abroad. If he does go, he cannot marry ; if he doesn't, he can. The discussion of this is to carry us through three acts ! There is, literally, nothing else, except an elderly French lady, who has had three husbands already and is now in search of a fourth. There is not an incident in the whole piece that would delay a modern dramatist one puff of his cigar ; and yet such is

U

the reality of these common clothes when a true-bred
Venetian puts them on that a full house is kept in roars
of laughter for three ample hours. And Benini, as Sior
Momolo, is superb. He is at once the butt and wag of
the whole party. He is the one on whom every one
relies ; to whom every one appeals ; whose genial discretion
sets everything straight. He presides at the supper :
never shall I forget the roar of laughter which went off
when he stood up and helped the macaroni. I think he
marries, in the end ; but, if not, you are quite consoled
by the feeling that marriage would destroy his general
usefulness and make him just an ordinary member of
society. Sundry marriages, however, certainly crown
the story, including one for the old French madame ;
and the play winds up with a dance, into which its
characters glide as ragged rascals from rugged rocks
into gently washing waves. A French company would
probably have made it too smooth and faultless ; with
an English company it would almost certainly have
degenerated into a romp ; but these Italians, while delight-
ing the eye with their movements, while expressing in
them the fullness of a dancer's joy, tempered the whole
with a jolt here and there, a trodden toe, and an apology,
in such wise that those two exacting masters, Truth and
Beauty, were successfully served.

Of other dialect companies, I remember that of the
Milanese actor, Ferravilla. Ferravilla himself is a very
clever humourist indeed, and is a man of all-round ability,
writing his own plays—as often happens, in these cases.
I cannot say, however, that the chief specimen I saw,
' Spos per Rider ' seemed to me to rise above the level of
a pot-boiler. Another and shorter piece, however, gave
Ferravilla the opportunity for some very amusing antics.
He was the chief of a pair of scoundrels who live by their
wits, pretending to tell fortunes. Arrived in a certain

part of the country, they come across a strayed and
fallen father of a family ; kidnap him, find out all the
local secrets, and retail them to marvelling ears.   In a
performance with a make-believe telephone to the spirits
Ferravilla was delightfully comic ; so, again, in the
table-turning, his long lanky figure, bending over the
table and pretending to hold it down while really
inciting it to rise.   Finally, the secret is detected,
and the country-folk assemble in force with stout
cudgels and an outwardly pacific air to the séance.
Tecoppa (Ferravilla) has his suspicions and an especial
eye on one stout individual with a particularly stout
stick.   ' As I was saying, the wonders that I am going to
. . . Won't you put your stick down, sir ? . . . are far
beyond anything that ever, either in this world or . . .
Surely, you'd like to put your stick down, sir ! ' and so
on.   Not very profound, but good rollicking sort of fun.

The only other thing I remember about this company
was a farce, ' El pneu Camerier,' announced as a translation from the French.   This was dialect enough for me.
A waiter ?—yes !   But what sort of waiter ?   However,
two minutes was enough to make it clear that this was
our old friend ' Whitebait at Greenwich.'   How it came
to them through the French, I do not know.   They played
it very amusingly, though Ferravilla was not of the cast.

On the whole, although entertained by Ferravilla's
acting, I had not received any profound impression.   The
praises, however, that I had heard and read showered
upon him made me doubt the accuracy of my judgment,
and I welcome the opportunity of hearing him again.

Three or four years afterwards, I was by great good
fortune passing through Florence when four performances
—more than usually extraordinary [1]—by him were

---

[1] One hardly ever gets a performance in Italy that is not a
' rappresentazione strordinaria.'

announced. He has made his money, and the director of the Niccolini at Florence had to go down on his knees to him (praying with joined hands, is the Italian phrase) to get him to come out of his retirement. Nothing was needed but that Ferravilla should trot out a few of his well-known characters and scenes for the public to applaud rapturously. It is a difficult atmosphere to judge an actor in. In the first play he chose, which was ' Spos per Rider,' my impression was exactly repeated. I would not change a line of what I wrote. But in the course of four different parts, I came to a better understanding of his powers as an actor. His make-up is wonderful, certainly. The personality is carried into every detail of his manners, gait, and gesture—even touch of his costume. I saw him twice as a young man and twice as an old one ; and, inasmuch as I am told he is a little past sixty the swinging, almost flapping, limbs of Belfaccini are more remarkable than the quaint shuffling of Sor Pannera. There is, to me, just a touch of mannerism about him at times—particularly in a gesture of taking off his hat—which was common to two of his characters. Their numbers have probably told on him ; and he has allowed several of them to make use of Ferravilla's stock of tricks. For all that, they are personalities ; there is no need to state that they are amusing. He succeeds in making his audience laugh : that is not, in itself, a great feat ; but he makes them laugh in the right way and at the right thing ; which is. He always keeps command of his public. He does not simply set in motion a current of mirth which goes on and on, creating laughter at anything or everything wise, witty, or wicked, so that the play only has to keep moving for the audience to keep laughing. Every touch goes home ; and I am convinced that if he stopped suddenly in his acting and broke to them, with tears, his mother's

Photograph by

FERRAVILLA

Nunes Vais,
Florence

death, they would weep as heartily as they had laughed.

To describe the thing that touched me most : one of his pieces was an old man, who recounts to his niece how his doctor has recommended him a little music in the evenings for cheerfulness' sake, and who totters to the piano and plays and sings. This, as a piece of characterisation, certainly deserves a place beside Novelli's young priest, in 'Divogando'; and, perhaps, is even more simply profound. The reality of the old fellow, neither a stage saint nor a piece of artificial decrepitude, but a dear old chap of the real world, with some humour and a touch of acidity, in about the proportions of the oil and vinegar in a well-composed salad ; and—to carry on the simile of the salad—the green about him, if not actually growing, fresh and juicy still. As a conception, it was perfect : as a piece of acting it was only less than perfect in that, while imitating deliciously the quavering and breaking of the voice, he played and sang with a little too much certainty for a man of his years ; and the evidence of it was that, when he began to speak again, his voice was too strong at first and he had to tone it down. He must be a musician of no mean order ; his touch on the piano is surer and finer than that of many a successful player of to-day.

With all this praise, there must be a note of doubt at the end. The succession of characters which he represents are the entertainment ; and the surrounding circumstances and personages are only introduced to show these characters in action. His plays he mostly writes himself—that is to say, he conceives the character, adds what is necessary to exhibit it in action, and brings the whole thing to an end, when he judges that it has lasted long enough. All this is not drama : and that acting, properly so called, can exist without drama, I gravely doubt. The actor, properly so called, subserves something

which is not himself or the character he represents.
He is part—as in real life, man is part—of the scenes
strenuous or joyful, of his family, his nation, his time ;
and even if he be an Augustus or a Napoleon, he will be
found, when history is written, to be a part of an issue which
his birth did not open and his death did not conclude.
So that the actor's art, in comedy or tragedy, is to exhibit
character in relation to things which are in themselves, if
not greater morally, at least more massive, more durable,
than itself.   In so doing, the art becomes a great one : as
the art of Michelangelo, chiselling hard blocks of stone,
is a great one, in comparison with that of the clay-
modelling ' sculptors ' of the present day.   The materials
that Ferravilla used are too plastic : he is too easily
master of them.   Therefore, I fear that, when this
generation has passed away, the picture of his memory
will be hung not with actors, like Garrick and Salvini,
but with society entertainers, like Corney Grain.

I will pass now to a well-known Neapolitan company,
that of Pantalena.   This certainly impressed me more
favourably than the Florentine company, to which I have
more than once referred.   I cannot help wondering
whether this is in any way due to the fact that I understood less of what was going on.   Of the play which I saw
the first night, having already noted that the last act was
the return from a wedding, I will add that the chief
character was a cobbler.   He was not the cobbler I
knew in Naples.   I don't say that he was, necessarily,
therefore, untrue to life ; but I do say that he was less
interesting.   This cobbler was like some blacksmith
—burly, portly ; and he walked with a waddle, with
his stomach thrown out ; said not much, and said it
tersely and dryly : a sort of Touchstone in cobbling.   My
cobbler was a little Jew : dry and wizened ; but he had
dried to a sort of india-rubber, and his smile and his

ankles were as elastic as a boy's. I was cross, irritable, and
definite, I know, when I brought him a pair of shoes to
sole; but you might as well have tried to spear a jelly-fish
as fix him to any particular price. The cunning and
yet the humour of it! I knew I was taken in, or was
going to be; and yet I was powerless either to resent or
resist. Here, again, I think that Nature beat the mirror.
One other thing I noted—I cannot think it is a mere
coincidence in both this and the next play—namely, that
just where a situation promised to become interesting
something is done to throw the interest away. Here, two
young lovers, whose marriage has just been forbidden,
find themselves in a room, the door of which opens on
the street. A procession is passing; while the others
are occupied in looking at it, he proposes to her an
elopement. She resists; but, overcome by emotion, throws
herself on her knees at a chair, sobbing, just at the moment
when the Cross is being borne by, and the others are on
their knees, too. Now the contrast here—the broken-
hearted girl and the commonplace devotees: outwardly
the same, so different inwardly—is admirable; and if
the curtain had come down here, it would have been very
effective. But the cobbler father comes along, sees that
she is crying, makes her get up, and the scene ends with
them in each other's arms. Like a glass smashed to atoms,
the charm and significance of the scene are gone.

And now I come gladly to a play which has rather
more in it than most of them, and has made a corresponding success. But it will be noted that the added element,
which made the play draw, does not consist of what is
local and characteristic, but of themes common to other
theatres and other times. ' Il soggetto del dramma è un
fatto commune, un vecchio fatto di cronaca '[1] admits the

---

[1] 'The subject of the play is a common fact; an old incident
oft told.'

'Messaggero,' while giving unstinted praise to the play. The dramatic episode—that is, this common fact—finds its base, and the reason of its development, in its surroundings; and the two are interwoven so as to form ' a wonderful and harmonious sobriety.' I will not, for a moment, contradict the ' Messenger ': I will only suggest that it is the presence of the common fact which raised —as it undoubtedly did raise—this play above its fellows; relegating for once these superficial details of life to their proper place, as accidental adornments of one of the strong themes that make men act and feel.

Assunta Spina is the name of the mistress of a laundry. She has a lover who has, in a fit of temper, ill-treated her, and she has sought redress in the courts. But she loves him still, in her own strange way; and, brought into the witness-box, she whirls round and does her best to save him. Nevertheless, the case being clear, he is condemned to two years' imprisonment. Now she hopes that he may be kept in Naples, where they might have seen each other; instead, he is sent elsewhere. But a worthless young officer of the court, one Federigo Funelli, offers to secure the imprisonment of Michele in Naples, if she will pay him with the only guerdon that she can give or he care to receive. She hesitates, refuses, then gives way. For a time, she remains his mistress; but he tires of her, and we see her preparing for what she fully expects will be her final supper, her final interview, with her gentleman lover. She has dismissed her girls, laid the table, and is moving restlessly about the stage when there violently enters not Federigo, but Michele! The great, hearty, but common and impulsive, fellow greets her as if she was all his; pats her, looks round the room, looks at the table—two plates! How did she ever know he was to be there? Sniffs the savoury mess (some

favourite Neapolitan dainty, no doubt)—his favourite
dish! It is powerful, pathetic to a degree; but it is
'Tristi Amori' over again. Maddened by his kindness,
she breaks out 'Don't, don't! I don't deserve it!' Then
follows her confession and his fury. But, listen! There
is a step outside, the whistling of some trivial air. Terrified
by the threats of the man, Assunta crouches in a corner,
and in a moment the wretched betrayer is a heap upon
the floor, and the avenged lover is in flight. Then, in
a moment, drawn by the cries, come the populace and the
guards. These bend over the body, look round the room.
From her corner, like some strange beast out of the
darkness, the girl uncoils herself and comes forward:
'I killed him for revenge!' The end should have been an
impressive one, but is marred by a piece of stupidity,
which is the evil genius of the dialect theatre. There are
two guards, who figure earlier in the play, to give a character-
contrast : one, a Neapolitan, gallant and gay ; the other,
an Abruzzese, taciturn, but sentimental. These details are
very well in the body of the play, but had better have
been spared at the end. The Neapolitan takes the girl
out, and the Abruzzese is left behind. And the scene,
which should end when the fate of the main characters
has declared itself, is drawn out for this policeman to
display his local character in maudling over the corpse.
I spoke of this to a young Sicilian, with whom I had
several interesting conversations, and his reply was
so very convincing, from his point of view ; so very
unsatisfactory, from mine. 'Oh, but,' he said, 'it must
be so ! There are always two guards ; and one goes out
with the prisoner and one is left behind with the body.'
True, for life which goes on perpetually ; where action
leads to action, scene to scene, and day and night, month
and year, begin and determine nothing. But for the
stage, it would be just as much and just as little to the

point to say that worms always come to eat a dead body—if you leave it there long enough.

Nevertheless, the play was a good instance of how effective local colour may be, if the main composition is strong enough. The opening scene in the ante-room of the court, the coming and going, the cries of the ushers, the plaintive little voice of the match-seller, all made a masterly and enduring picture. So, again, the scenes in the laundry were admirably real : all the more, because they were not the object of the play. The acting was good, although I did not think Michele quite rose to his part. But the mainstay of the whole thing was the girl, quite a new actress, who played the part of Assunta. She was a Neapolitan character, perhaps, but she had the mysterious personality which would have served— say, Floria Tosca—just as well. She attracted you, and yet you did not like her. She left the impression that none of her inconsistent actions were unnatural, and yet that you could foresee nothing that she could do ; and made up that picture of deliberate selfishness, and impulsive self-sacrifice, which only a woman can show without seeming incredible, and which for that very reason sometimes makes her startlingly real.[1]

A note on the audience and their reception of the play. These are from the ' Tribuna ' and the ' Messaggero,' respectively :—

' The new drama of " Salvatore di Giacomo " was received by the enormous audience, which thronged the Nazionale, as a real triumph. The author and the interpreters had more than applause ; interminable ovations.'

' Rarely has an audience so imposing, both for numbers and elegance, risen as one man to applaud, with such conviction, with such enthusiasm, a dramatic work.'

This was of the opening night, and I do not need to

[1] A. Magnetti was her name   I think it deserves a record.

remind my English readers of the special quality of the
audience at any first production. I was there on the
third. I saw at once that the audience, both for numbers
and elegance, was a remarkable one—for a dialect theatre !
The house was about as full as an English theatre some
ten days before the close of a long run, and some of
the fashionable people who generally spent their nights
applauding Dina Galli had found their way there. The
piece was very well received, as it deserved to be ; but
there was none of that profound emotion that these
extracts would have led one to expect—had one not
known and made the needful allowance beforehand for
the critics' point of view.

It is without a certain, though an unintentional,
appropriateness that I have kept till the last the most
recently formed dialect company : to wit—the Florentine.
It will be something of a shock to the average tourist
in Italy, to be told that the Florentines speak a dialect ;
for, is not the ' Lingua Toscana ' our ideal of pure Italian
speech ? And, is not Florence Tuscany's head—the intellectual centre which guides and governs all ? Nevertheless, it
is true ; for Tuscan speech contains words not found in
the written language of the day ; and the ' Bocca Toscana '
has marked—I wish I could say pleasurably marked—
peculiarities. Frankly, then, Florentine dialect is ugly.
Yet—though, perhaps, it is the prejudice born of an early
affection—to the writer's ears, it has a fine and masculine
sound : the ugliness of the strong man to whom, in spite
of it, the ladies show favour. I suppose that of all the
tokens which, in the collecting-cabinet of an Englishman's
mèmory, stand for the Italian cities he has visited, that
which represents Florence is stamped the deepest and
clearest. If he has entered at all through the gates of
art and history into the life of the past, the figures of
Dante, Savonarola, and Lorenzo the Magnificent, mean

more to him than any other poet, preacher, or prince, that Italy ever nurtured. He found it easier, while within their walls, to fill again the Bargello or San Marco with the personages that thronged them aforetime ; and, as he sits in his English arm-chair, he finds the buildings themselves the easiest to reproduce as pictures on the wall, or as realities in the hollows of the fire.

Impressions, ineffaceable like these, may be safely left till the end. They would be of little use to the writer of the dialect theatre : but, though different, are none the less deep ; and, though deep, the most easily aroused, and with the most difficulty resigned.

Sometimes a wide indefinite landscape, a morning breeze, and a bright though not cloudless sky, recall a walk along the Lido or repeat the Adriatic's whispered speech. But, oftener far, some building against the deep blue of a winter's sky suggests the tower of the old Bargello ; or the vibrating of pines, high overhead, brings back some old villa garden, or leads us walking in the woods above Fiesole. Memories of Florence, however, are not confined to towers and trees ; are not shut up in any medieval prison or laid to sleep in any disused palace chamber : they are active, living, of to-day.

Hearty hand-shakes, where good fellowship was stained —would it were never worse stained !—with the moist coolness of Mother Earth ; gazings into eyes that were like summer waters ; the watching of figures that in colour outblazoned the shield of the Medici and matched the lily in pose : hours of honest, if not over-profitable, toil in the workshop, shoulder to shoulder with master and man : the hum of deep voices in the old Piazza on market days ; comings and goings where the dust of disappointment was sometimes laid with tears ; and, above all, of one erect and grey-haired woman's form, which if honesty and goodwill had needed a monument

in this city of great things, might well have been set as
their emblem on a pedestal, from which it would
have looked neither up nor down; for she feared no
one, flattered no one, and yet was loved and honoured
by all.

These are my memories of Florence, but on such
the theatre cannot subsist. They are too powerful,
and blot it out. When we are again aware of the
foot-lights and the proscenium, we are conscious also of
a thinner atmosphere and more artificial people. These
figures of the Florentine theatre are wonderful imitations;
but they are imitations, and the stories that link them
together have not the holding force of great art. I was
fortunate in viewing the *pièce de résistance* of the
theatre, ' Acqua Cheta ' (Still Waters), of Augusto Novelli.
Perhaps, I should have been unfortunate had I not heard
it, seeing that it has been played over three hundred
times in the course of two years. If that should suggest
a great success, let me invite a comparison with the blank-
verse play of ' La Cena delle Beffe,' which has been played,
in one year in its native country, about four hundred
times.[1] ' Acqua Cheta ' is certainly more play-like
(dramatic, in our sense, will not do) than most of its
fellows ; and it is to this, and not to its reality, that it
owes its success. A lodger—a stranger—comes to take up
his abode in the family of a Florentine cab-driver. This,
and your introduction to the cab-driver's wife and two
daughters, and a carpenter—who is in love with one of
them, but whom the parents reject—form the first act. In
Act II. there is a pretty scene in the back-garden of this
rather exceptionally favoured ' veturino.'[2] First, we
have the lodger in his shirt-sleeves, reading ' Dante ' to

[1] Not to speak of its being translated into French, and played with
great success by Sarah Bernhardt.
[2] Do the cabbies have such delightful gardens in real life, I wonder!

the women of the family, who make absurd comments.
I have already made my objections to this scene : but,
as a scene, it is one of the best in any of these plays. Next,
he appears in more ample costume, to take them out for
the evening, and plans an elopement with the younger
daughter. The stage is thus left free for the elder
daughter and her carpenter, who, surprised by the return
of the family, mounts a tree ; overhears the conversations
which ensue, and throws things on the talkers' heads :
events which, of course, daily occur in Florentine gardens,
but are entirely new to the boards of the theatre ! In
the last act, the elopement has apparently taken place,
and the family are in tears ; but, no ! The sterling but
rejected carpenter appears, and, with much condescension,
discloses the part of beneficent deity that he has played.
After that, general ' brouhaha ' of satisfaction. Everybody
who needs it is forgiven, and everybody who desires it is
married.

There is no doubt that the play is acted with a great
deal of spirit. The part of Ulisse (not a bad name for
a cab-driver) is one of Niccòli's best parts ; the carpenter
acted by him who, I suppose, would be the ' brillante ' of
the company, is an exceedingly good performance ; and
his love, the elder daughter, exactly such a well-seasoned
delicacy as might be expected to penetrate to his palate
through the sprinkling of sawdust. And there is an
exceedingly funny scene : not, however, much above
the level of pantomime humour, when the reporter of
the ' Fieramosca ' is hovering round the outskirts of the
harassed family trying to pick up copy. If the house
was not full, the laughter was hearty. Subsequent
visits to the same company did not do more than rob the
favourable impression which had preceded them. That
which at first seemed a genuine creation, arising out of
a particular part, was then perceived to be a trick that

was part of the personality of the actor himself. The
impression was absolutely destroyed by repetition. It
was one of the cases where it may be possible to have
too much of a good thing !

I have short notes on sundry other plays, but they
would add little to what has been said. Only one shall
be noticed : a play—or rather a part, for it all hinged on
the one character—by a writer of the un-Italian name of
Moser. The incidents are, to a certain extent, historical.
Beco Sudiccio is a kind of less fortunate Hans Sachs, who
lived in Florence in the eighteenth century. In the
play, he is tricked in his business by an unscrupulous
brother. Then he goes blind. The brother makes love to
his wife, while he, poor wretch, makes existence tolerable
for himself by composing ballads with the aid of a girl,
who acts as a sort of secretary and general help to him.
The picture of patient, but acute, misery; his suspicions
of his wife, his attempts to get the girl mentioned above to
betray to his sightless eyes what is going on ; his catching
the wife in the act of replacing money which she has stolen
and he has missed ;—all these come back to the memory
with penetrating vividness, though they date from nearly
a year ago. The strange way that the actor's face had
altered, the moral as well as physical misery expressed
in the drawn cheeks and sightless eyes ; the tense attitude
of listening ; the grip of the hands on the woman when
he has caught her, reminding one of Stevenson's blind
beggar in the ' Treasure Island ' : with these, and a score
of other touches, the Florentine musician of a past day
rose into a life more distinct, more active, more spiritually
real, than that which informed the stage-carpenters,
coal-heavers, cab-drivers of to-day. So much so, that I
was not in the least surprised, when I mentioned the
performance tentatively to a leading critic, to hear that
it was a wholly inferior one, wanting in reality ; unworthy

to take rank with its author's other creations ; not to speak of sundry others, by others of those who hold a candle to the charms of Her Majesty, the Dialect Theatre.

This company is at an end, and there are no more of its class to succeed. Who follows ? And we go down to consult the weather-beaten old clerk who sells tickets for the Goldoni. 'Who next ?—Tina di Lorenzo ! What ! The Signore has never heard her ?—Never ? Is it possible ? Ah ! Tina di Lorenzo, Tina . . .' And, released at last, somewhat past lunch-time, we go away with a double appetite for ' pasta-faggioli ' and Tina.

CHAPTER VI

THEATRES AND AUDIENCES.   DIVAGANDO

THIS chapter might have conceivably been divided, allowing to each part a separate head. But for reasons which I do not feel bound to explain, I prefer to follow the example of certain distinguished musicians : and, instead of keeping the last two movements separate and affording the public a space for breathing and comment, hurry on my ' largo appassionato ' into a final ' presto diavoloso.' And lest, when the chapter is finished, the reader should be tempted to describe the terms as exaggerated ones, I hereby warn him that they must not be taken too literally, and that we merely mean that a practice which has the sanction of the high masters of harmony, cannot be blameworthy in such a humdrum account as this.

To begin with the actual theatres, then—for we can have the theatre without the audience, never the audience without the theatre—they, while they show a far greater diversity among themselves than is found among those of our own country, have some common features which distinguish them from these. In the first place, the auditorium is much larger than with us : its holding capacity relatively less. The bottom gallery comes down to the ground, and all the galleries are rather narrow— often no more than two seats deep—and they are generally entirely taken up with boxes, until you come to the top tier, or 'loggione,' which corresponds to our gallery. The floor of the house is generally seated to only two-thirds of its extent, and the back part is reserved for standing room; this and the 'loggione' being the only places that cannot be booked. Two tickets are needed, one for entrance, which admits also to the pit, the other for your reserved seat.

The relative size of the theatres gives much greater airiness and coolness. It is rare to find an Italian theatre too hot. Sometimes in the depth of winter they are bitterly cold. I do not think, as a rule, that their acoustic properties are good, and was struck by the difference made by changing from the back rows of the stalls to the boxes, only a few feet behind and above them. I am speaking of one particular theatre, the Goldoni in Venice; but I suspect that the remark is true of others besides. The decorations are often very simple, and, sometimes, in cheaper theatres or in out of way places, the curtain is nothing better than a sheet of advertisements. But when the style is a little more elaborate, the effect is often very good, and the Fenice in Venice is, without exception, the most beautiful house I know. The weak point of an Italian theatre, from a decorator's point of view, is its comparative formlessness, arising from the equal height and the uniform division of the tiers; but in this case a royal—a really royal—box, with a gothic arched canopy above it, set right opposite to the proscenium, somewhat takes off from this. And for the rest, the theatre is decorated as a bride, the paintings which cover its ceiling and galleries are works of art individually, and harmonious in general effect; while the tall curtains of grey-green velvet, patterned with fleur-de-lys, have an elegance and a distinction of their own: whether hanging in graceful folds or slowly swinging

together to shut in the death or apotheosis of some hero
of opera or tragic poem, with whose doings this most
aristocratic of play-houses is usually concerned.   The
only strange thing is that there is no carpet on the
floor : the lack giving the impression—to an English eye,
at least—of a finely dressed lady who has come out
without her shoes.

But the variety in Italian play-houses, among themselves, is even greater than their difference from our own.
The Manzoni at Milan—perhaps, the most important
prose theatre in Italy—has a particularly broad stage ;
the tiers being segments of a very large circle, giving an
effect unlike that of any other theatre I know.   The
Dal Verme, of the same city, where I saw the performances
of Benelli's tragedies, is a huge place, something of a
miniature Albert Hall, with only two galleries, but these
unusually deep ones, the upper one of which is devoted
to rows of seats.   In Venice, the theatres are not numerous :
only four to a population of 180,000.   But the Goldoni is
a pretty, if simply decorated, building ; while the Malibran,
the only other one used for plays, spells nothing but
ugliness and dilapidation : with tawdry Egyptian paintings on its great ceiling and wide galleries, which, from
their state of preservation, might well be relics of some
former occupation, if an advertisement curtain, upon
which the same decorative motives are introduced, did
not throw doubt on the supposition.

Most of my going was naturally to the Goldoni.   The
plays varied ; the audiences were wonderfully constant.
I think that the subscription habit prevailed there to a
greater extent than at any other theatre I know, and,
by consequence, the faces soon became familiar to one
who had, during the entr'actes, little to distract him from
their observation.   I remember, in particular, a small
hunch-back who, with rather a dour, sad face, always

sat towards the front of the 'poltrone.' He seemed to know everybody, and was greeted warmly by all ; though I did not see that he bestowed any very gracious smiles in return. He seemed to be treated as a sort of moral beggar, lacking, by no fault of his own, in life a most precious possession—the joy of living—which was freely and without thought of recompense flung out to him by those who were richer than he. Another noticeable person was a tall, fair man, with a beard something the shape of that usually worn by an Assyrian god ; though I hardly know whether he would have been pleased or offended by the comparison. He was hardly a handsome man ; but, for all that, as inimitable old Hobbes hath it, ' satisfied with his own share.' His manner of taking his seat, turning round to look at those behind, standing up at the end of the act and running his hand through his hair, marked him out as one whose self-conceit probably rendered him easy to live with. I often wondered what manner of a man he was. He bore a resemblance to a certain stage doctor I had seen ; but he was not on that account to be set down as a medico, any more than his beard was to proclaim him a descendant of Tiglath-Pileser.

When I began to go with friends, I learnt by degrees the names of the people in the boxes, and certain juicy bits of scandal floated around my ears : the very dashing lady, whose husband has grey hair ; her reasons for marrying him, and those of their acquaintances for not acknowledging the union. There is plenty of such talk in most cities, and Venice is no more exempt than her neighbours. I was fortunate—perhaps, I should have been unfortunate had it been otherwise—in seeing the two great Venetian beauties, who, though ' attempate ' (touched by the hand of Time), still hold their own against the generation following. I confess to having found the Contessa Morosini almost worthy the praise that has been showered upon her, as she sat, dressed in a dark but penetrating red, and crowned with a black hat whose circle could not have been described twice over along the front of one of the Goldoni boxes, and which therefore, properly and appropriately, no doubt limited her companion to one of much more modest size.

These are details. The character of the audience in the mass is a special one. Its members are not absorbed with a purely theatrical enjoyment. Neither do they go, like the Milanese, to show off their fine persons and their fine wits. They do interest themselves in the spectacle; but their main pleasure, I believe, is in the excuse it gives them for enjoying each other's company. Conversation during the entr'actes has an especial importance: not that its quality is unusually brilliant, but because the pleasure of the talkers is unusually great.

A Venetian audience is the most indulgent I know, unless—and it is, perhaps, a large exception—there is anything which touches their regional pride. If anything in the play seems to them, as Venetians, a public offence; or, in the way it is presented to them, a public slight; if they are offered matters more fit for those of Geneva, or inferior singers to those who have delighted the ears of Milan: then the genial, indulgent company of other nights becomes a collection of Rhadamanthine furies. Another characteristic of a Venetian audience is its sensuality. In one play that I witnessed, the leading actress is proceeding to go to bed, when the fall of the curtain happily cuts the matter short. Never shall I forget the thrill that went round, partly of realisation, partly of anticipation, when the lady, a well-known and much admired actress, took off her outer garment. There was a drawing in of the breath all round as if every man in the gallery had had a lemon applied to his lips.

But if the interiors and the audiences were interesting so were the exteriors too : I do not mean the entrances, or façades ; for the latter are ordinary enough in most cases ; and the former—at least, some of them—almost squalid in their simplicity. The land approach to the Fenice alone has any architectural character : the entrance colonnade being something half-way between the porch of a house in Westbourne Terrace and the portico of St. Paul's. But go to some point of vantage which commands the approach by water at the time the play ends ; watch the throng, coloured by the dresses of the ladies which are cloaked but half, and for form's sake only, from the gentle touch of the soft spring evening air ; watch the strange shapes of the black gondolas silhouetted against the brightness of the water, now seen in all their graceful length, now foreshortened so as to suggest some weird beast of the water ; watch the bending forms of the rowers ; hear the cries of their loud voices, and between the pauses, an ever-persisting under-current from the waiting crowd. Watch the graceful groups made by the latter as its members step one by one on board, laying a light touch on the arm of the gondolier, and see the mass grow thinner as the gondolas by twos and threes, to the rhythmic beat of the oar and dream-like cries of ' Stai O ! ' diminish and disappear down the windings of the canal. You will not come away saying that the fascination of Venice is all a myth or a memory, or go back for her romance to the days of Foscari or the verse of Byron. And if you are among the privileged ; have your gondola waiting for you, and have only to step on board and yield yourself up to delicious repose ? Still less is the delight imaginary. Never shall I forget, perhaps my only gondola-ride home from the theatre, after four hours of lowering tragedy which bore hardly on a mind vexed and a body travel-worn. Gondoliers

in Venice vary : with some, the craft has that poetry of
motion with which it is always credited ; with others it
has the hesitation of a crab and the jerkiness of a damp
firework.   This man was a past master of his art.   In
him, power and grace were combined.   We lay back on
our cushions and saw the houses glide past us ; the sharp
angles of the water streets deftly give themselves a double
twist so as to graze, but not touch, the sides of our boat
as they squeezed themselves by, and we reached home
in the space of a bird's flight, without seeming to have
stirred from the spot where we laid ourselves down to rest.

But one needs not to be among the luxurious to enjoy
the treasures that the sea's presence brings.   They are
not stored in far-away archives or rained into the rich
purses only :   they are minted down into current coin and
pass through the poorest hands.

Take the steamer down the Grand Canal, and the
churning of the screw, divided by the stoppages, pene-
trated with the ' 'giò ' ' 'mò,' ' 'trò ' of the capitano,
becomes the metre of a lyric song, which tells of the
romance that the moon saw, the wind wafted, and the
waters bore on their bosom years ago—nay, which they
bear e'en now.   Come by land, and the deep shadows
of the winding calle will be pregnant of strange shapes ;
begotten of fancy, true, but just one whit nearer to us
than the fancies of the theatre.   This mixture of land
and sea, what strange things it brings about !   Surely,
nothing could be more weird than the motion of the
lantern (nothing of the boat being visible), passing, like
some huge belated glow-worm, across the other end of a
campo ;   unless it should be to pass the bridge and look
far away into the shadows on the water : shadows which,
quite unlike those on land, seem to enlarge and deepen
that wherein they fall, making a few square feet of water-
surface significant with multitudinous forms—the opening

into another world! There are such varied themes upon which Fancy can play. She is always striking her lute, always finding an answering chord. Sometimes these, the semi-phantom-like shapes and shadows, beget a like unreality; and brain grows full of monstrous creatures and flaring wheels, like a chapter in Ezekiel. Sometimes, again, we see the arcades as arcades, the quays as quays, and we people them with the *dramatis personæ* of some story: oddly enough, making our dreams further off and less real, when their inhabitants are of this actual world. Some parts of no very striking features are more suggestive than others. One little piece, near La Fenice, always took toll of me. There is a straight piece towards the Canal, with a garden on one side and the high wall of the theatre on the other; then a sharp turn to the left along the water, under a very low arcade with flat roof and short round columns; next, to the right, over the bridge: and then look back! If you do not see a gay procession coming along, and a pair of men with daggers dash out from the dark shadows behind . . . you do not deserve to be in Venice, or you deserve to be somewhere else, far above this clothes-wearing and dagger-wielding world.

At this time of night, and with the exaltation begotten of theatre-going still in the veins, the whole visible world wears a new aspect. We are raised or changed into another atmosphere from that which we occupy by day; and to resume it suddenly and casually is a difficulty and a shock. I well remember, one night, after having accompanied a friend to her house beyond the Grand Canal, walking to one of the 'traghetti' at which, if the Fates be propitious, a rower may be found. I passed two men who were caroling at the tops of their powerful voices, . . . something about turning the night into day. I walked past them, and thought I heard them go by the

turning as I stood sniffing the fresh breeze which tells of
the Grand Canal.   But, no; they followed me down to
the 'traghetto' and came across with me.   Their voices
were deafening ; and yet, looking at the high walls of the
palaces and the wide surface of the waters, whose ripples
bore the lamps half a mile distant to our very feet, they
seemed no more than were appropriate to the place and
time.   Like the mask and the buskin of Greek tragedy,
they gave a suitable largeness to the whole.   And when,
as I stepped out of the gondola, they stopped their song,
and gave me an orderly everyday ' Good night !' it seemed,
really, as if Prince Hamlet had interrupted his soliloquy
to inquire whether his boots were blacked, or the Landgraf
broken in upon the reception of Elizabeth's suitors by
scratching his beard with his sceptre.

This perpetual, unforgettable presence of the waters
outside has sometimes a reflex on things within.   Nowhere,
I believe, did D'Annunzio's play of ' La Nave ' (The
Ship) meet with a better reception.   It is the play
wherein the origin of the Italian state is figured in the
launching of a ship : and the time and place chosen, are
those very lagoons into whose mud-banks the first
piles were being driven, and upon them the first frail huts
raised, ere ever St. Mark was housed under his five
soaring domes, or the Campanile of St. George lighted
the wanderer at sea.   The play is not good to read ; and
all foreigners who saw it declared that the performers
screeched and screamed at them through five interminable hours.   But its success was undoubted.   The
people thronged. The press applauded.   It needed not
that the idea should be worked out with the intuition
of a great poet.   The right key-note had been struck,
and the harmonies were supplied by the listeners themselves.   I, however, remember, myself, a ' Serata,' at which
I was present, and which brought home to me, more than

anything else, the power which the early history of her birth, from the waves, has over the son of Venice of to-day. It is a little difficult to use an English word to describe it. Performance, it hardly was ; entertainment, in the ordinary acceptation of the term, still less. A Triestine poet had come to recite his verses on the origin of Venice, and the sons of Venice had gathered together to hear. Faultlessly dressed, the men in their black coats and white shirt-fronts, the women with their stiff bodices and unwrinkled gloves, with folded hands, they sat, while— like a procession led on by the easy pace of the heroic couplet—the figures in the richly tricked tale marched past : and, from the gloom of night, the waste mud-banks, the struggles with hostile and barbarian hordes, as a miracle that city arose, which still flashes on the face of the globe as it spins past the sun. And all these pictures, divided and punctuated by the shorter rhythm of the trumpets, which declared, in honour of the dear city, things which had only their arrogance to make them sublime ; [1] rhythm placidly taken up and replied to by the bending of the heads and the muffled beating of the kid gloves. We have heard that the fantastic tricks of men make the angels to weep. We, in our modern way, may wonder whether those angels have any sense of humour ! Surely, any that overlooked that spectacle might have felt tears to be superfluous—nay, verily out of place ! for had they not—they, God's inter-mediaries—the best means of knowing that those whom comfort and peace had thus made ridiculous, stress and trial would easily again make sublime ? [2]

---

[1] 'Ciò che vuole Venezia vuole Iddio' (the will of Venice is the will of God), was a line written down afterwards. There were others to match.

[2] No one will deny the justness of the prophecy who has read the history of the Siege of Venice in '49 and her seventeen months' resistance, single-handed, to the whole Austrian power.

The cities, as we have seen, differ immensely among themselves; and others, for theatrical purposes, are preferred. Venetian audiences are not 'good audiences'? Perhaps not. Partly, I think, because they bring too much with them to the spectacle. Others, if they have not their failings, lack something of their charm. It is rather a jump to Milan where modern streets and much business effectually conceal the romance of the past. They are practical people, the Milanese; and they show it in their behaviour at the theatre. They are too much occupied with the concerns of everyday to be carried far away into romance or the past. Alert they are as critics, but without the special theatrical jargon; fashionable, but with a mind to prove that fashion and wit, once so fast married, are not, even in this day of easy separations, permanently divorced. He who appears in Milan must be as technically perfect as may be. If the prima attrice's hair is coming down, if a placard on the stage is crooked, if a sight is ridiculous or a sound inappropriate, no amount of fervour or pathos in the actors will make the young man in the stalls forget the fact. During the scene on the tower, mentioned in a preceding chapter, a shadow was seen to pass restlessly to and fro behind the battlements. ' The comet!' whispers one young gentleman behind me.[1] ' He says " Give me thy lips!"' but she only offers him her ear to kiss,' was another perfectly legitimate comment on a badly managed piece of stage business.

By one of those paradoxical contrasts in which Italy is peculiarly rich, I have to thank Milan for a sensation which I ought to have received anywhere else than within her walls. The Teatro Olimpia is a building which in our country would have very little claim to be called

---

[1] A distinguished visitor was about this time making its appearance in the sky at early morn.

a theatre at all. It has just one flat floor, square in shape, with—round it and slightly raised—one tier of boxes, between which and the seats of the pit stands a row of tables at which refreshments are served. Behind the boxes runs a great broad corridor, on the other side of which is a space divided, for the most part, into offices, refreshment-rooms, &c., but which in one place was put to a use different from any that we think of in connection with the precious room available within a theatre's walls. Possibly, lack of light suggested the experiment; possibly, simply that 'furia' for imitating something which is ingrained in every Italian heart. All I know is, that, wandering out from my place in the midst of an audience neither ample nor fashionable, and sniffing like a terrier down the long gallery, I found myself, unaware, in the bowels of the earth. Stalactites,

> Like snow or silver or long diamond spires
> Hung downward, raining forth a doubtful light.

Maidenhair-fern and moss clothed raggedly the limestone rocks, whose blackened sides were worn here and there into holes; while somewhere deep in their recesses, a tiny thread of water trickled and fell into a basin beneath. It was such a place as Wotan might have chosen for evoking the form of the unwilling Erda. One looked round more than half expecting to see the python-like roots of Ygdrasil striking downwards through the floor, and the shadowy figures of the Norns spinning their fateful line in the hollows far away. One looked, looked in vain, and then—with what surprise no one who had not experienced such a sensation can conceive—through an arch which should have disclosed the vista of some primeval river, the eye was dimly, incredulously, aware of waiters hurrying to and fro with trays and glasses, and men and women in twentieth-century

costumes, taking their ease ; and the ear, straining, made
out the confused and meaningless murmur of modern
speech. They seemed figures in a dream ; the senses
were obstinate, and it was a little while ere they would
order the dream-created beings to give place to the
flesh-and-blood personages of everyday.

Florence has a wealth of theatres, of which I have
seen many and forgotten some. After the large opera-
house, and a huge building called the Politeama
Fiorentino, there is the Pergola—itself, perhaps, nearly
the size of Drury Lane—fashionable, but comparatively
rarely used. There I saw La Duse play. But the
ordinary theatre for prose, the Niccolini, lies in a narrow
street only a few steps away from the north side of the
cathedral. Oh, those evenings at the Niccolini ! Never,
I think, did I hear acting under happier surroundings.
How one remembers the long stairs, the two magnificent
beadles at the top, whose uniform and staves seemed to
suggest an introduction to some other time or social state ;
and, finally, the trim, small, red theatre, with its audience
keen, alert, complete. Going into the Goldoni at Venice
you looked about for a friend. Going into the Niccolini
that seemed superfluous. Your ticket for the night
admitted you to a brotherhood of intellect : to a club
whose other members, like yourself, had no idea but to
appreciate or enjoy with their wits that which the wit
of the author had set before them.

There is another theatre in Florence, among the most
distinctive that I have seen, known as the Politeama
Nazionale (formerly Arena). When a theatre is described
as a Politeama it may be taken for granted that it is in
some way remarkable either for size or eccentricity. In
this case, the old title described it sufficiently well. It
is a low-roofed building with a broad stage, only one
deep-seated gallery, behind which the boxes are. It is

rarely full, and none of the seats are numbered. It was of this place that a Florentine friend said to me that it was the most republican theatre in the world. La Pergola was aristocratic; the Teatro Nazionale was for the 'basso popolo.' But at the Arena, you would have in one part a duchess surrounded by her circle; and a few rows off, a washer-woman in the midst of hers; and neither's presence would be in any way disturbing to the other.

I have seen more plays in Venice than in Florence, I suppose in proportion of three to one; but in the latter city the experiences have been as picturesque and as varied as in the former. We lived—the reader will perhaps forgive the personal note; we are on the theme ' divagando,' now—in a little villa high above the city, on the San Miniato side. Half an hour by tram, which goes right out along the river and then coasts, winding, up the hillside; and about the same to a practised walker who is not afraid of such a gentle slope as the ' Erta Canin'! It was half the treat—the childish word is, for once, justified—after the bright theatre, the sound of many voices, the spectacle of harassing fortunes, or the sound of full-throated laughter—to plunge into the lighted street, then cross the more gloomy piazza, then, from a series of uncouth lanes—like Dante diving into the shadowy wood to climb the mount of purgatory—to gather breath and attack the hill beyond. How it drew all taint of impure air from the lungs, all troubled thought from the head! And, looking back on the sleeping city and the great ancient dome towering like a guardian angel above it, one became aware of the insignificance of all our petty personal cares; and passed through the gates of sleep, caring no more, either that Hydaspes has not married Nerissa in the play, or Giovanni failed to order the wood in real life.

I remember especially the night when Novelli—with a ghastly realism of which I could have spared something—played the part of Hamlet, passing out into the street to find it raining. Clear and fine it had been when we had entered in; but . . . had the catastrophe of his death acted as a charge of gunpowder, and brought down rain from clear sky? No matter, it was the very thing we wanted; and with heedless joy we slushed into puddles ankle-deep, and held up our faces to the rain. How consoling was the contact with this simple, primeval element which swells the rivers, washes the house-tops, and makes the cabbages to grow! With such fancies, half unconscious, half expressed, I was pluming myself; had arrived at the bottom of the hill; was preparing to mount, when . . . horror of horrors, what was that? Had mine eyes cracked with looking on the spectacle of so many deaths, or was my brain—a well-worn metaphor becoming literal for once—taking fire? Was the air—to quote our friend Archibaldo—filled with flittings of my fiery soul? For filled with fiery flittings it was, in some sort. About and around they wavered, checked, disappeared, kindled again, in a wild and bewildering dance. Suddenly, the explanation came to me: fireflies! They had not been seen before that year, and the rain was the last place in which to expect them. Yet the drenching waters, that would have put out an earthly light, made no difference to theirs; and they threaded merrily among the water-strings like spirits of the air untouched and undimmed. How, when the blood is up, such effects as these are impressive and convincing! I recollect with what gusto I recounted it all to my sister the next day; recollect how, when, the night following, the lamp declined to be extinguished and persisted in flickering, with a series of weird pops that dimly suggested the dying sounds of the great actor,

I called her back and answered her sleepy grumble with
' Look here, you've got Novelli dying in the room next
to you ! ' and how she told me afterwards that she had not
slept a wink all night.

There is another theatre in Florence, which does not
open till rains and storms are, broadly speaking, things
of the past—until spring has laid aside her girlish quips—
and lasts until autumn has rendered up her golden fruits
into the harvester's hand. It lies in one of the long
streets on the south side of the Arno, and is called the
Arena (not Teatro) Goldoni. In form, it is something
like a Roman theatre, with a good sized proscenium,
the platea being on the ground itself—only one tier at the
back, if my memory serves me—and a gallery above it, by
which the spectators pass to and fro. The entrance from
the street is undistinctive, and the vestibule a low, squalid,
open space, filthy with matter and frightful with sound ;
choked up by screaming boys, vagabond paper-sellers,
conversational idlers, and spectators doubtful which way
to proceed. Once inside, we betake ourselves to our
numbered seats on the floor of the house, and listen to
the cries of the boys, modified to exactly the same extent
as those of a set of politicians on taking office, who line
the gallery at the back. It was about half-past four, and
the hot sun of midday had but a little while since ceased
to pour his rays into the cup which the roofless building
made. A touch of his hand still lingered on the upper
eastern wall. The place felt hot as a bakehouse in which
the fire has just gone out. The audience settled ; the
air cooled ; the play began. The boys who a moment
before had been screaming and squalling like demons
—or politicians—were now in a moment transformed,
and sat with hands folded, rapt, enthralled. The
drama—it was a play of Sardou's—developed with
tragic intensity. The air cooled to a balmy sweetness.

Night fell. The candles, lit in great masses on either side of the stage, guttered in the slight breeze, which curled round the pillars but did not reach our faces. The tragedy became more intense : the darkness deepened : and it was under the reopened eyes of the immortal stars that the last lurid glow of the mimic suicide was seen.

My impressions in the northern theatres seemed chiefly of picturesque details and people in the mass. Towards the south, the people about me seemed to individualise once more. In Venice, I had formed no Italian acquaintance-ship through constantly going to the theatres. A delightful Russian, with whom I conversed in (mutually) execrable French; a very self-satisfied Hungarian,' e basta.' But in Rome, I talked to various people, and made one friend. He was a charming young Sicilian, and had two characteristics which distinguished him from Italians in general—spectacles and a soft voice. We had several discussions on theatrical matters, and he was the most delightful disputant I ever knew, always ending the conversation, if we did not agree, with a placid but not disinterested shrug, and a ' What would you have ? '—' It all lies in the point of view,' or some such phrase, delivered with a smile which was as conclusive as it was charming. With his quiet and serious air, his tact, and his spectacles, it was hard to remember that he was a student from the Liceo, little more than half my age. My friend, Giulio Anca (he is hardly likely to have the chance of resenting the term) and I met first at the Manzoni, where we exchanged a few words ; afterwards, at the Metastasio, where conversation flowed more easily. Man's instincts are odd things. Meet an individual once, without an introduction, and you never think of going beyond ' Please pass me the salt.' Meet him again, and you find yourself pouring out to him your shooting exploits and your love affairs. A previous look and a pause do wonders. Even Hamlet was not roused to action before the ghost's second appearance ; but after that, he dis-embodied three human souls. But there was another reason here. The atmosphere of this theatre (to which I have referred already) had, I suppose, something to say in the matter. The fact of tumbling in and taking the first seat that chance may offer makes man something more of a republican ; for the mere occupation of so many square inches of leather with your hams gives none of the arrogance of a fixed tenure ; whereas the process of taking your seat days before-hand, after having carefully considered its advantages for sight and sound, and the discussion of the play in prospect with a circle of friends, all tend to create the feeling of property, to elevate into the Englishman's castle, the site of which you are, albeit, merely temporarily, seised. And woe betide the hardy free-lance who tries to gain access to you across the waters of silence or the portcullis of frowns wherewith you have guarded it round !

But Rome, if a city of present interests, is a place of memories as well : and the habit of remembering through the day and out-of-doors becomes persistent and will not desert us by night in the theatre. I shall not easily forget the feelings with which, seated in the platea of the Valle, I waited for the rise of the curtain after the lapse of a dozen years. What a contrast ! The last time, I had seen a man towering, stupendous, masterful, saddening us, yet exalting us, with the gloomy melodrama of ' La Morte Civile.' Now it was a woman, light, dainty, supple, who frisked like a butterfly, yet like a magnet endured. Should they have come on to the stage together, never, I suppose, had two such opposites been seen engaged in the same task. But this is, after all, the way of the stage. Bricklayers have a family-likeness ; lawyers or horse-dealers, a type of mouth by which they may be recognised ; chess-players, a forehead, which if they lack they are so much the lesser men. But actors ! They may—nay, must—be equal in variety to the parts they play. Some graceful, some stately ; some clumsy and powerful ; some very *frou-frous*—fair and dark, tall and short, moving or comic, quiet or volatile—they still adorn a corner of the house of that art which is only one whit less varied than Nature herself.

Rome, while having no theatre of the size of the Dal Verme or the splendour of the Fenice, is peculiarly rich in good houses of a moderate size. Noteworthy among them is the Nazionale, in the street of that name : a legacy of one of the abortive attempts to found a permanent theatre : left, in a sense, like some embalmed body from which the spirit has departed ; or rather perhaps (for it is constantly in use), into which another or others have entered. It stands just at a bend in the road, looking down the street and away over the piazza Venezia. I remember—such strange effects does the contrast between the mimic and the real world provide for us, sometimes—coming out one morning from taking tickets, to see a stately funeral winding up the road. I stood on the step and watched. The sight was a splendid one. Soldiers and banners, cavalry and carriages, came up the straight road and bent round the curve. I remember in the midst of the procession there passed great landaus full to overflowing of flowers. Then a space, and then a tiny fragment of a flag was borne by—relic of some dearly bought Italian victory. The man was a Senator ; but had, it seemed, served his country in other ways as well. So I looked outward on Death and his pomp, whom I was to see within, in his own bare rags, but a few hours later ; could I say which of the two was to impress me as the most real ?

The house was fairly full one night when I was there—

the first of a well-advertised piece; but in general, the plays, while I was in the city, were not such as to attract great audiences. Still more is this true of the Manzoni (to which reference has already been made); though there, in a performance of 'L'Aiglon,' I saw one of the finest pieces of acting, of its kind, that I have ever come across. With the wealth of (apparently) unnecessary talent in Italy, one is tempted to picture a corresponding amount of disappointed ambition, a series of sad histories of those who—

> Go mad and beat their wives,
> Plunge, after shocking lives,
> Razors and carving knives
> Into their gizzards.

Yet, in fact, I never heard it suggested that the player in Italy was particularly addicted to suicide, or was otherwise anything but as merry a fellow as poverty and hard labour would allow him to be.

In one way—for the theatre-goer, at least—Rome does not take the best advantage of her possessions. In Venice, the charm is everywhere. In Florence, on the way to her theatres, some one of her great buildings or noble squares is sure to be passed. But in Rome, the play-goer may go and return without one of the great giants of passed days raising a head to peer at him. The fountain of Trevi, the one of her monuments most often to be encountered, is but a poor echo of the sea. Nevertheless, one of her great things, and that in some ways the most marvellous of all, may have to be met. I remember the first time I was hastening, late and flustered, astray after so many years' absence from the great city, to find my way towards the Valle and Dina Galli. Suddenly, at a turn of the road, I was in the piazza, over which the huge Pantheon loomed. Its stately porch with its many columns, its huge dome behind; there they stood over the flickering lamps of the piazza, awful and reserved as of yore. I paused, gathered courage, and stole past—as a boy slinks out in search of mischief past the form of his revered parent dozing in an ample arm-chair.

The days are growing hotter and the nights less cool. The judas-trees have bloomed, and scattered on the ground those dainty fragments which, like the remains of an ethereal paper-chase, are daily swept into their baskets by the terretsrial 'spazzini.' There are fewer strangers in the streets; less flowers on the Scala di Spagna. Midday hoists her 'Vietato l'Egresso' during four solid hours, and a couch, a book, and the lightest of clothes behind the shut 'Persiane' hold us in imperious, if not violent, constraint. Summer is upon us! Let us away to the country! Water we cry for; fresh breezes, mountain slopes, and an air that makes climbing a delight. A touch of the freshness which shall release our prisoned faculties, and make all things—as if seen through the magic spectacles of old fairy tales—seem unchanged, yet alive with new wonders. What delight in a daisy when the air is fresh! When it is surcharged and heavy, what gloom in a rose! Man's mood is the only thing that matters? Yes! For, among all Nature, he only can be coarse, gloomy, or depressed.

My experience of really country theatres is confined to the lakes or places near them, and they group themselves round Como, Arona, Maderno: one for each of the three great lakes, though they are not all three equally well known. My hotel at Como was in a lofty building, with the restaurant on the ground floor, and the bedrooms on the top, and nothing apparently in between: reminding one distantly of the elongated Alice, in 'Wonderland,' whose head passed out of communication with her feet. I had travelled right through, from London; reached

Como about six, dined, and gone out to the spectacle. How expect to enjoy the pathos of . . . or the refined witticism of . . . No, reader, set thy heart at rest; it was nothing but our old friend ' Charley's Aunt.' And I laughed: head aching, limbs shaking, with the journey, how I laughed! The two older men were splendid. I never saw anything like the insinuation of Spettigue. His performance has wiped out all recollection of the London actor who played the part. But the Aunt himself was the root of the whole matter. He was a tall slender fellow, with a long pale face. He did not rollick through it like Penley, but just put all the grace and gravity—and they were considerable—into it, of which he was capable. I shall never forget his grave curtsy—a curtsy of which any dancer might have been proud—with this ridiculous calf's face at the top of it, and a pair of trousers at the bottom. The thing was suffocating, because all the time, you felt a lurking sense that you ought not to laugh. It was only when the end came that there was a certain puzzling inappropriateness. When in the final scene, this graceful curtsy-making youth was confronted by a fat, common, middle-class actress, the boot was on the wrong leg. Imagination was called upon as witness that she was the perfection of Spanish grace, and her impersonator, a clumsy boy from whom his borrowed plumes must be ignominiously stripped. And it was called upon in vain.

On my way back from my last Italian journey, tempted by the announcement in a Treves guide,[1] ' Teatro Sociale Molto Grazioso,' I was tempted to pass a night or two at Arona. I cannot say, on general grounds, that I in any way fell foul of the inducement which had drawn me thither. There is no place better than Arona for seeing the lake. After a perfectly serene morning had lured

---

[1] The Italian Baedeker.

me some miles over its glassy surface, a gale sprang up
and put my back and thighs to a test that I had not
bargained for.   In the afternoon, unaware of the particular ' lion ' of the place, I set off to stretch my stiffening
limbs uphill.   The genial climate, beauty of the scene,
the exhilaration produced by the near prospect of a
performance ' Molto Grazioso,' predisposed the mind to
receive, with calmness, any marvellous event.   That
much must be conceded.   Otherwise I find it difficult
to explain why I did not turn tail and run downhill
with a piercing scream, on perceiving, rearing itself over
the neighbouring eminence, the head of a man who bore
the same proportions thereto, as an ordinary man to a
dinner-table.   Even as it was, I felt a little surprise, and
a doubt in which terms or what language to address the
monster.   Then, again, how had he come there ?   The
attitude was not that of a man walking ; and if he had
descended from the skies the fact could hardly, even
in my dreamy frame of mind, have escaped my notice.
The only solution seemed to be that he had come up
from below : a suggestion which, besides throwing a
doubt on the physical safety of the ground, suggested
a moral one as to the character of the personage
himself.   As I was making these reflections, I was
slowly moving on, and, exactly as I moved, the figure
rose into view.   Surely, there was something strange
and suggestive about the repose of the attitude !
Surely . . . ' Why, it is a statue ! '   The truth was so
simple that it had eluded the subtlety of the most modern
Odysseus.   I had thought of angels from the sky, demons
from the inferno ; while stalwart, substantial bronze,
wrought out by the hand of man, had never occurred to me.
     Nothing at the theatre was so strikingly effective
as this unlooked-for appearance of San Carlo Borromeo.
Not to speak of the fact that the personages were

represented by actors of the average size, the plays were more ordinary than the acting was unremarkable. 'Molto Grazioso?' I hardly think it. It was that style of performance whose very merit deletes it from the mind. If it had been worse it had been ridiculous; if better, remarkable. But it steadily travelled down the beaten road of commonplace: pausing, no doubt, for a jest or a tale here and there; but no incident made the passer-by give heed, or delay for a hand-shake the speed of his journey.

I think I have said that it has not been my fortune to see any of the really popular performances which still linger on in parts of Italy: performances, that is, in which the people themselves take part. The lowest in the professional scale took place in a region where one had very little right to expect a theatre at all. It is a strange thing, seeing how much our countrymen travel, that to not more than one Englishman in ten thousand is the Lago di Garda anything more than a name. I suppose you would have as good a chance of meeting a countryman in the wilds of Sahara, the fastnesses of the Himalayas, or among the bitter polar snows, than by the placid shores of this accessible lake. As we fly past it on our way from Milan to Venice, we see a blue sheet stretched out to the north of us, and lazily ask its name. But few think of descending to those stateliest and sweetest of inland Italian waters; of gazing on her for whom the blood spilt on her shores has only seemed to make her richer than her sisters in fruit and flowers.

> I sometimes think that never blows so red
> The rose, as where some buried Cæsar bled.

Perhaps the spirit of a thousand of rank and file is as rich in fertility as that of one great man. Perhaps the warm hills more warm, the dark earth more dark, with

the blood of the slain, may have inspired some gifted
native pen to a perfect expression of such a fancy as that
which they whispered faintly, elusively, to an English
traveller who climbed the steep slopes behind Maderno,
towards that rocky barrier, along which Garibaldi and his
' cacciatori ' passed ; while at every step the landscape
widened, the flowers grew more dainty, the sky more
serene.   The violets spoke to him of patience and
endurance ; the laurels promised reward to action ; the
bocca-di-neve[1] opened their white lips to sing their
treble chant of freedom, honour, and devotion ; while the
deepening sunset warmed the slopes of Castrozza and
gilded St. Martin's tower.   It is a land where all seems
large and full of power.   The long wide lake ; Monte
Baldo with its endless ridge ; the masses of olive wood
and oak copse ; the smooth stretching shores ; the armies
of well-drilled vines.   It is splendid ; it is fertile ; it is
full of light.   And yet it seems to have on the spirit the
effect of twilight after a well-used day.   The deeds of
the past seem to enter into and possess the soul.   The
splendours of the present gain mastery over the eye, and
the mind seems to pass onward into a night of memories,
where neither darkness nor sleep disturb the tranquillity
of our dreams.

If, however, we chance to find ourselves on the
Riviera side, we shall need to go a little way from the
shore to indulge in such reflections as these.   The succession of villages along the well-protected strip that lies
between the mountains and the shore has become linked
together by a chain of hotels, pensions, villas.   The
Austrian has returned and reconquered in peace that
which was won from him by war.   The hotels are arranged
to suit German usage.   All the blandishments of the
shops are addressed to the Austrian predilection.   ' Feine

---

[1] Christmas rose.

Küche' replaces 'Ottima Cucina' in the humblest of
eating-houses. German is spoken by all hotel servants,
and shares with the native language the duty of the street
announcements. One has the impression of being in
some district of Germany, into which a large colony of
Italians has been imported to do menial service.

The Germanisation is, however, higher, the nearer we
go towards Italy. Move towards Austria, and, little by
little, the villages become more simple and more native :
tue explanation of the apparent paradox being that,
owing to military reasons, the roads along the lake are
not linked up : and you cannot get from Riva to Gardone
without going round by Desenzano, or driving (at some
expense) through the Idro valley. It was in one of these
further villages that we were camped ; where you could
go out for a walk, so to speak, in Italy on the one side,
or in Germany on the other. But the place where our
performance took place was just a little higher up, and
as much in Italy as if it had been buried in the recesses
of the Apennines.[1]

It was not, however, our only visit to the theatre.
An operatic performance was announced at Brescia, with
which the Riviera was connected by a steam train :
one of those little winding railways which, instead
of being kept severely apart behind set barriers, trot
pleasantly along interminably winding roads, in the
course of which the train stops to look at the violets, or
is brought up by an unusually large cow. I remember
once travelling by this very line, having to pass through
a village on market-day, the streets of which were lined
with rows on rows of white oxen. Placid, patient, they
waited as we grunted and sneezed past them, the tips
of their horns so near that to have looked out would

---

[1] The Germanisation has spread since those days : I doubt whether
Toscolano is as primitive now.

have been to have risked leaving one's eyeball neatly stuck on one of their points.

The long slow, journey out ; a wash, lunch ; a walk about the pleasant little town, including a visit, for duty's sake, to her museum, where endless and priceless Byzantine treasures were said to be reposing : all this was no bad preparation for our one musical treat of the season. Never did theatre seem so stupendous, never the stately apartments of an Italian provincial audience more imposing ; never did indifferent music have a more impressive, if a slightly mysterious, sound. I can see now the hands of the women, over which their gloves might have been made ; their faces, over which their expressions might have been stretched : both motionless, alike, whether Maurizio waved his sword in triumph, or poor Adrienna grovelled in agony on the ground. Yes, the spectacle had been made interesting. But the midnight return ? Never, I believe, did I know two such interminable hours. It was as if the method, but not the delight, of music had been applied to the roadway. All the stages were demi-semi quavers, each as lengthy as a semibreve. Nothing was done but was repeated ; and when repetition would seem to have exhausted itself, a large ' da capo ' rolled out again the same interminable chain. The time seemed so long that all hope of reaching our destination had gone—nay, we ceased to believe that we had any destination at all ! We were simply travellers in the void—nineteenth-century Melchizedeks— for whom the secret of perpetual motion had been solved. And it was with a feeling of absolute incredulity that we heard the name of our station hoarsely cried out in the execrable dialect of the place.

Our performance at Toscolano—so the village adorned by a Teatro Sociale was called—was of a very different order. It had for a background nothing but the serene waters and bright skies of the lake. It brought—for all the promise of ' blood-and-thunder ' contained in the words ' Vendetta Montenegriana—laughter to our lips instead of tears to our eyes ; and, instead of sinking us in a crowd, it raised us to a pinnacle of worldly greatness that I have never since occupied. When I came—needless excursion !—to take tickets in the morning, I was greeted by a respectful voice calling out ' Due poltrone per il Signore,' and the owner thereof, with a bow, which seemed to belong properly to an emperor's equerry, handed me over to a second official, who, in turn, conducted me to the box-office, where, further, with compliments which seemed disproportionate to the benefits received or conferred, my money was taken and my ticket presented to me. It mattered not to me that the entrance was dingy ; the box-office, a hole cut in woodwork from which the paint had long ago disappeared ; our ticket a mere scrap of paper ; and the liveries that clothed my obsequious servants, not more lovely or well-ordered than the flowers of speech that bloomed from their earthy lips. No matter ! If in stately hall, so many gorgeous heralds had presented to me a large and illumined address, and the cheers from a thousand throats had shaken the roof, I doubt whether I should have felt the same glow of pride and satisfaction.

If we were kings, we soon found that the old saying Uneasy lies the head ' was the first state maxim that we should have to apply. Doubtless, in all good faith and in a desire to do us honour, our equerries of the morning had given us seats in the very front row (they could hardly have had any sinister design, for none other of the ' poltrone ' were occupied). And arriving late—I believe they waited for us—our first sensation was that of the largest brass instrument of the orchestra squirting his clamour into our ears. We moved further back—giving the most tactful excuse we could to the equerries in question, who hastened to know what was our reason for finding fault with their arrangements—and satisfied ourselves that at ten rows back the movements of the orchestra, which had only been tremendous before, were really amusing and interesting. Its members amounted to about a dozen in all. It had no conductor, but was led, as in a quartet, by the first violin—a cheerful, round-faced old fellow, with deformed feet, who nodded his signal to the rest of the band as if the whole thing was an excellent joke : as indeed, rightly taken, I believe it was. We listened to their braying, and perused the birre and aperitivi which the curtain recommended to our notice before it rolled itself up. Then the fun began. Performances must have been rare in Toscolano, for certainly the audience were not in a critical frame of mind. The leading actor was very tall and lanky, with a beak like a vulture's. He had a peculiar way of sitting with his right elbow on the table and curving his large, flat hand over so as to completely hide his face ; but, on the whole, he was most effective when erect ; his feet and hands distributed in various parts of the limited stage, his raucous voice calling upon the enemy to come on, and at the same time warning him of the disastrous consequences of so doing.

The leading lady, by the universal testimony of her companions on the stage, was young, charming, and oppressed. They were right, no doubt ; for they had closer opportunities of observing her than we had : but I confess that the only remarkable thing that I could perceive about her was that she had the most appalling cold that ever choked a hearty voice into quasi-dumbness. Its sound seemed far distant ; or, rather, coming from beneath innumerable swathes of shawl. And the frequency with which she buried her head in her hands might have been attributed to overpowering emotion if a simpler explanation had not been that it gave her a convenient opportunity of blowing her nose. At this distance of time, the only performance which stands out among the minor characters is that of the bishop, who defied the villain, reproved the hero when his courage failed him, and finally murmured a blessing over the heads of the happy pair. We appreciated his good intentions, but could not understand a word he said. However, a very little reflection convinced us that he was a local light hastily pressed into the service on the failure of the original exponent of the part. Though a child by the side of the hero, he was, in an ordinary world, a comparatively tall man : taller, at any rate, than he whose vestments he wore. And when he threw up his hands to heaven—which favourite gesture he performed, keeping the arms and the body rigid at an angle of about a hundred and thirty-five degrees, and bringing the arms into the perpendicular—he disclosed a large interval between sock and frock, painfully prominent from the distinguished position in which we sat. And yet, with all these absurdities—aye, and a hundred more which the feather-broom of sleep had dusted from the memory ere the clock struck one—there was a go and a life about the performance which held us, in spite of its absurdities. It was real, though grotesque ; and I am sure that, were I to travel to-day in Montenegro, it would be a bitter disillusion to find that her heroes comparatively rarely exceeded six foot nine ; that maidenly grief and bronchial affection were not always synonymous ; and that bishops occasionally wore clothes which fitted them as correctly as those of other men. And, if the first purpose of the stage is to be convincing and real, what more is to be said ?

What more, indeed ? Fancy's question, lightly cast

forth, has echoed against the hard rocks of common-sense, reminding us of how far we have strayed from that which we came out for to see. Yet, after all, does it matter ? It may be a mistake on principle ; but did we come to the theatre to learn principles ? Was it not rather to receive instruction in the noble art of amusement ; to rest ourselves for a moment among the do-as-you-likes ; to draw a passing, and, all too short, satisfaction from the fruit that falls and the breezes that blow. And, further—if excuse must needs be offered—we are critics, anecdotists ; not spectators. And if a play—according to our English notions, at least—ought to end crisply and concisely, there is no reason why this wandering review should be executed like a malefactor, or vanish, like Mephistopheles, in a fizzle of false fire.

I have tried—with what success he alone can be the judge—to let the reader hear the magic voice of Novelli, look upon La Duse's classic form, feel the sparkling wit and beauty of Tina di Lorenzo, or the girlish charm of Dina Galli. To freeze him with the tragedy of ' La Cena,' fire him with the patriotic fervour of ' Romanticismo,' and supply that relief of frivolity, which even the stern artistic Greek admitted, with the fantasies of ' La Commedia della Peste.'

These, each in its due time. And afterwards, since all this means theatre-going—and theatre-going too often spells exhaustion and an aching head—we have tried—and again to his judgment we submit ourselves—to relieve and refresh him by a breath of fresh mountain air, a wide view out over a shining lake, a gossipy word or two with some humdrum mortal like ourselves. Perhaps he has had no anxieties stirred, felt no grief or expectation, has not seen the mimic personages suffer, or has not suffered with them. In that case this last chapter has become unnecessary, but not, we hope, on that account to be condemned. But if the journey has been a profitable or an interesting one, none the less, like other mortal things, by law immutable it must have its end. Like a guide, who, the dangers of valley and crag being passed, accompanies his party for comradeship's sake out on to the broad plain, the writer has followed on, needlessly, a little way. Perhaps, too far. He recognises that his strict business is over ; admits that the pictures, such as they are, are painted ; and the tale is told. And now, lest comradeship should become familiarity and attention assiduity, with a bow and a hope of employment on some future occasion, he humbly and gratefully takes his leave.

APPENDICES

A.—Popular Plays

(The authority for the main part of this appendix is Alessandro d'Ancona's great work on the origins of the Italian Drama.)

1. *Maggi, or Popular Plays of Tuscany.*

These are performed in honour of Spring, in May; hence the name. They are to be met with to-day in the country villages round Pisa and Lucca. Orzignano, Asciano, Papiano, and Malina are among the names given. They are in rhymed stanzas (specimens of which are given by d'Ancona), and the verse is accompanied by a kind of music called a cantilena —low, persistent, and full of repetition. They were generally verse versions of previous writings, either theatrical or romantic: some taken from Metastasio, others from the 'Orlando,' or the 'Gerusalemme.' They dated from pre-Renaissance times, and were unaffected by the classical movement. Saracens, Turks, Charles the Great, &c., are their personages; but the heroes of Argos and Mycenæ find no place in them.

Nevertheless, d'Ancona mentions one, called ' The Burning of Troy,' whose author he has met: a bricklayer in Asciano, by name, Domenico Barsotti. In their nature, these plays approached more nearly to the Spanish than to the English theatre : their object being the display of incident rather than character. 'Rather than the illustration of a passion in its origin, in its working out, and in its result, the Maggio has for its object the representation of extraordinary events,' d'Ancona says. It is said that the division into acts and scenes on the Spanish stage only took place in 1533. It can therefore hardly have been earlier here.

In old days—and, indeed, up to the beginning of the nineteenth century (1808 is the date given)—the theatres were booths or platforms in the open air. Changes of scene were made—as in pre-Shakespearean days—by a verbal announcement, or the hanging up of a card. The actor came forward to the front, spoke his lines, and then retired or sat down until it was his turn to speak again.

The actors were *contadini* (country folk); the female parts were generally taken by men. I am not quite clear whether this practice still prevails. D'Ancona speaks of 'Those worthy farm-hands, who, from love of religious and chivalrous traditions, without any other reward than internal satisfaction and the applause of their fellows, with toil and study represent heroes,' &c.

Shade of Philostrate ! How it makes one think of those—

' Hard-handed men that work in Athens here,
   Which never laboured in their minds till now,
   And now have toiled their unbreathed memories
   With this same play.'

2. *The Sicilian Religious Plays.*

These are of comparatively late origin—about 1550. They developed from the ordinary drama, instead of giving rise to it—as in Tuscany and the north. Though their first origins were literary, they seem to have become a popular spectacle from the point of view of the performers. The following is the description of a performance on the day of San Giuseppe (St. Joseph) ('D'Ancona,' ii. 261) :—

The Holy Family appear on their journey into Egypt and seek shelter in an inn. Richer travellers come, and the party are turned out to make room for them. Fury of the populace (the spectators). The members of the Carpenters' Guild (under whose auspices the play is performed) rise from among the audience and fly to the aid of the Holy Family. This seems the most ' popular ' of any performance of which we have been able to find a trace.

Elsewhere D'Ancona says : ' Symbolic processions were in use in Sicily from very ancient times.' This sentence suggests that this, and not the literary development put forward above, may have been the true origin of the religious play, although, apparently, D'Ancona does not take that view.

B.—THE SCHEME OF SIGR. EDOARDO BOUTET FOR CREATING THE IDEAL ACTOR

(The reader will easily understand that he can have only the bare bones here ; for the whole thing was flung across the table at a torrential pace to the writer by a man who had no syllabus, and professed never to write anything down).

He professes to have two (I should have said, three) departments :—

1. *Historical* (*three courses*).
   (a) Classical theatre.
   (b) Italian theatre.
   (c) Medieval and modern theatre of other nations.

> Spanish, French, English, German, and Scandinavian (I think the names were given me in this order) all traced from origin downwards. This series necessarily more summarily.

2. *The Theory of Representation.*
He takes the practical aids to the actor's art, and gives a historical course on them.
   (a) Scenery and stage property.
   (b) Make-up.
   (c) Costume.

3. (He makes this a part of No. 2. I should call it a separate department.)

    (*a*) Instruction in practical stage-craft
    (*b*) Facial expression.
    (*c*) Voice-production and delivery.
    (*d*) Gesture, posture, &c.

He then takes a character of Shakespeare and goes through it with his pupil minutely, making him think out the essential character from the actions or words. He then makes the pupil go back, and indicate all the surroundings by which the character should be shown of scenery, make-up, costume, so that every minute detail shall be in harmony with the character as deduced. He then makes him recite, suiting the action to the word, and the word to the action.

C.—Of Certain Actors and Actresses

(These are mostly taken from writers on the Italian stage elsewhere referred to : I preferred not to create confusion by putting them along with my own impressions, in the text).

La Duse.—Jarro's observations about her are not always favourable. Elaborating the criticism already mentioned in the text, he likens her to a famous singer (whose name I have down in my notes as Albani[1]) who made herself insupportable by the breaking-up of her phrases to such an extent that she lengthened the operas in which she sang by three-quarters of an hour. He says this is all the more extraordinary in the actress, as she at first showed an inclination towards a too rapid diction. I confess to having noticed the latter defect, if anything, rather than the former.

Notices her as forcing the low tones of her voice, and giving vent to ugly guttural sounds. This, I am bound to say, I have never noticed, but it might be a defect more apparent to an Italian than to an Englishman.

He speaks of her as 'la donna nervosa,' and suggests her suitability for representing the character of Cleopatra, for

---

[1] Certainly not the Albani so well known in England.

this very reason. Elsewhere he accuses her of being ultra-modern. The critic is not very consistent here. His study of Cleopatra is very interesting, especially where he combats the idea that the part ought to be played by a big woman. His discussion on the modern style is too long to quote and not apropos here : but I cannot resist one sentence which for crispness and truth I have not seen surpassed : ' We tire of perfection on the ground that it is out of date. We fall in love with defects. Not by any means because they are new but because it is a novelty to give them the name of perfection.' How much of our modern music, drama, or decorative art, could be tried by that touchstone, and found to be of pure gold ?

Tina di Lorenzo.—Of this actress he records that she is of a naturally sad temperament : easily discouraged ; and has had more than one impulse to leave the stage altogether. It is not what one would have expected either from her acting or from the accounts of the admiration that has been showered on her ever since she was seventeen. On this head, the critic waxes wrath with the lovers : who, he says, generally end by blowing out their brains, supposing they have any. And again, to the critics : 'Don't deafen her with your trumpets, which are certainly not those of the Judgment.' She studies her parts by reading them aloud before the looking-glass and noting the expression of her face meanwhile. Born in September, 1872.

Ferravilla.—Joint founder (in 1870) of the Milanese Theatre with one Arrighi. He began as *amorosa*, but was not a great success (his face now hardly looks as if he would be). A chance of his having to take a part at a moment's notice gave him his opportunity as a comic and character actor. The rest seems to have been plain sailing.

It is recorded that when a portrait was wanted of a man recently dead, Ferravilla, who knew him well, made up to represent him and sat : and the portrait so evolved was a complete success.

Jarro says that he speaks pure Italian with the exception of a slight peculiarity of accent, and is not to be classed with the true dialect actors or those of a limited scope. He may be right. Personally, I think he is. But Ferravilla is so generally spoken of as a dialect actor, that I have thought it better to introduce him under that head.

Novelli.—(*a*) Anecdotes from Jarro.—He started off, a raw youth of seventeen, with sixpence and abundance of hopes. His few possessions were in a small trunk. At the first inn at which he stayed, the landlord, none too sure of his customer, locked him in. Novelli climbed out of the window, leaving his trunk behind. Then he went to the padrone of the diligence by means of which he proposed to join a travelling company at a city some miles distant and demanded a place. 'Very good, the price of a place is . . . ' 'Oh, I don't propose to pay you in cash : I shall give you a charge on all my worldly possessions.' 'Well, bring them along.' 'I can't. They are locked in my room at the . . . But this is what you will do. You will pay my bill and bring my possessions here and I will give you a charge on them and on my future earnings. You will be quite safe ! ' And this astounding proposition was actually carried out : arrived at the end of his diligence drive Novelli found that he had still a river to cross. This he managed, somehow or other, without payment : sought the head of the company, and announced the fact that he had come to join it. They took him ! When they came to play at Florence, the audiences hooted him, and it was with the greatest difficulty that he could make himself heard. Finally, in a pause in the uproar, he said quite quietly, 'Dunque—Io non devo vivere ? ' (I am not to be allowed to live, then ?) Living and acting being the same things to him. The audience were struck with the calm persistence of the boy : they gave him a hearing and, finally, made a popular favourite of him.

Being taken prisoner in the war, and sent back on exchange, blindfolded, he filled his pockets with sand : and made a hole in them, so that the sand would enable him to trace the way. Unfortunately, however, there immediately followed a heavy fall of rain !

He was for four years in the company of a certain Pietriboni, and afterwards with L. Bellotti-Bon, who had a great reputation as a manager and for whom his illustrious pupil cherishes a most affectionate respect. He eked out his scanty salary at one time by making wigs. The picture given is of a man of immense determination, entire devotion to his art, inordinate conceit ; and, so long as this flattered, easy good-nature.

(*b*) Remarks from the addenda to the French edition of ' Le Pere Lebonnard,' by J. Aicard.

1. By the author.—' I have a feeling of infinite gratitude towards this extraordinary comedian. . . . Never was the word creation more justly applied than here . . . (and the piece had already been played by Antoine twelve years before !) . . . as long as there is a Novelli there will be a living Lebonnard. Thanks to Novelli, this old Lebonnard is a true son who continues to give me all possible satisfaction. Thanks to Novelli the name of Lebonnard will never be effaced from the story of the stage throughout the world. Modesty makes me say that *without Novelli my piece would not have had this good fortune.* But pride bids me claim that it has been able to inspire Novelli, a man and an artist, body and soul, able to conceive the real and the ideal.

2. The public.—A medal struck at Toulon bore the inscription—

> ' TO ERMETI NOVELLI
> THE INCOMPARABLE ARTIST
> WHO HAS CAUSED TO BE ACCLAIMED
> THROUGHOUT THE ENTIRE WORLD
> THE PÈRE LEBONNARD.
> OF OUR CITIZEN
> JEAN AICARD '

3. An actor.—Silvain, who succeeded him in the part.

> The cry of all humanity,
>   Where pain and pleasure have their turns,
>   In the true Drama smiles and burns
> Like life itself alternately.
> The two-faced mask of Verity
>   Whose pleasure smiles, whose longing yearns,
>   Frederick, how happy he who learns,
> This mask to wear alternately

Sock, shoe or buskin thou didst don.
Lekain and Pasquin, in thy leash,
    Thou couldst the human soul command.
Novelli, thou that path art on !
Melpomene and Thalia, each
    Beside to lead thee by thy hand.

In plain prose, Novelli is following the steps of Frederick
Lemaitre. To say this of an actor in France is like comparing
him to David Garrick in England.

D.—ABNORMAL ' CURTAINS '

The conclusions to two modern plays which correspond
to the conditions of a favourite Italian form of ending—as,
for instance, that of ' La Crisi.'

1. *Don.*—(This did not survive the first night.) (Don is a
chivalrous young fellow, who, to relieve Mrs. Thomset from
embarrassment, has put himself in a compromising position
with regard to her : being all the while engaged to Anne.
The theme of the whole play is the difficulties that this gets
him into with the conventional world.)

As Thomset and his wife go out, the Canon gives one
quick glance from Don to Anne, and then follows the first two
out. Don is standing with his back to the fire down stage
right. Anne is standing by the left of the window, more
than three-quarters of the stage away from him. There is
a pause : Don looks intently at her but does not stir. Her
eyes are on the ground : slowly she raises them and looks
at him, but still he does not move. Without taking her
eyes off him she takes a slow and almost uncertain step forward : then moves more quickly and firmly : then breaks
into a run and with a sort of gasp or half-exclamation, tumbles
into his arms. He moves his arms and takes a half-step
forward just in time to catch her. Quick curtain.

2. *Denton, Lab.*—(The point of this sketch—it is no more—

is the situation of a wealthy man with strong but common-sense Tory views, who, as it happens, has been given by his doctors three months in which to die; with a valet who, unknown to him, is a distinguished labour leader, and has been asked to contest the local borough in opposition to his master's son. As a preliminary to this he finds it necessary to resign his position of valet, which he has held for a goodly number of years. The master tells him the state of his health, and he agrees, politics or no politics, to 'see the thing through.')

As he goes out, his master says that the parson is coming to dinner. 'Very good, Sir' says Denton, 'then I'll put out your second-best dress-coat.' Exit Denton. There is a considerable pause during which the master walks slowly up and down the room: then goes to the window and draws aside the curtains. The red light of the blast-furnaces, whose gradual approach to the Hall has been a topic of conversation during the interview, breaks in, flooding the room. The man stands with his back to the audience lost in contemplation of the sight.

The curtain slowly falls.

E.—THE ZEPHYR IN LOVE

(From Act III. of ' Les Bouffons.')

The breeze that imperceptibly
Flutters the leaves of yonder tree,
A zephyr's soul! whose history
An old Magician told to me.
One day this zephyr, musing, dreaming,
    Found an old Burg within whose dead
Memorial walls, with tresses gleaming,
    Sat a maiden spinning thread.

Her eyes had almost ta'en the blue
Of skies that he had wandered through:
Her fingers, that would range anew
Her folded cloak, the buckle drew

With such a touch, so light, so true,
So supple, aye and dainty too,
That the enamoured zephyr flew
Curvetting around as dancers do.
Spendthrift of vows, and apt deceiver,
    Having but touched that golden head,
Peasant he found, but queen he'll leave her,
    The maiden spinning thread.

Henceforth she had perpetually
A lover whom she could not see.
And he had full content to be
The loving, yet unknown. And she,
When her fair eyes burned inwardly
Desiring something : swiftly he
Sought out the song birds in the tree ;
The scented flowers that decked the lea.
The butterfly, the forest gloom,
The field, the park, Earth's grassy loom,
Gave him their colour, glow, perfume,
And he would cast them in her room.
Lilac and Marjoram and Roses,
    Myrtle and Thyme, he softly spread
Under the window, where reposes
    The maid who spins the thread.

Sometimes to far Provence he went
To fetch the heavy orange scent.
He mended nature's every rent.
He sighed the cold nights warm, and bent
The mountain snows, till they had lent
Their freshness to the summer spent.
And when she sits a-reading breathes
With ready lip to turn the leaves ;
When on her bed she lays her down,
The curtains lightly back are blown ;
Then, bending, with his breath he draws
A daintier being out of hers.
Long time he marks with wild unrest
The light hand on the rounded breast,

Then, overcome, his fever hot
In kisses slakes : she blushing not.
But ha ! one day a fair lord fain,
 With a gay plume on his head,
Young, handsome, and of Acquitaine,
 For the maid who spins the thread.

His beauty and the gifts he brought
Won favour at the youthful court.
And after fair words murmuring,
They spoke of marriage and a ring.
What can a sweet-voiced zephyr do
Against these noble lords who strew
Pearls, sapphires, rubies ? Down he pours
A tempest on the castle towers.
Wall, spire and turret fairly rock.
For days the old stones feel the shock.
Within the very church he goes.
Now east, now west, now north he blows.
That none may cast a rose that day,
Their every leaf he strips away.
That none may speak the word divine,
He tries to dry the holy wine.
And when above the wedding bell
Would sound, it only rings a knell.
Yet foiled, he speeds with bitter cry,
To gather all his company.
Two awful years around they fly :
And the men fear, and the crops die.
The great Burg as a whisp of hay
They'll scatter next. But why delay ?
What's lying here ? A cradle, yea,
A dainty babe ! And mutely pray
The mother's lips against the day
When friends shall fail, and skies grow grey.
And the beauty of love triumphant seeing,
 He bent and blessed that tiny head.
Yielding at once his hate and being
 To the mother spinning thread.

F.—THE ITALIAN LANGUAGE

The following statement was made to me by Signor Onorato Roux, which is interesting as coming from a writer of distinction who is himself a civil servant, and therefore belonging to the higher walks of the great class of *impiegati*, to which his observation refers. The word *impiegato* is the literal equivalent of the French *employé* : but its sense in Italy is not so wide. It includes clerks and officials whether in government offices, or banks and the like, but does not include the labouring man. This class is an enormous one in Italy—far larger, relatively, than with us : and Signor Roux says that a new language is being constructed among its members by each talking in his own dialect, and that the resultant is simply a huge hybrid of all the dialects in Italy which is destined in time to swamp pure Italian even as a literary mode of expression. I give this opinion on the authority of a man who has high—though not, I should say, a popular—reputation as an author : who is certainly speaking of things within his cognisance. Nevertheless, I cherish the hope that it is perhaps the ultra-purist in him that is speaking and that things are not really so bad as he believes.

INDEX

' Acqua Cheta,' 274, 301

Acting, art of, in Italy, different training needed for the, 243 ; elements affecting, 237

——, Italian, executive force of, 212, 213

——, schools of, 13, Appendix B.

——, styles of, their difference, 218

Action, suspension of, between the acts, 109

Actor, the, conditions of his art, 236 ; nature of his art, 237

——, character of, 258

——, English, his powers of interpretation, 212

——, French, 255

——, ideal, the, 13 ; Appendix B

——, Italian, his use of gesture, 244 ; of facial expression, 245 ; elocution, 246 ; fast speaking of, 247 ; conversational character of his delivery at times, 248 ; lowness at times, 249 ; his personal movements, 250 ; inability to drudge, 254 ; rarely word perfect, 254 ; his strongest department, 255 ; his weakest, 256

——, leading, 19, 257

—— manager, 22 ; reforms concerning by, the Compania Argentina, 20

Actress, character, 258

Ailgi, part of, in ' La Figlia di Jorio,' 209

' Amore dei tre Re, L',' 150, 164 ; described, 165 ; criticised, 164, 166, 167, 170, 171 ; translations from, 167, 170, 171

Arena, 317

Arena Goldoni, 320

Arlecchino, 3, 219

Arona, performances at, 326

Art, great periods of, 26

Arte, Teatro d'. See Teatro

Assunta Spina, 296

Audiences, at Florence, 317 ; Milan, 309, 315 ; Rome, 18, 321 ; Venice, 309, 314

' Avventura in Viaggio, Un,' 36

Baghetti, 193, 194, 261

' Beco Sudicio,' 303

Bellotti-Bon, 12, Appendix C

Benelli, Sem, 19, 148, 307 ; future of, 149 ; his work criticised, 149, 172

Benini, Ferruccio, 221, 281, 287 ; personal appearance described, 288 ; his best parts, 288

Bernhardt, Sarah, 178

Bordelli, Ada, 260

Borelli, Lyda, 187

' Bouffons, Les,' 144, 183, 247 ; Appendix E.

Boutet, Edoardo, 13, 19, Appendix B

Bracco, Roberto, 17, 36, 79, 192

Bragaglia, Signorina, 211

Brescia, 27 ; operatic performance at, 330

Brighella, part of, in Venetian comedy, 3

Browning, his treatment of art, 60
'Bugiardo, Il,' 281, 288
'Buona Figliuola, La,' 262;
  described, 128; criticised, 130
Business, lack of, on the Italian
  stage, 249, 250
Butti, E. A., 98

'CANTICO dei Cantici, Il,' 120
'Capo Comici,' 24; unione dei.
  See Unione
Carignano. See Companie
Catholicism, Italian attitude to-
  wards, 119
'Cavalleria Rusticana,' 210
Cavalotti, Felice, 17, 120
'Cena delle Beffe, La,' 21, 301,
  335; described, 150; transla-
  tions from, 153; criticised,
  162
'Charley's Aunt,' 326
Church, the, 5, 29, ; attitude of,
  towards divorce, 119
Cobbler, on the stage and in real
  life, 294
'Come le Foglie,' 69, 87, 192;
  compared with Macbeth, 70;
  with Molière, 71; aphorisms
  from, 72; description of, 73;
  characters in, 77
Comedy, the first Italian, 5
Commedia, meaning explained, 34
'Commedia della Peste, La,' 8,
  39, 192, 263, 335; described,
  131; criticised, 134; trans-
  lations from, 135
Como, performance at, 326
Compagnie :
  Ando'-Paoli-Gandusio, 263
  Argentina, 19, 21, 22, 216;
    its reforms, 265; acting of,
    266; staging of, 267
  Benini, 287
  Carignano, 14
  Dina Galli, 264
  Manzoni, 16
  Metastasio, 17
  Pantalena, 294
  Virgillio Talli, 261, 268
Companies, dialect, question of
  their antiquity, 270; alleged
  advantages, 272, 286

Companies, Italian, their composi-
  tion, 257; want of unity, 259;
  exceptions to this, 261, 263, 264
Conventions. See Stage
Corriere della Sera, La, 14
Country life : English, 26;
  Italian, 39
Courts, local, 5
'Crisi, La,' 38, 44, 246, 253;
  translations from, 103
Critic, Italian, 275
'Cuculo, Il,' 41, 101

'DAME aux Camellias, La,' 177
De Sanctis, Alfredo, 203
Dialect :
  Florentine, 299
  Milanese, 281, 287
  Neapolitan, 294
  Sicilian, 210
  Venetian, 281
—— play. See Play
Dialects, diminishing force of, 271 ;
  more marked among the lower
  orders, 282 ; probable influence
  on the language, Appendix F
'Diana of Ephesus, 122, 203,
  204
D'Annunzio, Gabriele, 55 ; special
  nature of his characterisation,
  57 ; material character of his
  themes, 61 ; his prose plays,
  57 ; his verse plays, 62
——, Gabriellino, 266
'Di Lorenzo, La.' See Di Lorenzo,
  Tina
Di Lorenzo, Tina, 82, 185, 304,
  335, Appendix C
Director, reforms of the Compania Argentina, with regard
  to the, 20
'Diritti dell Anima,' 46
'Divagando,' monologue by Novelli, 227, 293
Drama, wherein consisting, 293
——, Italian, the, 5 ; intellectual
  character of, 37 ; humour in,
  35 ; sources of materials for,
  123 ; psychological nature of,
  244
Dramma, meaning of, 34
Dress, in modern life, 251 ; its
  value on the stage, 252

Duse, Eleonora, 11, 56, 244, 317, 335, Appendix C; characteristics of her acting, 176; her Marguerite Gautier, 177; nature with regard to her style, 178; her Monna Vanna, 178; her comedy, 179; personal description of, 181; sense of mystery surrounding, 190
Duse, La. *See* Duse, Eleonora

EAR, quickness of the Italian' 249
Elocution, 246, 283
' End of Sodom, The,' 205
Endings of plays. *See* Plays
English Reviewer's opinion of Giacosa. *See* Giacosa
Englishman, his mode of self-expression in conversation, 240

FACIAL expression, its use in conversation, 241, 242; on the stage, 245
Falconi, Armando, 217
Family traditions, their use in training the actor, 11
Farce, subservient to comedy in Italy, 35, 252
Farces, 35
Farsa, 34
Farulli, Ugo, 266
Favre, Gina, 144, 183, 193, 216, 259, 261; her variety, 183; her playing of a man's part, 183; her elocution, 184, 247
Favre, La. *See* Favre, Gina
Ferrara, 5
Ferravilla, Edoardo, 221, 271, 281, 290; his different characters, 292; doubts as to his position as an actor, 293; anecdotes of, Appendix C
' Fiamme nell' Ombra,' 216
'Figlia di Jorio, La,'209; described, 63; translations from, 65
Florence, 5, 14; life in the suburbs of, 318. *See also* Audiences and Teatro.
Foreign plays on the Italian stage, 23

Fra due Guanciali, 38
French, translations from the, 17; imitations of the, 37
GALLI, Dina, 196, 324, 335; her performance of Mlle: Josette, 196; in ' La Sfumatura,' 198; her dancing, 199
Gandusio, 219
Garavaglia, A., 259
Garavaglia, Ferruccio, 144, 204; his Hamlet, 205; his elocution, 246
Garrick, David, 294, Appendix C
Gazzettino, The, of Venice, 7
Genova, 8
German theatrical works. *See* Theatrical works
Gestures, use of, in ordinary life, 240, 241; in oratory or on the stage, 244
Giacosa, Giuseppe, 17, 68; his knowledge of stage-craft, 69; English Reviewer's opinion of, 69
Giannini, Olga, 195
' Gioconda, La,' 57
Giovannini, Alberto, 101, 213, 262; his Sennuccio, 214; his acting in La Tignola, 215
Goldoni, 14, 17; influence of, on a modern play, 122; his women, 180
Goldoni, Casa di, 14
Gondoliers, 310
Grain, Corney, 294
Grammatica, Emma, 184; Irma, 184, 246
Grand Canal, Venice, the, 311, 312
Grasso, Giovanni, 210; his Alfio, 211; his Othello, 211

HEROD Antipas, character of, in ' Salome,' 209
History of the Renaissance. *See* Renaissance

' INFIDELE,' 82, 218; description of, 82
Irving, H. B., compared to Garavaglia, 205; his Hamlet, 205; his hands, 245 *n.*
——, Henry, 30 *n.*

Italian, the, his love of dissertation, 45, 62 ; attitude towards Catholicism, 119 ; general character, 239 : manner in conversation, 240; 'every I. a born actor,' 242 ; man of thought rather than action, 249 ; his regional pride, 275
—— lady : social conventions with regard to, 81 ; her dress, 251
—— woman, treatment of in verse, 173, 174
Italian actor, see Actor; I. comedy, see Comedy ; I. country life, see Country life ; I. critic, see Critic ; I: drama, see Drama ; I. ear, see Ear ; I. language, see Language; I. people, see People ; I. plays, see Plays ; I. theatre, see Theatre ; I. voices, see Voices ; I. writers, see Writers

JONSON, Ben, compared with Shakespeare, 273
Juvenile lead, 257, 258

KEAN, Edmund, 236 ; his performance of Othello, 211

LAGO di Garda, The, 328 ; Riviera of, 329 ; Germanisation of, 330
Lamberti, character of, in 'Romanticismo,' 216
Language, the Italian, Appendix F
Lavedan, Henri, 40
Leading actor. See Actor.
'Lecouvreur, Adrienne,' 182
'Lettre d'Amore,' 120
Local colour, when effective, 298
'Locandiera, La,' 179 ; described, 180
London, 7
Lotti, R., 193, 261
Lover, the, on Italian and English stage, 256

MACHIAVELLI, 5
Madame Sans-Gêne, 182
Mademoiselle Josette, 196, 217

'Maison d'Argile, La,' 203
'Malefico Anello,' ll, 38, 45
Mantova, 5
Manzoni, Teatro. See Teatro
Maria, Febo, 16
'Marito in Campagna, Il,' 194
'Marquis de Priola, Le,' 40
Melato, La. See Melato, Maria
Melato, Maria, 82, 192, 262
Meredith, 79
Messaggero, The, criticisms by, 296, 298
Metastasio, Teatro. See Teatro
Metodo, Il, 121
'Midsummer Night's Dream,' its performance by the Compania Argentina, 22
Milan, 8, 11, 14, 27 and see Audiences and Teatro
Mirandolina, part of, in 'La Locandièra,' performance of, by La Duse, 179
Mirror to nature, holding up the, 244, 272, 279
Mise-en-scène the, in an Italian theatre, 17
Mission of the theatre, the true, 282
'Modella, La,' 38, 188
Modena, Gustavo, 12, 200
Modern life, its tendency towards specialisation, 173
'Moglie del Dottore, La,' 38 ; described, 113 ; translations from, 115 ; criticised, 116
Moglie Ideale, La,' 102
'Monastery, The,' 80
'Monna Vanna,' 177
'Monsieur Codomat,' 203
'Morte Civile, La,' 117, 322 ; described, 118
M.P., Italian, on the stage, 29

NAPLES, 6, 11, 14
Nature in art : In what it truly consists, 279
'Nave, La,' 56, 313
Nazionale, Museo, in Rome, 280
Nazionale. See Teatro
'Nel Paese della Fortuna,' 98
Niccòli, A., 302
'Non fare ad Altri,' 36
Northern and Southern races contrasted, 62

Novelli, Augusto, 301
——, Ermete, 14, 220, 221, 272, 319; his face, mobility of, 224; his voice, 231; freedom from tricks, 230; his Louis XI, 225, 232; Shylock, 225; Hamlet, 225; Papà Lebonnard, 226, Appendix C; 'Divagando,' 227; Travetti, 232; compared with French actors, 226; anecdotes of, Appendix C

OFFICIALS, &c., their effect on the stage, 29
Openings of plays. *See* Plays
'Othello,' third act of, played by the Sicilians, 210
Othello, the, of Giovanni Grasso, 211

PALADINI, Ettore, 193, 216, 261
Palmarini, Ugo, 246
Panhard, character of, in 'Mademoiselle Josette,' 217
Pantalena. *See* Companie
Paoli, Evelina, 56, 82, 190, 244
Paoli, La. *See* Paoli, Evelina
Papà Eccellenza, 38, 93
—— Lebonnard, 226, Appendix C
Paris, 7
Parisian atmosphere, its impossibility in Italy, 177
'Patto d'Alleanza, Il,' 23
People, the Italian, in an earlier stage than the English, 124
Permanent theatre. *See* Theatre
'Petite Chocolatière, La,' 263
'Piccola Fonte, La,' 192; described, 84; translations from, 85
Più Forte, Il, 69
Players, Italian, 175
Plays, openings of, 40, 55; endings of, 43, 55; middle, 55; problem, 45; verse, 130
——, dialect, 10; plots of, their superficiality, 272; possibility of their disappearance, 286
——, Italian, 46; influence of national life on, 28; classified, 34; gloomy character of, 99
——, popular, 3; Appendix A

Playwright, art of the, 28; difficulty of judging a foreign, 39
Politeama Florentino, 317;
—— Nazionale, 317
Popular plays. *See* Plays
Praga, Marco, as president of the Società degli Autori, 23; as author, 44, 102, 253
Prompter, his prominence in Italian theatres, 254
Prosa, Scena di, 39, 40
Prose theatre. *See* Theatre

RASI, Luigi, 13, 131
Real life, contrasted with the dialect play, 277
'Regina, La,' 39; described, 124; criticised, 127
Regional pride, 275, 309
'Reiter, La.' *See* Reiter, Virginia
Reiter, Virginia, 12, 182
'Renaissance, History of the,' by Addington Symonds, 2
Riccardi, Re, 23, 24
'Romanticismo,' 39, 69, 216, 335; described, 93; the oath in, 95, 147
Rome, 5, 6, 11, 13, 14, 15, 321, 322; theatres of, 323; funeral procession in the via Nazionale, 323; monuments apart from the theatres, 324; summer in, 325
Rossi, La. *See* Rossi, Luciana
Rossi, Luciana, 193, 261; her dancing, 194
Rouchon, Jean, character of, in 'La Maison d'Argile,' 203
Rovetta, Gerolamo, 17, 92

'SALOME,' 188
Salvini, Gustavo, 202
——, Tommaso, 294; his lecture on Gustavo Modena, 200; his views on acting as an art, 201
San Carlo Borromeo, statue of, 327
Sardou, 320
Scarpetta, 271
'Scena a soggetto musicale,' 292
Scena di prosa. *See* Prosa
Schools of acting. *See* Acting

Sea, its influence on the Theatre in Venice, 313

Secolo, Il, of Milan, 176

'Second Mrs. Tanqueray, The,' 46

'Sfumatura, La,' 198

Shakespeare, 71 ; compared with Ben Jonson, 273

Sichel, 217

Sicilian in the audience, 321

Sicilian players, the, 210

Signorina Josette. *See* 'Mademoiselle Josette.'

Sleeping Fury, The, in the Museo Nazionale at Rome, 280

Smoke in an Italian theatre, 18

Società degli Autori Italiani, 23

Society, local, 6

' Spos per Rider,' 290, 292

Stabili, compagnie. *See* Compagnie

Stage, the, 1

——, the Italian, 2 ; how affected by public life, 25

—— conventions, 40, 279

Stenterello, 3

Style in acting. *See* Acting

Style in art generally, 235

Subscriptions at the Theatre, 285, 307

Talli, Virgillio, 12, 192, 217 ; his company, 261

Tanqueray, Paula, played by Italia Vitaliani, 195

' Tantalising Tommy,' 264

Teatro :
 Dal Verme (Milan), 307, 323
 D'Arte, 14
 Fenice, La (Venice), 306, 312
 Goldoni (Venice), 306, 307
 Malibran (Venice), 307
 Manzoni (Milan), 14, 307
 Manzoni (Rome), 16, 321
 Metastasio (Rome), 17, 120, 321
 Nazionale (Florence), 318
 Nazionale (Rome), 14, 323
 Olympia (Milan), 315
 Pergola, La (Florence), 317
 Valle (Rome), 14, 16, 322, 324
 See also Arena, Politeama

Tecoppa, character of, 291

Terry, Ellen, her Beatrice, 179

Testoni, Alfredo, 110

Theatre, the, 1, 3, 5 ; true view of, 30, 276

——, dialect, 4, 11, 270

——, Italian, 3

——, permanent, 10, 18

——, prose, 4

Theatres, Italian, described, 305

Theatres of :
 Arona, 327
 Brescia, 331
 Como, 326
 Toscolano, 331
 See also Arena, Politeama, Tetaro

Theatrical works : English, 23 ; French, 23 ; German, 23 ; Scandinavian, 23

' Tignola, La,' 150 ; described, 171 ; criticised, 172

' Titus Andronicus,' 62

Toscolano, performance at, 331

Touring system, the, 10

Tragedia, meaning of, 34

Tribuna, La, criticisms by, 298

' Tristano e Isolda,' described, 144 ; criticised, 144, 146 ; translations from, 146

Turin, 11, 14, 15

Tyrant prince, in Italy, in former days, 5

' Ultimo Doge, L',' 8, 263

' Una delle Ultime Sere di Carnivale,' 288, 289

' Unione dei Capo Comici, L',' 22

Valle, Teatro. *See* Teatro

Venice, 6, 7, 8, 11, 14 ; the siege of, 27 ; on the stage, 287 ; poem on the origin of, 314 ; acquaintances at the theatres in, 321

Venetian audiences. *See* Audiences:

—— dialect, *See* Dialect

Vitaliani, Italia, 195

Voice, its use in conversation, 240, 241, 248

Voices, English and Italian compared, 243

'WHITEBAIT at Greenwich,' 35, 291
Writer, dramatic, proper objects of his study, 34

Writers, Italian, 33. Their imitations of the French 37

ZACCONI, Ermete, 220, 221, 222, 281
Zago, 281

THE END